Alexander Mackenzie's
Voyage to the
Pacific Ocean
in 1793

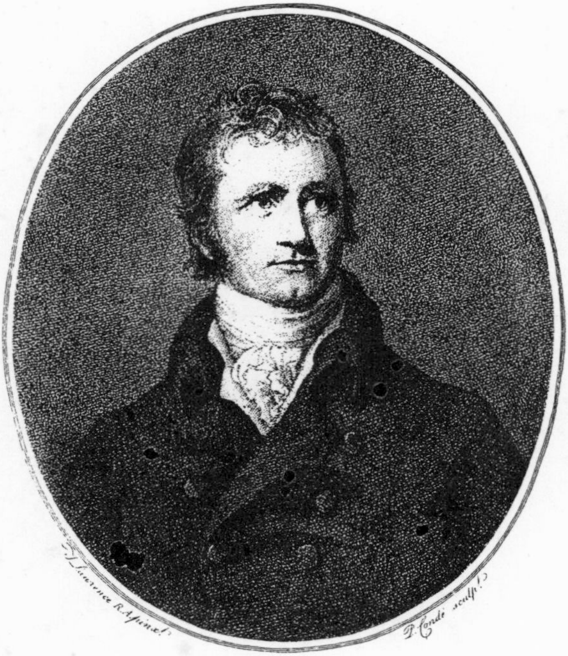

ALEXANDER MACKENZIE Esqr.

Alexander Mackenzie's Voyage to the Pacific Ocean in 1793

by *Alexander Mackenzie, Esq.*

Historical introduction and footnotes by
Milo Milton Quaife

The Citadel Press, New York

Publisher's Note

This is one of a series of books devoted to telling the story of the American frontier and of the lives of the men and women who were the pioneers in shaping the American West. These are the intimate memoirs, journals, autobiographies, and other writings that provide the basic source material for an understanding of the rise of the American nation. For, basically, the story of the expanding frontier is the story of the United States.

Contents

Historical Introduction

Historical Introduction

ELEVEN men slept on a rock at the edge of the Pacific Ocean, the night of July 21, 1793. Three of the little party were Indians. Of the eight white men, six were French-Canadian voyageurs; two were Scottish adventurers and explorers. Hostile Indians swarmed around. Whether any of the party would live to witness another sunset, was a matter of grave doubt. On the morning of the twenty-second, the leader, after patiently taking repeated astronomical observations, the while his men clamored for instant departure, concocted some red paint by mixing vermilion with hot grease, and traced on the smooth side of the rock this inscription: *Alexander Mackenzie, from Canada, by land, the twenty-second of July, one thousand seven hundred and ninety-three.* This done, the eleven men entered their canoe and with swift paddle strokes of the brawny voyageurs vanished from the scene. Who they were, and what the significance of the rude inscription left by their leader, this book undertakes to relate.

In doing so, the scene shifts from the Far Southwest, to whose exploitation the annual

Historical Introduction

Lakeside Classics volumes have for several years been devoted, to the Canadian Northwest. The change of climate and of physical scene accomplished thereby is great indeed—from the thirst and tropic heat of the deserts of Arizona, New Mexico, and Chihuahua to the towering mountains, gigantic trees, and torrential rivers of the Northwest Coast. One factor remains common to both scenes, however; the daring enterprise of the sturdy adventurers who first essayed the task of winning them to civilization.

The period of exploration of the American continent initiated by the fateful voyage of Christopher Columbus in 1492 has reached its termination within the memory of men still living. No gigantic rivers or lofty mountain ranges remain to be discovered; the face of the continent has been mapped. High on the roll of immortals who performed the tremendous enterprise stands the name of Alexander Mackenzie, to whose second great voyage of exploration the present volume is devoted.

Mackenzie was a Scot, of Highland stock, a native of Stornoway, a town in Lewis, the largest island of the Hebrides. Strangely enough, having in view his subsequent prominence, the date of his birth can only be approximately fixed as about the year 1758.

Historical Introduction

For centuries Scotsmen have gone out from their native land to the far corners of the earth in search of fame and fortune. In particular were they attracted to Canada in the decades following the British conquest of New France. The chief commercial business of Canada in this period was the fur trade, over which the Scots ere long acquired a thorough-going dominance. About the close of the American Revolution a number of the leading merchants of Canada associated themselves under the name of the North West Company, with headquarters at Montreal. Thereafter for forty years (until its amalgamation with the Hudson's Bay Company in 1821) the "Great Company," as it was familiarly known, dominated the commercial life of Canada. Independent traders continued to afford a measure of competition, however, while individual rivalries within the Company resulted in a number of secessions and consequent reorganizations. Although Mackenzie's career is chiefly associated with that of the Great Company, under whose auspices his explorations were performed, he was at two distinct periods and for several years identified with the opposition to it.

The date of Mackenzie's migration to Canada, like that of his birth, is unknown. A letter still preserved discloses that he was there in 1778, and contains indications that he had come out at least two years earlier, when he was probably about eighteen years of age. In 1779 he entered the employ of John Gregory of Montreal, a prominent merchant of the town. When the North West Company was organized in the winter of 1783–84, Gregory held aloof, and for some years headed the rival firm of Gregory, McLeod, and Company, more familiarly known as the "Little Company." After a brief, but strenuous rivalry, the two concerns were amalgamated by a reorganization of the North West Company effected in 1787. Until 1784 Mackenzie was employed as a clerk in the Montreal establishment of Gregory. During this period he won the confidence of his employer, and in the year noted he was sent to Detroit in charge of a trading adventure. Here he remained for upwards of a year. Save the broad fact itself, nothing of his activities during this period has been preserved, although the Detroit local records are remarkably complete and ample.

Two prominent traders who opposed the organization of the North West Company in 1783–84 were Peter Pond and Peter Pangman. Pond soon joined the organization, however, and by reason of his great energy and his accumulated store of experience in the trade, became for a time one of its foremost leaders. Pangman, on the contrary, went down to Montreal from the Upper Country and there persuaded Gregory and his partner, McLeod, to organize the "Little Company" and embark upon that career of competition with the larger organization which has already been noted. It was an unequal competition, for in addition to greater capital, the adherents of the North West Company numbered most of the men of experience and outstanding ability in the trade. It is a significant testimonial of the character of Mackenzie that, despite his youth and lack of capital, Gregory should decide to admit him to a partnership in his "New Company," on condition that he proceed to the Far Northwest, there to lead in person the opposition to the "Northwesters."

It was an ordeal calculated to test to the utmost the metal of the young partner. The interior headquarters of the fur trade was Grand Portage on the northwest side of Lake Superior. Hither the "wintering" partners from the interior came once a year to bring out their winter's harvest of furs for transportation to Montreal, and to procure the new supply of trade goods for the ensuing year. Here for a brief period high carnival was held by partners and voyageurs alike, the while the exchange of supplies was effected and the program of operations for the coming year formulated. Grand Portage was the westernmost destination of the men from Montreal, the easternmost of the traders from the interior. For six years following his arrival at Grand Portage, in the spring of 1785, Mackenzie was not to venture eastward of this "last outpost of civilization." For two years, as one of the partners in the "Little Company," he bore his part in a struggle which he himself subsequently characterized as "the severest ever known in that part of the world." It was a ruinous competition for all concerned, and in 1787, one of the partners having meanwhile been slain by Peter Pond, an amalgamation of the rival organizations was effected by the procedure of admitting the members of the "Little Company" to partnerships in the North West concern.

Thereby, in 1787, Mackenzie, probably not yet thirty years of age, became a partner in the famous Great Company. For two years he had directed with success the operations of his firm in the Churchill River district. In the reorganization of activities following the union, he was assigned to the most important department of trade of all

the interior region, the Athabaska district.
His predecessor in this region, and indeed
the first man to extend the fur trade to it,
was the tempestuous Peter Pond. Although
Pond again returned to the district and was
still a partner in the Company, it seems to
have been more or less tacitly assumed that
the younger trader was the dominant figure
in the scene. Before long, Pond retired from
the Company. Pond had established his headquarters on the Athabaska River, about
forty miles above Lake Athabaska. Close at
hand was the great river (the Peace) coming
out of the West and disappearing into the
North, whose source and whose destination
were alike matters of mystery. The ambition
to solve the twin mysteries was conceived
during Mackenzie's first season on the Athabaska. In its pursuit he was to emerge from
the humdrum rôle of trader and win un-
dying fame as one of the world's great
explorers.

In 1492 Columbus had undesignedly stum-
bled upon the outlying islands of a New
World, and now for three hundred years an
eager search had been conducted for a pass-
ageway leading through or around the American continent and on to the fabled Indies. In
pursuit of such a quest John Smith had ascended the James River to the falls where

now is the city of Richmond; Jacques Cartier had explored the St. Lawrence; Henry Hudson, the Hudson River; Jean Nicolet had penetrated to Wisconsin in 1634; and Louis Jolliet had descended the Mississippi in 1673. In pursuit of the same quest, a century later still, Mackenzie was to descend the Mackenzie River to the Arctic in 1789, and four years later, by way of the Peace River to cross the mountains to the Pacific in 1793.

In preparation for the first of these explorations, he went down with the furs to Rainy Lake in 1788, where he persuaded his cousin, Roderick Mackenzie, to return to Athabaska with him. Roderick was needed to guide the affairs of the department while Alexander should be absent on the projected exploration. Roderick had come to Canada in 1784 and had entered the employ of Gregory, McLeod, and Company. Like Alexander, he had been in the Far Northwest since 1785. He was now to become the close associate of his older and (subsequently) more famous cousin; and although himself no explorer, he was to coöperate usefully and effectually in making possible the exploits of the latter.

On returning to his station, Mackenzie decided to abandon the post which Pond had established and to remove his headquarters to the shore of Lake Athabaska. To Roderick was entrusted the task of building the new post, on which the name Fort Chipewyan was bestowed. Substantially erected, and furnished as adequately as the available resources permitted, Fort Chipewyan remained for six years Mackenzie's headquarters. From this center his two great explorations—to the Arctic in 1789 and to the Pacific in 1793—were conducted.

Since our present interest in the first of these is but incidental, but few words will be devoted to it. With all preparations completed, Mackenzie left Fort Chipewyan, June 3, 1789, in a birch-bark canoe. His party included one German and four French voyageurs; the wives of two of the Frenchmen; and an Indian known as "English Chief," who was attended by two wives and several male followers. The Indian men were to serve as interpreters and hunters, while the wives of the "English Chief" would perform much of the camp drudgery. As far as Great Slave Lake, Mackenzie was accompanied also by one Leroux, a French employee of the Company who had served under Pond before Mackenzie came into the Athabaska country. On July 12, Mackenzie reached the Arctic Ocean, although he seems not at the moment to have recognized it. Exactly two months later, he was back at Fort Chipewyan. In 102 days he had journeyed 3000 miles, and had fixed his name upon the great river of the north. He had proved that there was no Northwest Passage south of the latitude of its mouth, and he quite correctly concluded that there could be no practicable one in a higher latitude. Precisely how clearly the geographical bearings of his exploration were comprehended by Mackenzie, is still a matter of uncertainty. His own account emphasizes chiefly the negative result of the non-existence of a Northwest Passage to the Pacific; while the name he gave to his river—River Disappointment—seems to indicate that he had entertained high hope that the Pacific Ocean rather than the Arctic, would prove to be the goal of his exploration.

Back at Fort Chipewyan again, Mackenzie undoubtedly reflected much upon his voyage, with whose results he was far from satisfied. In particular, he realized keenly his own defects as an explorer. Not only had he lacked the "necessary books and instruments," as he subsequently wrote, but he also felt himself "deficient in the sciences of astronomy and navigation." Before renewing his effort to solve the geographical problem of finding the way to the Pacific, he determined to remedy this defect.

Historical Introduction

The opportunity came in 1791, when he procured his first leave of absence since he had entered the Northwest in 1785. Leaving the faithful Roderick in charge of his department, Mackenzie went east to Montreal, and from there to London, where he passed the winter of 1791–92. The principal purpose of his sojourn was to obtain such scientific instruction as would qualify him to make observations correctly—in particular to master the difficult problem of determining longitude. Although he had explored one of the great rivers of the world, and London was the world's chief center of interest in geographical discovery, for a characteristic reason Mackenzie's presence passed unnoticed: "Not having been furnished with proper instruments to ascertain the longitude on my first expedition," he wrote at a later time, "I made myself but little known during my residence in London."

Mackenzie left London in April, 1792, and five months later was again at his home station, Fort Chipewyan. Although the great world of London had not noted his presence, we may be sure that Mackenzie had not omitted to procure all the information available there concerning the Northwest Coast. The active exploration of this region had really begun with the voyage up the coast of the Spaniard, Juan Perez, in 1774. Five years later Quadra, another Spaniard, had explored much of the coast of present-day British Columbia, while in 1778 Captain James Cook, representing the British government, had sailed northward along the coast to, and around, the Alaskan Peninsula, vainly seeking a channel leading to the eastward. Other voyages had been made to the coast during the ensuing years, chiefly in search of skins of the sea otter, from which some further geographical information had resulted. Finally, in 1792 Vancouver began an exhaustive three-year examination of the coast from San Francisco to Bering Sea. Of these various activities and the knowledge resulting from them, Mackenzie must have inquired with eager interest, since he was returning to Fort Chipewyan with the definite project of seeking the Pacific by ascending the Peace River to the mountains and crossing thence to some coastward-flowing river which might be descended to the sea.

To facilitate the performance of the journey, which must be completed in a single season, Mackenzie planned to winter at an advance base, as far up the Peace as practicable, and from this point launch his exploration proper as early in the spring of 1793 as the weather might permit. On October 10,

Historical Introduction

"having made every necessary preparation," he departed from Fort Chipewyan for his projected winter station, and with this departure his journal of the "voyage" begins. Since this journal is before the reader in the pages that follow, we need note here merely the most salient facts recorded in it. A single twenty-five-foot canoe bore the ten members of the party and all their equipage for a journey of unknown duration and extent. Besides the leader himself the party numbered six French voyageurs (two of them had accompanied Mackenzie to the Arctic in 1789), Alexander Mackay, Mackenzie's trusted lieutenant, and two Indian guides whose qualifications for the enterprise were more than dubious. The journey was begun from the wintering station on May 9, 1793, and by May 31 they were at the forks of the Peace in the heart of the mountains. An aged Indian encountered on the journey to this point had told Mackenzie that by ascending the south fork (Parsnip River) to its source a portage might be effected to a river which flowed into the sea. With much danger and hardship this was accomplished, and June 17 found them on the north fork of the great, and hitherto undiscovered, Fraser River. They began its descent under the two mistaken ideas that it was the "Great River of the West"—the Columbia—and that it was susceptible of canoe navigation. The reports of natives encountered along the way convinced Mackenzie that the further descent of the Fraser was impracticable, and on June 23 he abandoned the effort in favor of an overland trail across the mountains, of which the Indians had informed him. Retracing their way to the Blackwater and ascending that stream, the explorers cached their canoe and on July 4, heavily laden with food and equipment, began the overland journey. The triumphant culmination of the enterprise, registered in Mackenzie's vermilion-hued inscription of July 22 on the rock beside the ocean, we have already noted. For the first time in history, a white man had crossed the American continent north of Spanish Mexico. Compared with the outward voyage, the return voyage was made with relative ease. On August 24 the winter camp was reached, from which they had departed on May 9. "Here my voyages of discovery terminate," wrote Mackenzie, and here, appropriately, he terminates his journal. Despite hardships and dangers beyond his power adequately to describe, he had received the reward of his labors in the knowledge that "they were crowned with success."

Historical Introduction

Of Mackenzie's later career some information may be appropriately recorded. The pathway of achievement is not unattended with difficulties. The winter of 1793–94 Mackenzie passed at Fort Chipewyan in a despondent state of mind. The dreary routine of his remote fur trade station had lost its attraction for him. In the spring he went down the Grand Portage, and at the meeting of the partners there, was appointed agent of the Company, with station at Montreal. Here he resided until 1805, although in the interval he spent a considerable period of time in England, where in 1801 his narrative of his discoveries was finally published. In 1805, he left Canada for good, to spend his remaining years in his native land. Here in 1812 he married a kinswoman, Geddes Mackenzie, and on her estate in Inverness-shire he resided until his death, in March, 1820.

To the narrative of his discoveries Mackenzie gave the strangely inaccurate title *Voyages from Montreal on the River St. Laurence, through the continent of North America to the Frozen and Pacific Oceans, in the years 1789 and 1793.* The journals of the two explorations are prefaced by a history of the fur trade of Canada which long remained a useful work of reference. The exploration of

Historical Introduction

1793 is subtitled *Journal of a Second Voyage,* *etc*. Only this journal (comprising pages 121 to 397 inclusive, of the original edition) is reproduced in our present volume. Under these circumstances, the propriety of supplying a new title seems obvious, and equally obvious is the one supplied, *Alexander Mackenzie's Voyage to the Pacific Ocean in 1793.* A deplorable degree of editorial carelessness characterizes the printing of the original edition, which concludes with an extensive list of errata. These corrections we have incorporated in the text of the narrative, and in addition have rectified numerous other errors not included in the editor's list. We have also supplied the descriptive chapter heads which are listed in the table of contents, and the footnotes to which the signature "Ed." is appended. Apart from these corrections and additions, the text of Mackenzie's original edition of 1801 is reproduced verbatim.

That Mackenzie's mastery of the wilderness exceeded his mastery of the pen will be apparent to the reader of his journal. It recites a great chapter in the annals of world exploration, and the contents are, therefore, of enduring interest and importance. A skillful narrator, however, might easily have presented the story in more captivating fashion; indeed, with the material at Mackenzie's command, a classic of world literature might have been produced. To demand this of Mackenzie, however, would be unreasonable. The world's great men of achievement have not seldom been inept in the art of narration. Yet, reflecting on such a narrative as that of Alexander Henry, Mackenzie's predecessor in the Far Northwest (reproduced as *The Lakeside Classics* volume for 1921), we may regret that the narrative skill of the latter was not shared more fully by our present journalist.

As one of Canada's foremost figures, Mackenzie's career has been frequently related. His narrative has been many times reprinted, and a tradition exists to the effect that a French translation of it was ordered to be made by Napoleon Bonaparte. The latest edition of it was issued by the Radisson Society of Toronto in 1927, under the editorship of Professor C. W. Colby.

M. M. Quaife

Detroit Public Library,
    June, 1931.

xxix

VOYAGES

FROM

MONTREAL,

ON THE RIVER ST. LAURENCE,

THROUGH THE

CONTINENT OF NORTH AMERICA,

TO THE

FROZEN AND PACIFIC OCEANS:

In the Years 1789 *and* 1793.

WITH A PRELIMINARY ACCOUNT

OF THE RISE, PROGRESS, AND PRESENT STATE OF

THE FUR TRADE

OF THAT COUNTRY.

ILLUSTRATED WITH MAPS.

BY ALEXANDER MACKENZIE, ESQ.

LONDON:

PRINTED FOR T CADELL, JUN. AND W. DAVIES, STRAND; COBBETT AND MORGAN.
PALL-MALL; AND W. CREECH, AT EDINBURGH.

BY R. NOBLE, OLD-BAILEY.

M.DCCC.I.

TO

HIS MOST SACRED MAJESTY

GEORGE THE THIRD,

THIS VOLUME IS INSCRIBED,

BY HIS MAJESTY'S MOST FAITHFUL SUBJECT,

AND DEVOTED SERVANT,

ALEXANDER MACKENZIE.

Preface to
the Original Edition

———

ON presenting this Volume to my
Country, it is not necessary to enter
into a particular account of those
voyages whose journals form the principal
part of it, as they will be found, I trust, to
explain themselves. It appears, however, to
be a duty, which the Public have a right to
expect from me, to state the reasons which
have influenced me in delaying the publica-
tion of them.

It has been asserted, that a misunderstand-
ing between a person high in office and myself, was the cause of this procrastination. It
has also been propagated, that it was occasioned by that precaution which the policy
of commerce will sometimes suggest; but
they are both equally devoid of foundation.
The one is an idle tale; and there could be no
solid reason for concealing the circumstances
of discoveries, whose arrangements and prosecution were so honourable to my associates
and myself, at whose expence they were
undertaken. The delay actually arose from

the very active and busy mode of life in which I was engaged since the voyages have been completed; and when, at length, the opportunity arrived, the apprehension of presenting myself to the Public in the character of an Author, for which the course and occupations of my life have by no means qualified me, made me hesitate in committing my papers to the Press; being much better calculated to perform the voyages, arduous as they might be, than to write an account of them. However, they are now offered to the Public with the submission that becomes me.

I was led, at an early period of life, by commercial views, to the country North-West of Lake Superior, in North America, and being endowed by Nature with an inquisitive mind and enterprising spirit; possessing also a constitution and frame of body equal to the most arduous undertakings, and being familiar with toilsome exertions in the prosecution of mercantile pursuits, I not only contemplated the practicability of penetrating across the continent of America, but was confident in the qualifications, as I was animated by the desire, to undertake the perilous enterprize.

The general utility of such a discovery, has been universally acknowledged; while the

wishes of my particular friends and commercial associates, that I should proceed in the
pursuit of it, contributed to quicken the execution of this favourite project of my own ambition: and as the completion of it extends the
boundaries of geographic science, and adds
new countries to the realms of British commerce, the danger I have encountered, and the
toils I have suffered, have found their recom-
pence; nor will the many tedious and weary
days, or the gloomy and inclement nights
which I have passed, have been passed in vain.

The first voyage has settled the dubious
point of a practicable North-West passage;
and I trust, that it has set that long agitated
question at rest, and extinguished the dis-
putes respecting it for ever. An enlarged
discussion of that subject will be found to
occupy the concluding pages of this volume.

In this voyage, I was not only without the
necessary books and instruments, but also
felt myself deficient in the sciences of astronomy and navigation: I did not hesitate,
therefore, to undertake a winter's voyage to
this country, in order to procure the one and
acquire the other. These objects being accomplished, I returned, to determine the
practicability of a commercial communication through the continent of North America,
between the Atlantic and Pacific Oceans,

which is proved by my second journal. Nor do I hesitate to declare my decided opinion, that very great and essential advantages may be derived by extending our trade from one sea to the other.

Some account of the fur trade of Canada from that country, of the native inhabitants, and of the extensive districts connected with it, forms a preliminary discourse, which will, I trust, prove interesting to a nation whose general policy is blended with, and whose prosperity is supported by, the pursuits of commerce. It will also qualify the reader to pursue the succeeding voyages with superior intelligence and satisfaction.

These voyages will not, I fear, afford the variety that may be expected from them; and that which they offered to the eye, is not of a nature to be effectually transferred to the page. Mountains and vallies, the dreary waste, and wide-spreading forests, the lakes and rivers succeed each other in general description; and, except on the coasts of the Pacific Ocean, where the villages were permanent, and the inhabitants in a great measure stationary, small bands of wandering Indians are the only people whom I shall introduce to the acquaintance of my readers.

The beaver and the buffalo, the moose-deer and the elk, which are the principal animals to be found in these countries, are already so familiar to the naturalists of Europe, and have been so often as well as correctly described in their works, that the bare mention of them, as they enlivened the landscape, or were hunted for food; with a cursory account of the soil, the course and navigation of lakes and rivers, and their various produce, is all that can be reasonably expected from me.

I do not possess the science of the naturalist; and even if the qualifications of that character had been attained by me, its curious spirit would not have been gratified. I could not stop to dig into the earth, over whose surface I was compelled to pass with rapid steps; nor could I turn aside to collect the plants which nature might have scattered on the way, when my thoughts were anxiously employed in making provision for the day that was passing over me. I had to encounter perils by land and perils by water; to watch the savage who was our guide, or to guard against those of his tribe who might meditate our destruction. I had, also, the passions and fears of others to control and subdue. To day I had to assuage the rising discontents, and on the morrow to cheer the fainting spirits, of the people who accompanied me. The toil of our navigation was incessant, and oftentimes extreme; and in our progress over land we had no protection from the severity of the elements, and possessed no accommodations or conveniences but such as could be contained in the burden on our shoulders, which aggravated the toils of our march, and added to the wearisomeness of our way.

Though the events which compose my journals may have little in themselves to strike the imagination of those who love to be astonished, or to gratify the curiosity of such as are enamoured of romantic adventures; nevertheless, when it is considered that I explored those waters which had never before borne any other vessel than the canoe of the savage; and traversed those deserts where an European had never before presented himself to the eye of its swarthy natives; when to these considerations are added the important objects which were pursued, with the dangers that were encountered, and the difficulties that were surmounted to attain them, this work will, I flatter myself, be found to excite an interest, and conciliate regard, in the minds of those who peruse it.

The general map which illustrates this volume, is reduced by Mr. Arrowsmith from his three-sheet map of North-America, with the latest discoveries, which he is about to republish. His professional abilities are well known, and no encomium of mine will advance the general and merited opinion of them.

Before I conclude, I must beg leave to inform my readers, that they are not to expect the charms of embellished narrative, or animated description; the approbation due to simplicity and to truth is all I presume to claim; and I am not without the hope that this claim will be allowed me. I have described whatever I saw with the impressions of the moment which presented it to me. The successive circumstances of my progress are related without exaggeration or display. I have seldom allowed myself to wander into conjecture; and whenever conjecture has been indulged, it will be found, I trust, to be accompanied with the temper of a man who is not disposed to think too highly of himself: and if at any time I have delivered myself with confidence, it will appear, I hope, to be on those subjects which, from the habits and experience of my life, will justify an unreserved communication of my opinions. I am not a candidate for literary fame: at the same time, I cannot but indulge the hope that this volume, with all its imperfections, will not be thought unworthy the attention of the scientific geographer; and that, by unfolding countries hitherto unexplored, and which, I presume, may now be considered as a part of the British dominions, it will be received as a faithful tribute to the prosperity of my country.

ALEXANDER MACKENZIE

LONDON,
November 30, 1801.

Alexander Mackenzie's Voyage to the Pacific Ocean in 1793

A Map of
Mackenzies Track.
from
FORT CHIPEWYAN
to the
PACIFIC OCEAN
in 1793.

PACIFIC OCEAN

ROCKY MOUNTAIN INDIANS

NANSCUD DENEES or IND.

Carrying Place Portage

SLOCA... INDIANS

Wet Road & Rapid

NAGAILER INDIANS

ATNAH NATION

Columbia River

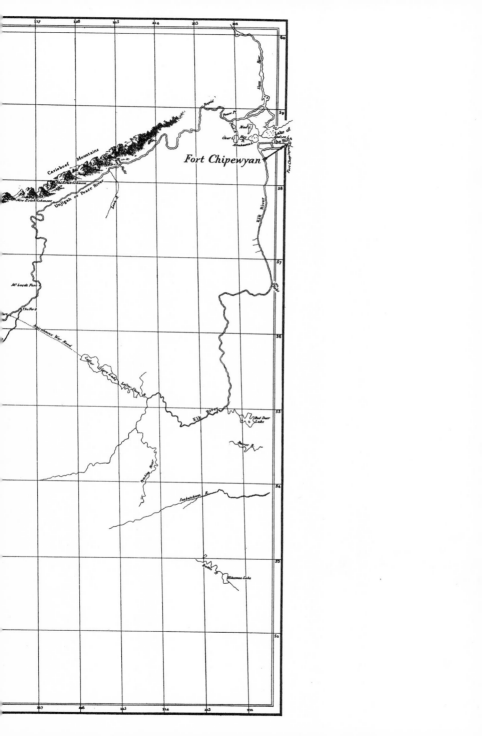

Fort Chipewyan

Journal of a
Second Voyage, &c.

───

Chapter 1

*Leave Fort Chepewyan. Proceed to the Peace River. State
of the Lakes. Arrive at Peace Point. The reason assigned
for its name. The weather cold. Arrive at the Falls.
Description of the country. Land at the Fort, called
The Old Establishment. The principal building destroyed by fire. Course of the river. Arrive at another
fort. Some account of the natives. Depart from thence.
Course of the river continued. It divides into two
branches. Proceed along the principal one. Land at the
place of our winter's residence. Account of its circumstances and inhabitants, &c. Preparations for
erecting a fort, &c., &c. Table of the weather. Broke
the thermometer. Frost sets in. Description of birds.*

October 10, 1792.

HAVING made every necessary preparation, I left Fort Chepewyan, to
proceed up the Peace River. I had
resolved to go as far as our most distant
settlement, which would occupy the remaining part of the season, it being the route
by which I proposed to attempt my next

3

discovery, across the mountains from the source of that river; for whatever distance I could reach this fall, would be a proportionate advancement of my voyage.

In consequence of this design, I left the establishment of Fort Chepewyan, in charge of Mr. Roderic Mackenzie,[1] accompanied by two canoes laden with the necessary articles for trade: we accordingly steered West for one of the branches that communicates with the Peace River, called the Pine River; at the entrance of which we waited for the other canoes, in order to take some supplies from them, as I had reason to apprehend they would not be able to keep up with us. We entered the Peace River at seven in the morning of the 12th, taking a Westerly

[1] Roderick Mackenzie, cousin and associate of Alexander, was a native of Scotland, who came to Canada in 1784. The following year he left Montreal for the far Northwest, where in 1788 he built Fort Chipewyan on Lake Athabaska. He remained in charge here during the absence of Alexander on the latter's explorations of 1789 and 1793. In 1799 he became a partner in the North West Company. In 1806 he retired from the fur trade. The latter portion of his life was passed in Lower Canada, where he died, Aug. 15, 1844. He devoted much effort to gathering materials upon the history of the fur trade, and some of these were published by L. R. Masson in *Bourgeois de la Compagnie du Nordouest* (Quebec, 2 vols., 1889). Mackenzie died, Aug. 15, 1844.—ED.

course. It is evident, that all the land between it and the Lake of the Hills, as far as
the Elk River, is formed by the quantity of
earth and mud, which is carried down by
the streams of those two great rivers. In
this space there are several lakes. The lake,
Clear Water, which is the deepest, Lake
Vassieu, and the Athabasca Lake, which is
the largest of the three, and whose denomination in the Knistineaux language, implies,
a flat low, swampy country, subject to
inundations. The two last lakes are now so
shallow, that, from the cause just mentioned,
there is every reason to expect, that in a few
years, they will have exchanged their
character and become extensive forests.

This country is so level, that, at some
seasons, it is entirely overflowed, which accounts for the periodical influx and reflux of
the waters between the Lake of the Hills and
the Peace River.

On the 13th at noon we came to the Peace
Point; from which, according to the report
of my interpreter, the river derives its name;
it was the spot where the Knisteneaux and
Beaver Indians settled their dispute; the real
name of the river and point being that of the
land which was the object of contention.

When this country was formerly invaded
by the Knisteneaux, they found the Beaver

5

Indians inhabiting the land about Portage la Loche; and the adjoining tribe were those whom they called slaves. They drove both these tribes before them; when the latter proceeded down the river from the Lake of the Hills, in consequence of which that part of it obtained the name of the Slave River. The former proceeded up the river; and when the Knisteneaux made peace with them, this place was settled to be the boundary.

We continued our voyage, and I did not find the current so strong in this river as I had been induced to believe, though this, perhaps, was not the period to form a correct notion of that circumstance, as well as of the breadth, the water being very low; so that the stream has not appeared to me to be in any part that I have seen, more than a quarter of a mile wide.

The weather was cold and raw, so as to render our progress unpleasant; at the same time we did not relax in our expedition, and, at three on the afternoon of the 17th we arrived at the falls. The river at this place is about four hundred yards broad, and the fall about twenty feet high: the first carrying place is eight hundred paces in length, and the last, which is about a mile onwards, is something more than two thirds of that distance. Here we found several fires, from which circumstance we concluded, that the canoes destined for this quarter, which left the fort some days before us, could not be far a-head. The weather continued to be very cold, and the snow that fell during the night was several inches deep.

On the morning of the 18th, as soon as we got out of the draught of the fall, the wind being at North-East, and strong in our favour, we hoisted sail, which carried us on at a considerable rate against the current, and passed the Loon River before twelve o'clock; from thence we soon came along the Grande Isle, at the upper end of which we encamped for the night. It now froze very hard: indeed, it had so much the appearance of winter, that I began to entertain some alarm lest we might be stopped by the ice: we therefore set off at three o'clock in the morning of the 19th, and about eight we landed at the Old Establishment.[2]

The passage to this place from Athabasca having been surveyed by M. Vaudreuil, formerly in the Company's service, I did not think it necessary to give any particular attention to it; I shall, however, just observe, that the course in general from the Lake of the Hills to the falls, is Westerly, and as

[2] This had been built four years earlier by a trader named Boyer.—Ed.

much to the North as the South of it, from thence it is about West-South-West to this fort.

The country in general is low from our entrance of the river to the falls, and with the exception of a few open parts covered with grass, it is clothed with wood. Where the banks are very low the soil is good, being composed of the sediment of the river and putrefied leaves and vegetables. Where they are more elevated, they display a face of yellowish clay, mixed with small stones. On a line with the falls, and on either side of the river, there are said to be very extensive plains, which afford pasture to numerous herds of buffaloes. Our people a-head slept here last night, and, from their carelessness, the fire was communicated to and burned down, the large house, and was proceeding fast to the smaller buildings when we arrived to extinguish it.

We continued our voyage, the course of the river being South-West by West one mile and a quarter, South by East one mile, South-West by South three miles, West by South one mile, South-South-West two miles, South four miles, South-West seven miles and an half, South by West one mile, North-North-West two miles and an half, South five miles and a quarter, South-West one mile and an half, North-East by East three miles and an half, and South-East by East one mile.

We overtook Mr. Finlay, with his canoes, who was encamped near the fort of which he was going to take the charge, during the ensuing winter, and made every necessary preparative for a becoming appearance on our arrival the following morning. Although I had been since the year 1787 in the Athabasca country, I had never yet seen a single native of that part of it which we had now reached.

At six o'clock in the morning of the 20th, we landed before the house amidst the rejoicing and firing of the people, who were animated with the prospect of again indulging themselves in the luxury of rum, of which they had been deprived since the beginning of May; as it is a practice throughout the North-West, neither to sell or give any rum to the natives during the summer. There was at this time only one chief with his people, the other two being hourly expected with their bands; and on the 21st and 22d they all arrived except the war chief and fifteen men. As they very soon expressed their desire of the expected regale, I called them together, to the number of forty-two hunters, or men capable of bearing

arms, to offer some advice, which would be
equally advantageous to them and to us, and
I strengthened my admonition with a nine
gallon cask of reduced rum and a quantity of
tobacco. At the same time I observed, that
as I should not often visit them, I had
instanced a greater degree of liberality than
they had been accustomed to.

The number of people belonging to this
establishment amounts to about three
hundred, of which, sixty are hunters. Although they appear from their language to
be of the same stock as the Chepewyans,
they differ from them in appearance, manners, and customs, as they have adopted
those of their former enemies, the Knisteneaux: they speak their language, as well
as cut their hair, paint, and dress like them,
and possess their immoderate fondness for
liquor and tobacco. This description, however, can be applied only to the men, as the
women are less adorned even than those of
the Chepewyan tribes. We could not observe, without some degree of surprize, the
contrast between the neat and decent appearance of the men, and the nastiness of
the women. I am disposed, however, to
think that this circumstance is generally
owing to the extreme submission and abase-
ment of the latter: for I observed, that one of

the chiefs allowed two of his wives more liberty and familiarity than were accorded to the others, as well as a more becoming exterior, and their appearance was proportionably pleasing. I shall, however, take a future opportunity to speak more at large on this subject.

There were frequent changes of the weather in the course of the day, and it froze rather hard in the night. The thickness of the ice in the morning was a sufficient notice for me to proceed. I accordingly gave the natives such good counsel as might influence their behaviour, communicated my directions to Mr. Finlay for his future conduct, and took my leave under several vollies of musketry, on the morning of the 23d. I had already dispatched my loaded canoes two days before, with directions to continue their progress without waiting for me. Our course was South-South-East one mile and an half, South three quarters; East seven miles and an half, veering gradually to the West four miles and an half. South-East by South three miles, South-East three miles and an half, East-South-East to Long Point three miles, South-West one mile and a quarter, East by North four miles and three quarters, West three miles and an half, West-South-West one mile, East by South five miles

and an half, South three miles and three
quarters, South-East by South three miles,
East-South-East three miles, East-North-
East one mile, when there was a river that
flowed in on the right, East two miles and
an half, East-South-East half a mile, South-
East by South seven miles and an half,
South two miles, South-South-East three
miles and an half; in the course of which we
passed an island South by West, where a
rivulet flowed in on the right, one mile, East
one mile and an half, South five miles, South-
East by South four miles and an half, South-
West one mile, South-East by East four
miles and an half, West-South-West half a
mile, South-West six miles and three quarters, South-East by South one mile and an
half, South one mile and an half, South-East
by South two miles, South-West three quarters of a mile, South-East by South two
miles and an half, East by South one mile
and three quarters, South two miles, South-
East one mile and an half, South-South-East
half a mile, East by South two miles and an
half, North-East three miles, South-West by
West short distance to the establishment of
last year, East-North-East four miles, South-
South-East one mile and three quarters,
South half a mile, South-East by South
three quarters of a mile, North-East by East

one mile, South three miles, South-South-East one mile and three quarters, South by East four miles and an half, South-West three miles, South by East two miles, South by West one mile and an half, South-West two miles, South by West four miles and an half, South-West one mile and an half, and South by East three miles. Here we arrived at the forks of the river; the Eastern branch appearing to be not more than half the size of the Western one. We pursued the latter, in a course South-West by West six miles, and landed on the first of November at the place which was designed to be my winter residence[3]: indeed, the weather had been so cold and disagreeable, that I was more than once apprehensive of our being stopped by the ice, and, after all, it required the utmost exertions of which my men were capable to prevent it; so that on their arrival they were quite exhausted. Nor were their labours at an end, for there was not a single hut to receive us: it was, however, now in my power to feed and sustain them in a more comfortable manner.

December, 1792. We found two men here who had been sent forward last spring, for

[3]The site which had been selected for Mackenzie's winter quarters was near the present town of Peace River; it was about six miles up the Peace from the junction of Smoky River with that stream.—ED.

the purpose of squaring timber for the erection of an house, and cutting palisades, &c. to surround it. With them was the principal chief of the place, and about seventy men, who had been anxiously waiting for our arrival, and received us with every mark of satisfaction and regard which they could express. If we might judge from the quantity of powder that was wasted on our arrival, they certainly had not been in want of ammunition, at least during the summer.

The banks of the river, from the falls, are in general lofty, except at low woody points, accidentally formed in the manner I have already mentioned: they also displayed, in all their broken parts, a face of clay, intermixed with stone; in some places there likewise appeared a black mould.

In the summer of 1788, a small spot was cleared at the Old Establishment, which is situated on a bank thirty feet above the level of the river, and was sown with turnips, carrots, and parsnips. The first grew to a large size, and the others thrived very well. An experiment was also made with potatoes and cabbages, the former of which were successful; but for want of care the latter failed. The next winter the person who had undertaken this cultivation, suffered the potatoes, which had been collected for feed, to catch the frost, and none had been since brought to this place. There is not the least doubt but the soil would be very productive, if a proper attention was given to its preparation. In the fall of the year 1787, when I first arrived at Athabasca, Mr. Pond[4] was settled on the banks of the Elk River,[5] where he remained for three years, and had formed as fine a kitchen garden as I ever saw in Canada.

In addition to the wood which flourished below the fall, these banks produce the cypress tree, arrow-wood, and the thorn. On either side of the river, though invisible from it, are extensive plains, which abound in buffaloes, elks, wolves, foxes, and bears. At a considerable distance to the Westward, is an immense ridge of high land or mountains,

[4] Peter Pond, a native of Connecticut, was one of the most remarkable characters in the history of the Canadian fur trade. He was the first trader to penetrate the Athabaska region, to which he came almost a decade in advance of Mackenzie's advent. He was one of the organizers of the North West Company in 1783, and for several years thereafter a leading figure in its activities. Owing to unfortunate quarrels with rival traders, he withdrew from the Company in 1791, returning to his native state, where his declining years were spent.—ED.

[5] Better known as the Athabaska. Pond's establishment was some thirty miles above its debouchment into Lake Athabaska.—ED.

which take an oblique direction from below the falls, and are inhabited by great
numbers of deer, who are seldom disturbed,
but when the Indians go to hunt the beaver in those parts; and, being tired of the
flesh of the latter, vary their food with that
of the former. This ridge bears the name
of the Deer Mountain. Opposite to our
present situation, are beautiful meadows,
with various animals grazing on them, and
groves of poplars irregularly scattered over
them.

My tent was no sooner pitched, than I
summoned the Indians together, and gave
each of them about four inches of Brazil
tobacco, a dram of spirits, and lighted the
pipe. As they had been very troublesome to
my predecessor, I informed them that I had
heard of their misconduct, and was come
among them to inquire into the truth of it.
I added also that it would be an established
rule with me to treat them with kindness, if
their behaviour should be such as to deserve
it; but, at the same time, that I should be
equally severe if they failed in those returns
which I had a right to expect from them. I
then presented them with a quantity of rum,
which I recommended to be used with dis-
cretion; and added some tobacco, as a token
of peace. They, in return, made me the

fairest promises; and, having expressed the pride they felt on beholding me in their country, took their leave.

I now proceeded to examine my situation; and it was with great satisfaction I observed that the two men who had been sent hither some time before us, to cut and square timber for our future operations, had employed the intervening period with activity and skill. They had formed a sufficient quantity of palisades of eighteen feet long, and seven inches in diameter, to inclose a square spot of an hundred and twenty feet; they had also dug a ditch of three feet deep to receive them; and had prepared timber, planks, &c. for the erection of an house.

I was, however, so much occupied in settling matters with the Indians, and equipping them for their winter hunting, that I could not give my attention to any other object, till the 7th, when I set all hands at work to construct the fort, build the house, and form store-houses. On the preceding day the river began to run with ice, which we call the last of the navigation. On the 11th we had a South-West wind, with snow. On the 16th the ice stopped in the other fork, which was not above a league from us, across the intervening neck of land. The water in this branch continued to flow till the 22d, when

it was arrested also by the frost, so that we
had a passage across the river, which would
last to the latter end of the succeeding April.
This was a fortunate circumstance, as we
depended for our support upon what the
hunters could provide for us, and they had
been prevented by the running of the ice
from crossing the river. They now, however,
very shortly procured us as much fresh meat
as we required, though it was for some time
a toilsome business to my people, for as there
was not yet a sufficient quantity of snow to
run sledges, they were under the necessity of
loading themselves with the spoils of the
chase.

On the 27th the frost was so severe that
the axes of the workmen became almost as
brittle as glass. The weather was very various until the 2d of December, when my
Fahrenheit's thermometer was injured by an
accident, which rendered it altogether useless. The following table, therefore, from the
16th of November, to this unfortunate circumstance, is the only correct account of the
weather which I can offer.

In this situation, removed from all those
ready aids which add so much to the comfort, and indeed is a principal characteristic
of civilized life, I was under the necessity of
employing my judgment and experience in

Month and Year	Date	Hours A.M.	below o.	above o.	Wind	Weather	Hour	below o.	above o.	Wind	Weather	Hour P.M.	below o.	above o.	Wind	Weather	Remarks
1792 Nov.	16	8½		10	ESE	clear	12		14	ESE	clear	6		15	ESE	cloudy	
	17	8½		17	NW		12		20	NW		6		23	NW	ditto	
	18	9		19			12		21			6		14		clear	Strong wind.
	19	8		5		ditto	12		12		ditto	6		9		ditto	
	20	8½		4		cloudy	12		14		cloudy	6		19		cloudy	
	21	8		19		clear	12		25		clear	6		23	N.		At 10 last night 1 below o. River stopped.
	22	9	3	27	N.	ditto	12		29			6	1	28	N.E.		Ice drove, and water rises.
	23	8½		2		ditto	12		23	N.E.	ditto	6	2				Ice drove again.
	24	8				clear	12		23		clear	6	0				
	25	8	14			ditto	12	4				6	7				
	26	9	10		N.	ditto	12		2	N.		6				cloudy	Snowed last night 2 inches.
	27	8	2			ditto	12		2			6			N.	clear	
	28	8	16			ditto	12	3				6		1	1 SW	ditto	
	29	7½		4	S.	cloudy	12		13	S.	cloudy	6		7	S.	ditto	
	30	9		4			12		13			5		16		ditto	After dark, over cast.
Dec.	1	9		10			12		19	S.		5		24	S.	cloudy	Ditto, a little wind S. W.
	2	9		27	E.		12			S.E.		5			S.E.	ditto	Fell 3 inches snow last night.

accessory circumstances, by no means connected with the habits of my life, or the enterprise in which I was immediately engaged. I was now among a people who had no knowledge whatever of remedial application to those disorders and accidents to which man is liable in every part of the globe, in the distant wilderness, as in the peopled city. They had not the least acquaintance with that primitive medicine which consists in an experience of the healing virtues of herbs and plants, and is frequently found among uncivilized and savage nations. This circumstance now obliged me to be their physician and surgeon, as a woman with a swelled breast, which had been lacerated with flint stones for the cure of it, presented herself to my attention, and by cleanliness, poultices, and healing salve, I succeeded in producing a cure. One of my people also, who was at work in the woods, was attacked with a sudden pain near the first joint of his thumb, which disabled him from holding an axe. On examining his arm, I was astonished to find a narrow red stripe, about half an inch wide, from his thumb to his shoulder; the pain was violent, and accompanied with chilliness and shivering. This was a case that appeared to be beyond my skill, but it was necessary to do something towards relieving the mind of the patient, though I might be unsuccessful in removing his complaint. I accordingly prepared a kind of volatile liniment of rum and soap, with which I ordered his arm to be rubbed, but with little or no effect. He was in a raving state throughout the night, and the red stripe not only encreased, but was also accompanied with the appearance of several blotches on his body, and pains in his stomach: the propriety of taking some blood from him now occurred to me, and I ventured, from absolute necessity, to perform that operation for the first time, and with an effect that justified the treatment. The following night afforded him rest, and in a short time he regained his former health and activity.

I was very much surprised on walking in the woods at such an inclement period of the year, to be saluted with the singing of birds, while they seemed by their vivacity to be actuated by the invigorating power of a more genial season. Of these birds[6] the male was something less than the robin; part of his body is of a delicate fawn colour, and his neck, breast, and belly, of a deep scarlet; the wings are black, edged with fawn colour, and two white stripes running across them; the tail is variegated, and the head crowned with

[6] Apparently the White-winged Crossbill.—ED.

a tuft. The female is smaller than the male, and of a fawn colour throughout, except on the neck, which is enlivened by an hue of glossy yellow. I have no doubt but they are constant inhabitants of this climate, as well as some other small birds which we saw, of a grey colour.

Chapter 2

December 23, 1792.

I THIS day removed from the tent into the house which had been erected for me, and set all the men to begin the buildings intended for their own habitation. Materials sufficient to erect a range of five houses for them, of about seventeen by twelve feet, were already collected. It would be considered by the inhabitants of a milder climate, as a great evil, to be exposed to the

weather at this rigorous season of the year,
but these people are inured to it, and it is
necessary to describe in some measure the
hardships which they undergo without a
murmur, in order to convey a general notion
of them.

The men who were now with me, left this
place in the beginning of last May, and went
to the Rainy Lake in canoes, laden with
packs of fur, which, from the immense length
of the voyage, and other concurring circumstances, is a most severe trial of patience and perseverance: there they do not
remain a sufficient time for ordinary repose,
when they take a load of goods in exchange,
and proceed on their return, in a great measure, day and night. They had been arrived
near two months, and, all that time, had
been continually engaged in very toilsome
labour, with nothing more than a common
shed to protect them from the frost and
snow. Such is the life which these people
lead; and is continued with unremitting
exertion, till their strength is lost in premature old age.

The Canadians remarked, that the weather
we had on the 25th, 26th, and 27th of this
month, denoted such as we might expect in
the three succeeding months. On the 29th,
the wind being at North-East, and the

weather calm and cloudy, a rumbling noise was heard in the air like distant thunder, when the sky cleared away in the South-West; from whence there blew a perfect hurricane, which lasted till eight. Soon after it commenced, the atmosphere became so warm that it dissolved all the snow on the ground; even the ice was covered with water, and had the same appearance as when it is breaking up in the spring. From eight to nine the weather became calm, but immediately after a wind arose from the North-East with equal violence, with clouds, rain, and hail, which continued throughout the night and till the evening of the next day, when it turned to snow. One of the people who wintered at Fort Dauphin in the year 1780, when the smallpox first appeared there, informed me, that the weather there was of a similar description.

January 1, 1793. On the first day of January, my people, in conformity to the usual custom, awoke me at the break of day with the discharge of fire-arms, with which they congratulated the appearance of the new year. In return, they were treated with plenty of spirits, and when there is any flour, cakes are always added to their regales, which was the case on the present occasion.

Alexander Mackenzie

On my arrival here last fall, I found that one of the young Indians had lost the use of his right hand by the bursting of a gun, and that his thumb had been maimed in such a manner as to hang only by a small strip of flesh. Indeed, when he was brought to me, his wound was in such an offensive state, and emitted such a putrid smell, that it required all the resolution I possessed to examine it. His friends had done every thing in their power to relieve him; but as it consisted only in singing about him, and blowing upon his hand, the wound, as may be well imagined, had got into the deplorable state in which I found it. I was rather alarmed at the difficulty of the case, but as the young man's life was in a state of hazard, I was determined to risk my surgical reputation, and accordingly took him under my care. I immediately formed a poultice of bark, stripped from the roots of the spruce-fir, which I applied to the wound, having first washed it with the juice of the bark: this proved a very painful dressing: in a few days, however, the wound was clean, and the proud flesh around it destroyed. I wished very much in this state of the business to have separated the thumb from the hand, which I well knew must be effected before the cure could be performed;

but he would not consent to that operation, till, by the application of vitriol, the flesh by which the thumb was suspended, was shrivelled almost to a thread. When I had succeeded in this object, I perceived that the wound was closing rather faster than I desired. The salve I applied on the occasion was made of the Canadian balsam, wax, and tallow dropped from a burning candle into water. In short, I was so successful, that about Christmas my patient engaged in an hunting party, and brought me the tongue of an elk: nor was he finally ungrateful. When he left me I received the warmest acknowledgments, both from himself, and his relations with whom he departed, for my care of him. I certainly did not spare my time or attention on the occasion, as I regularly dressed his wound three times a day, during the course of a month.

On the 5th in the morning the weather was calm, clear, and very cold; the wind blew from the South-West, and in the course of the afternoon it began to thaw. I had already observed at Athabasca, that this wind never failed to bring us clear mild weather, whereas, when it blew from the opposite quarter, it produced snow. Here it is much more perceptible, for if it blows hard South-West for

four hours, a thaw is the consequence, and if
the wind is at North-East it brings sleet and
snow. To this cause it may be attributed,
that there is now so little snow in this part
of the world. These warm winds come off the
Pacific Ocean, which cannot, in a direct line,
be very far from us; the distance being so
short, that though they pass over mountains
covered with snow, there is not time for them
to cool.

There being several of the natives at the
house at this time, one of them, who had received an account of the death of his father,
proceeded in silence to his lodge, and began
to fire off his gun. As it was night, and such a
noise being so uncommon at such an hour,
especially when it was so often repeated, I
sent my interpreter to inquire into the cause
of it, when he was informed by the man himself, that this was a common custom with
them on the death of a near relation, and was
a warning to their friends not to approach, or
intrude upon them, as they were, in consequence of their loss, become careless of life.
The chief, to whom the deceased person was
also related, appeared with his war-cap on
his head, which is only worn on these solemn
occasions, or when preparing for battle, and
confirmed to me this singular custom of firing
guns, in order to express their grief for the

death of relations and friends.* The women alone indulge in tears on such occasions; the men considering it as a mark of pusillanimity and a want of fortitude to betray any personal tokens of sensibility or sorrow.

The Indians informed me, that they had been to hunt at a large lake, called by the Knisteneaux, the Slave Lake, which derived its name from that of its original inhabitants, who were called Slaves. They represented it as a large body of water, and that it lies about one hundred and twenty miles due East from this place. It is well known to the Knisteneaux, who are among the inhabitants of the plains on the banks of the Saskatchiwine river; for formerly, when they used to come to make war in this country, they came in their canoes to that lake, and left them there; from thence there is a beaten path all the way to the Fork, or East branch of this river, which was their war-road.

January, 10. Among the people who were now here, there were two Rocky Mountain Indians, who declared, that the people to

*When they are drinking together, they frequently present their guns to each other, when any of the parties have not other means of procuring rum. On such an occasion they always discharge their pieces, as a proof, I imagine, of their being in good order, and to determine the quantity of liquor they may propose to get in exchange for them.

whom we had given that denomination, are by no means entitled to it, and that their country has ever been in the vicinity of our present situation. They said, in support of their assertion, that these people were entirely ignorant of those parts which are adjacent to the mountain, as well as the navigation of the river; that the Beaver Indians had greatly encroached upon them, and would soon force them to retire to the foot of these mountains. They represented themselves as the only real natives of that country then with me: and added, that the country, and that part of the river that intervenes between this place and the mountains, bear much the same appearance as that around us; that the former abounds with animals, but that the course of the latter is interrupted, near, and in the mountains, by successive rapids and considerable falls. These men also informed me, that there is another great river towards the mid-day sun, whose current runs in that direction, and that the distance from it is not great across the mountains.

The natives brought me plenty of furs. The small quantity of snow, at this time, was particularly favourable for hunting the beaver, as from this circumstance, those animals could, with the greater facility, be traced from their lodges to their lurking-places.

Voyage to the Pacific Ocean

On the 12th our hunter arrived, having left his mother-in-law, who was lately become a widow with three small children, and in actual labour of a fourth. Her daughter related this circumstance to the women here, without the least appearance of concern, though she represented her as in a state of great danger, which probably might proceed from her being abandoned in this unnatural manner. At the same time without any apparent consciousness of her own barbarous negligence; if the poor abandoned woman should die, she would most probably lament her with great outcries, and, perhaps, cut off one or two joints of her fingers as tokens of her grief. The Indians, indeed, consider the state of a woman in labour as among the most trifling occurrences of corporal pain to which human nature is subject, and they may be, in some measure, justified in this apparent insensibility from the circumstances of that situation among themselves. It is by no means uncommon in the hasty removal of their camps from one position to another, for a woman to be taken in labour, to deliver herself in her way, without any assistance or notice from her associates in the journey, and to overtake them before they complete the arrangements of their evening station, with her newborn babe on her back.

I was this morning threatened with a very unpleasant event, which, however, I was fortunately enabled to control. Two young Indians being engaged in one of their games, a dispute ensued, which rose to such an height, that they drew their knives, and if I had not happened to have appeared, they would, I doubt not, have employed them to very bloody purposes. So violent was their rage, that after I had turned them both out of the house, and severely reprimanded them, they stood in the fort for at least half an hour, looking at each other with a most vindictive aspect, and in sullen silence.

The game which produced this state of bitter enmity, is called that of the Platter, from a principal article of it. The Indians play at it in the following manner.

The instruments of it consist of a platter, or dish, made of wood or bark, and six round or square, but flat pieces of metal, wood, or stone, whose sides or surfaces are of different colours. These are put into the dish, and after being for some time shaken together, are thrown into the air, and received again in the dish with considerable dexterity; when, by the number that are turned up of the same mark or colour, the game is regulated. If there should be equal numbers, the throw is not reckoned; if two or four, the platter changes hands.

Voyage to the Pacific Ocean

On the 13th, one of these people came to me, and presented in himself a curious example of Indian superstition. He requested me to furnish him with a remedy that might be applied to the joints of his legs and thighs, of which he had, in a great measure lost the use for five winters. This affliction he attributed to his cruelty about that time, when having found a wolf with two whelps in an old Beaver lodge, he set fire to it and consumed them.

The winter had been so mild, that the swans had but lately left us, and at this advanced period there was very little snow on the ground: it was, however, at this time a foot and a half in depth, in the environs of the establishment below this, which is at the distance of about seventy leagues.

On the 28th the Indians were now employed in making their snowshoes, as the snow had not hitherto fallen in sufficient quantity to render them necessary.

February, 2. The weather now became very cold, and it froze so hard in the night that my watch stopped; a circumstance that had never happened to this watch since my residence in the country.

There was a lodge of Indians here, who were absolutely starving with cold and hunger. They had lately lost a near relation, and had, according to custom, thrown away every thing belonging to them, and even exchanged the few articles of raiment which they possessed, in order, as I presume, to get rid of every thing that may bring the deceased to their remembrance. They also destroy every thing belonging to any deceased person, except what they consign to the grave with the late owner of them. We had some difficulty to make them comprehend that the debts of a man who dies should be discharged, if he left any furs behind him: but those who understand this principle of justice, and profess to adhere to it, never fail to prevent the appearance of any skins beyond such as may be necessary to satisfy the debts of their dead relation.

On the 8th I had an observation for the longitude. In the course of this day one of my men, who had been some time with the Indians, came to inform me that one of them had threatened to stab him; and on his preferring a complaint to the man with whom he now lived, and to whom I had given him in charge, he replied, that he had been very imprudent to play and quarrel with the young Indians out of his lodge, where no one would dare to come and quarrel with him; but that if he had lost his life where he had been, it would have been the consequence of his own folly. Thus, even among these children of nature, it appears that a man's house is his castle, where the protection of hospitality is rigidly maintained.

The hard frost which had prevailed from the beginning of February continued to the 16th of March, when the wind blowing from the South-West, the weather became mild.

On the 22d a wolf was so bold as to venture among the Indian lodges, and was very near carrying off a child.

I had another observation of Jupiter and his satellites for the longitude. On the 13th some geese were seen, and these birds are always considered as the harbingers of spring. On the 1st of April my hunters shot five of them. This was a much earlier period than I ever remember to have observed the visits of wild fowl in this part of the world. The weather had been mild for the last fortnight, and there was a promise of its continuance. On the 5th the snow had entirely disappeared.

At half past four this morning I was awakened to be informed that an Indian had been killed. I accordingly hastened to the camp, where I found two women employed in rolling up the dead body of a man, called the White Partridge, in a beaver robe, which I had lent him. He had received four mortal wounds from a dagger, two within the collar-bone, one in the left breast, and another in the small of the back, with two cuts across his head. The murderer, who had been my hunter throughout the winter, had fled; and it was pretended that several relations of the deceased were gone in pursuit of him. The history of this unfortunate event is as follows:—

These two men had been comrades for four years; the murderer had three wives; and the young man who was killed, becoming enamoured of one of them, the husband consented to yield her to him, with the reserved power of claiming her as his property, when it should be his pleasure. This connection was uninterrupted for near three years, when, whimsical as it may appear, the husband became jealous, and the public amour was suspended. The parties, however, made their private assignations, which caused the woman to be so ill treated by her husband, that the paramour was determined to take her away by force; and this project ended in his death. This is a very common practice among the Indians, and generally terminates in very serious and fatal quarrels. In consequence of this event all the Indians went away in great apparent hurry and confusion, and in the evening not one of them was to be seen about the fort.

The Beaver and Rocky Mountain Indians, who traded with us in this river, did not exceed an hundred and fifty men, capable of bearing arms; two thirds of whom call themselves Beaver Indians. The latter differ only from the former, as they have, more or less, imbibed the customs and manners of the Knisteneaux. As I have already observed they are passionately fond of liquor, and in the moments of their festivity will barter any thing they have in their possession for it.

March, 1793. Though the Beaver Indians made their peace with the Knisteneaux, at Peace Point, as already mentioned, yet they did not secure a state of amity from others of the same nation, who had driven away the natives of the Saskatchiwine and Missinipy Rivers, and joined at the head water of the latter, called the Beaver River: from thence they proceeded West by the Slave Lake just described, on their war excursions, which they often repeated, even till the Beaver Indians had procured arms, which was in the year 1782. If it so happened that they missed them, they proceeded Westward till they were certain of wreaking their vengeance on those of the Rocky Mountain, who being without arms, became an easy prey to their blind and savage fury. All the European articles they possessed, previous to the year

1780, were obtained from the Knisteneaux and Chepewyans, who brought them from Fort Churchill,[1] and for which they were made to pay an extravagant price.

As late as the year 1786, when the first traders from Canada arrived on the banks of this river, the natives employed bows and snares, but at present very little use is made of the former, and the latter are no longer known. They still entertain a great dread of their natural enemies, but they are since become so well armed, that the others now call them their allies. The men are in general of a comely appearance, and fond of personal decoration. The women are of a contrary disposition, and the slaves of the men: in common with all the Indian tribes polygamy is allowed among them. They are very subject to jealousy, and fatal consequences frequently result from the indulgence of that passion. But notwithstanding the vigilance and severity which is exercised by the

[1] Otherwise known as Prince of Wales Fort, the Hudson's Bay Company establishment at the mouth of Churchill River, on Hudson Bay. It was built in the years 1733–71, with walls of massive masonry upwards of forty feet thick and enclosing an area 310 by 317 feet. In 1782 it was captured by a French expedition under Admiral La Perouse. It was defended by forty cannon. The walls, fallen in parts, and the cannon are still to be seen.—Ed.

husband, it seldom happens that a woman is without her favourite, who, in the absence of the husband, exacts the same submission, and practises the same tyranny. And so premature is the tender passion, that it is sometimes known to invigorate so early a period of life as the age of eleven or twelve years. The women are not very prolific; a circumstance which may be attributed, in a great measure, to the hardships that they suffer, for except a few small dogs, they alone perform that labour which is allotted to beasts of burthen in other countries. It is not uncommon, while the men carry nothing but a gun, that their wives and daughters follow with such weighty burdens, that if they lay them down they cannot replace them, and that is a kindness which the men will not deign to perform; so that during their journeys they are frequently obliged to lean against a tree for a small portion of temporary relief. When they arrive at the place which their tyrants have chosen for their encampment, they arrange the whole in a few minutes, by forming a curve of poles, meeting at the top, and expanding into circles of twelve or fifteen feet diameter at the bottom, covered with dressed skins of the moose sewed together. During these preparations, the men sit down quietly to the enjoyment of their pipes, if they happen to have any tobacco. But not-withstanding this abject state of slavery and submission, the women have a considerable influence on the opinion of the men in every thing except their own domestic situation.

These Indians are excellent hunters, and their exercise in that capacity is so violent as to reduce them in general to a very meagre appearance. Their religion is of a very con-tracted nature, and I never witnessed any ceremony of devotion which they had not borrowed from the Knisteneaux, their feasts and fasts being in imitation of that people. They are more vicious and warlike than the Chepewyans, from whence they sprang, though they do not possess their selfishness, for while they have the means of purchasing their necessaries, they are liberal and gener-ous, but when those are exhausted they be-come arrant beggars: they are, however, re-markable for their honesty, for in the whole tribe there were only two women and a man who had been known to have swerved from that virtue, and they were considered as ob-jects of disregard and reprobation. They are afflicted with but few diseases, and their only remedies consist in binding the temples, pro-curing perspiration, singing, and blowing on the sick person, or affected part. When death overtakes any of them, their property, as I

have before observed, is sacrificed and destroyed; nor is there any failure of lamenta-
tion or mourning on such occasion: they who
are more nearly related to the departed person, black their faces, and sometimes cut off
their hair; they also pierce their arms with
knives and arrows. The grief of the females
is carried to a still greater excess; they not
only cut their hair, and cry and howl, but
they will sometimes, with the utmost delib-
eration, employ some sharp instrument to
separate the nail from the finger, and then
force back the flesh beyond the first joint,
which they immediately amputate. But this
extraordinary mark of affliction is only displayed on the death of a favourite son, an
husband, or a father. Many of the old women
have so often repeated this ceremony, that
they have not a complete finger remaining on
either hand. The women renew their lamentations at the graves of their departed rela-
tives for a long succession of years. They appear, in common with all the Indian tribes,
to be very fond of their children, but they
are as careless in their mode of swaddling
them in their infant state, as they are of their
own dress: the child is laid down on a board,
of about two feet long, covered with a bed of
moss, to which it is fastened by bandages, the
moss being changed as often as the occasion

requires. The chief of the nation had no less than nine wives, and children in proportion.

When traders first appeared among these people, the Canadians were treated with the utmost hospitality and attention; but they have, by their subsequent conduct, taught the natives to withdraw that respect from them, and sometimes to treat them with indignity. They differ very much from the Chepewyans and Knisteneaux, in the abhorrence they profess of any carnal communication between their women and the white people. They carry their love of gaming to excess; they will pursue it for a succession of days and nights, and no apprehension of ruin, nor influence of domestic affection, will restrain them from the indulgence of it. They are a quick, lively, active people, with a keen, penetrating, dark eye; and though they are very susceptible of anger, are as easily appeased. The males eradicate their beards, and the females their hair in every part, except their heads, where it is strong and black, and without a curl. There are many old men among them, but they are in general ignorant of the space in which they have been inhabitants of the earth, though one of them told me that he recollected sixty winters.

An Indian in some measure explained his age to me, by relating that he remembered the opposite hills and plains, now interspersed with groves of poplars, when they were covered with moss, and without any animal inhabitant but the rein-deer. By degrees, he said, the face of the country changed to its present appearance, when the elk came from the East, and was followed by the buffalo; the rein-deer then retired to the long range of high lands that, at a considerable distance, run parallel with this river.

April, 1793. On the 20th of April I had an observation of Jupiter and his satellites, for the longitude, and we were now visited by our summer companions the gnats and mosquitoes. On the other side of the river, which was yet covered with ice, the plains were delightful; the trees were budding, and many plants in blossom. Mr. Mackay[2] brought me a bunch of flowers of a pink colour, and a yellow button, encircled with six leaves of a light purple. The change in the appearance

[2]Alexander Mackay, Mackenzie's lieutenant on the expedition to the Pacific, entered the employ of the North West Company soon after its formation, and in 1804 achieved the coveted rank of partner in the Company. In 1810 he joined Astor's Pacific Fur Company and sailed that year for Astoria. He was one of the victims of the *Tonquin* Massacre the following year. His widow subsequently became the wife of Dr. John McLoughlin, famous leader of the Hudson's Bay Company in the Columbia River region.—ED.

of nature was as sudden as it was pleasing, for a few days only were passed away since the ground was covered with snow. On the 25th the river was cleared of the ice.

I now found that the death of the man called the White Partridge, had deranged all the plans which I had settled with the Indians for the spring hunting. They had assembled at some distance from the fort, and sent an embassy to me, to demand rum to drink, that they might have an opportunity of crying for their deceased brother. It would be considered as an extreme degradation in an Indian to weep when sober, but a state of intoxication sanctions all irregularities. On my refusal, they threatened to go to war, which, from motives of interest as well as humanity, we did our utmost to discourage; and as a second message was brought by persons of some weight among these people, and on whom I could depend, I thought it prudent to comply with the demand, on an express condition, that they would continue peaceably at home.

May, 1793. The month of April being now past, in the early part of which I was most busily employed in trading with the Indians, I ordered our old canoes to be repaired with bark, and added four new ones to them, when with the furs and provisions I had purchased,

six canoes were loaded and dispatched on the
8th of May for Fort Chepewyan. I had, however, retained six of the men who agreed to
accompany me on my projected voyage of discovery. I also engaged my hunters, and closed
the business of the year for the company by
writing my public and private dispatches.

Having ascertained, by various observations, the latitude of this place to be 56.9.
North, and longitude 117.35.15. West:—on
the 9th day of May, I found, that my acrom-
eter was one hour forty-six minutes slow to
apparent time; the mean going of it I had
found to be twenty-two seconds slow in
twenty-four hours. Having settled this point,
the canoe was put into the water: her dimensions were twenty-five feet long within,
exclusive of the curves of stem and stern,
twenty-six inches hold, and four feet nine
inches beam. At the same time she was so
light, that two men could carry her on a good
road three or four miles without resting. In
this slender vessel, we shipped provisions,
goods for presents, arms, ammunition, and
baggage, to the weight of three thousand
pounds, and an equipage of ten people; viz.
Alexander Mackay, Joseph Landry, Charles
Ducette,* François Beaulieux, Baptiste Bisson,

* Joseph Landry and Charles Ducette were with me
in my former voyage.

François Courtois, and Jacques Beauchamp, with two Indians as hunters and interpreters. One of them, when a boy, was used to be so idle, that he obtained the reputable name of Cancre, which he still possesses. With these persons I embarked at seven in the evening. My winter interpreter, with another person, whom I left here to take care of the fort, and supply the natives with ammunition during the summer, shed tears on the reflection of those dangers which we might encounter in our expedition, while my own people offered up their prayers that we might return in safety from it.

Chapter 3

Proceed on the voyage of discovery. Beautiful scenery. The canoe too heavily laden. The country in a state of combustion. Meet with an hunting party. State of the river, &c. Meet with Indians. See the tracks of bears, and one of their dens. Sentiment of an Indian. Junction of the Bear River. Appearance of the country. State of the river. Observe a fall of timber. Abundance of animals. See some bears. Come in sight of the rocky mountains. The canoe receives an injury and is repaired. Navigation dangerous. Rapids and falls. Succession of difficulties and dangers.

May, 1793.

THURSDAY, 9. We began our voyage with a course South by West against a strong current one mile and three quarters, South-West by South one mile, and landed before eight on an island for the night.

Friday, 10. The weather was clear and pleasant, though there was a keenness in the air; and at a quarter past three in the morning we continued our voyage, steering South-West three quarters of a mile, South-West by South one mile and a quarter, South three quarters of a mile, South-West by South one quarter of a mile, South-West by West one mile, South-West by South three miles, South by West three quarters of a mile,

and South-West one mile. The canoe being
strained from its having been very heavily
laden, became so leaky, that we were obliged
to land, unload, and gum it. As this circumstance took place about twelve, I had an
opportunity of taking an altitude, which
made our latitude 55. 58. 48.

When the canoe was repaired we continued
our course, steering South-West by West one
mile and an half, when I had the misfortune
to drop my pocket-compass into the water;
West half a mile, West-South-West four miles
and an half. Here, the banks are steep and
hilly, and in some parts undermined by the
river. Where the earth has given way, the
face of the cliffs discovers numerous strata,
consisting of reddish earth and small stones,
bitumen, and a greyish earth, below which,
near the water-edge, is a red stone. Water is-
sues from most of the banks, and the ground
on which it spreads is covered with a thin
white scurf, or particles of a saline substance:
there are several of these salt springs. At half
past six in the afternoon the young men
landed, when they killed an elk and wounded
a buffalo. In this spot we formed our encampment for the night.

From the place which we quitted this morning, the West side of the river displayed a
succession of the most beautiful scenery I

had ever beheld. The ground rises at intervals to a considerable height, and stretching inwards to a considerable distance: at every interval or pause in the rise, there is a very gently-ascending space or lawn, which is alternate with abrupt precipices to the summit of the whole, or, at least as far as the eye could distinguish. This magnificent theatre of nature has all the decorations which the trees and animals of the country can afford it: groves of poplars in every shape vary the scene; and their intervals are enlivened with vast herds of elks and buffaloes: the former choosing the steeps and uplands, and the latter preferring the plains. At this time the buffaloes were attended with their young ones who were frisking about them; and it appeared that the elks would soon exhibit the same enlivening circumstance. The whole country displayed an exuberant verdure; the trees that bear a blossom were advancing fast to that delightful appearance, and the velvet rind of their branches reflecting the oblique rays of a rising or setting sun, added a splendid gaiety to the scene, which no expressions of mine are qualified to describe. The East side of the river consists of a range of high land covered with the white spruce and the soft birch, while the banks abound with the alder and the willow. The water continued to rise, and the current being proportionably strong, we made a greater use of setting poles than paddles.

Saturday, 11. The weather was overcast. With a strong wind a-head, we embarked at four in the morning, and left all the fresh meat behind us, but the portion which had been assigned to the kettle; the canoe being already too heavily laden. Our course was West-South-West one mile, where a small river flowed in from the East, named *Quiscatina Sepy,* or River with the High Banks; West half a mile, South half a mile, South-West by West three quarters of a mile, West one mile and a quarter, South-West a quarter of a mile, South-South-West half a mile, and West by South a mile and an half. Here I took a meridian altitude, which gave 55. 56. 3. North latitude. We then proceeded West three miles and an half, West-South-West, where the whole plain was on fire, one mile, West one mile, and the wind so strong a-head, that it occasioned the canoe to take in water, and otherwise impeded our progress. Here we landed to take time, with the mean of three altitudes, which made the watch slow, 1. 42. 10 apparent time.

We now proceeded West-South-West, one mile and a quarter, where we found a chief of the Beaver Indians on an hunting party.

I remained, however, in my canoe, and though it was getting late, I did not choose to encamp with these people, lest the friends of my hunters might discourage them from proceeding on the voyage. We, therefore, continued our course, but several Indians kept company with us, running along the bank and conversing with my people, who were so attentive to them, that they drove the canoe on a stony flat, so that we were under the necessity of landing to repair the damages, and put up for the night, though very contrary to my wishes. My hunters obtained permission to proceed with some of these people to their lodges, on the promise of being back by the break of day; though I was not without some apprehension respecting them. The chief, however, and another man, as well as several people from the lodges, joined us, before we had completed the repair of the canoe; and they made out a melancholy story, that they had neither ammunition or tobacco sufficient for their necessary supply during the summer. I accordingly referred him to the Fort, where plenty of those articles were left in the care of my interpreter, by whom they would be abundantly furnished, if they were active and industrious in pursuing their occupations. I did not fail, on this occasion, to magnify the advantages of the present expedition; observing, at the same time, that its success would depend on the fidelity and conduct of the young men who were retained by me to hunt. The chief also proposed to borrow my canoe, in order to transport himself and family across the river: several plausible reasons, it is true, suggested themselves for resisting his proposition; but when I stated to him, that, as the canoe was intended for a voyage of such consequence, no woman could be permitted to be embarked in it, he acquiesced in the refusal. It was near twelve at night when he took his leave, after I had gratified him with a present of tobacco.

Sunday, 12. Some of the Indians passed the night with us, and I was informed by them, that, according to our mode of proceeding, we should, in ten days, get as far as the rocky mountains. The young men now returned, to my great satisfaction, and with the appearance of contentment: though I was not pleased when they dressed themselves in the clothes which I had given them before we left the Fort, as it betrayed some latent design.

At four in the morning we proceeded on our voyage, steering West three miles, including one of our course yesterday, North-West by

North four miles, West two miles and an half, North-West by West a mile and an half, North by East two miles, North-West by West one mile, and North-North-West three miles. After a continuation of our course to the North for a mile and an half, we landed for the night on an island several of the Indians visited us, but unattended by their women, who remained in their camp, which was at some distance from us.

The land on both sides of the river, during. the two last days, is very much elevated, but particularly in the latter part of it, and, on the Western side, presents in different places, white, steep, and lofty cliffs. Our view being confined by these circumstances, we did not see so many animals as on the 10th. Between these lofty boundaries, the river becomes narrow, and in a great measure free from islands; for we had passed only four: the stream, indeed, was not more than from two hundred to three hundred yards broad; whereas before these cliffs pressed upon it, its breadth was twice that extent and besprinkled with islands. We killed an elk, and fired several shots at animals from the canoe.

The greater part of this band being Rocky Mountain Indians, I endeavoured to obtain some intelligence of our intended route, but they all pleaded ignorance, and uniformly declared, that they knew nothing of the country beyond the first mountain: at the same time they were of opinion, that, from the strength of the current and the rapids, we should not get there by water; though they did not hesitate to express their surprise at the expedition we had already made.

I inquired, with some anxiety, after an old man who had already given me an account of the country beyond the limits of his tribe, and was very much disappointed at being informed, that he had not been seen for upwards of a moon. This man had been at war on another large river beyond the Rocky Mountain, and described to me a fork of it between the mountains; the Southern branch of which he directed me to take: from thence, he said, there was a carrying-place of about a day's march for a young man to get to the other river. To prove the truth of his relation, he consented, that his son, who had been with him in those parts, should accompany me; and he accordingly sent him to the Fort some days before my departure; but the preceding night he deserted with another young man, whose application to attend me as a hunter, being refused, he persuaded the other to leave me. I now thought it right to repeat to them what I had said to the chief of the first band, respecting the advantages which would be derived from the voyage, that the young men might be encouraged to remain with me; as without them I should not have attempted to proceed.

Monday, 13. The first object that presented itself to me this morning was the young man whom I have already mentioned, as having seduced away my intended guide. At any other time or place I should have chastised him for his past conduct, but in my situation it was necessary to pass over his offence, lest he should endeavour to exercise the same influence over those who were so essential to my service. Of the deserter he gave no satisfactory account, but continued to express his wish to attend me in his place, for which he did not possess any necessary qualifications.

The weather was cloudy, with an appearance of rain; and the Indians pressed me with great earnestness to pass the day with them, and hoped to prolong my stay among them by assuring me that the winter yet lingered in the rocky mountains: but my object was to lose no time, and having given the chief some tobacco for a small quantity of meat, we embarked at four, when my young men could not conceal their chagrin at parting with their friends, for so long a period as the voyage threatened to occupy. When I had assured them that in three moons we should return to them, we proceeded on our course, West-North-West half a mile, West-South-West one mile and an half, West by North three miles, North-West by West two miles and an half, South-West by West half a mile, South-South-West a mile and an half, and South-West a mile and a half. Here I had a meridian altitude, which gave 56. 17. 44. North latitude.

The last course continued a mile and an half, South by West three quarters of a mile, South-West by South three miles and an half, and West-South-West two miles and an half. Here the land lowered on both sides, with an increase of wood, and displayed great numbers of animals. The river also widened from three to five hundred yards, and was full of islands and flats. Having continued our course three miles, we made for the shore at seven, to pass the night.

At the place from whence we proceeded this morning, a river falls in from the North; there are also several islands, and many rivulets on either side, which are too small to deserve particular notice. We perceived along the river tracks of large bears, some of which were nine inches wide, and of a proportionate length. We saw one of their dens, or winter quarters, called *watee*, in an island, which was ten feet deep, five feet high, and six feet wide; but we had not yet seen one of those animals. The Indians entertain great apprehension of this kind of bear, which is called the grisly bear, and they never venture to attack it but in a party of at least three or four. Our hunters, though they had been much higher than this part of our voyage, by land, knew nothing of the river. One of them mentioned, that having been engaged in a war expedition, his party on their return made their canoes at some distance below us. The wind was North throughout the day, and at times blew with considerable violence.

The apprehensions which I had felt respecting the young men were not altogether groundless, for the eldest of them told me that his uncle had last night addressed him in the following manner:—"My nephew, your departure makes my heart painful. The white people may be said to rob us of you. They are about to conduct you into the midst of our enemies, and you may never more return to us. Were you not with the Chief,* I know not what I should do, but he requires your attendance, and you must follow him."

* These people, as well as all the natives on this side of Lake Winipic, give the mercantile agent that distinguished appellation.

Tuesday, 14. The weather was clear, and
the air sharp, when we embarked at half
past four. Our course was South by West one
mile and an half, South-West by South half
a mile, South-West. We here found it necessary to unload, and gum the canoe, in which
operation we lost an hour; when we proceeded on the last course one mile and an
half. I now took a meridian altitude, which
gave 56. 11. 19. North latitude, and continued to proceed West-South-West two miles
and an half. Here the Bear River, which
is of a large appearance, falls in from the
East; West three miles and an half, South-
South-West one mile and an half, and South-
West four miles and an half, when we encamped upon an island about seven in the
evening.

During the early part of the day, the current was not so strong as we had generally
found it, but towards the evening it became
very rapid, and was broken by numerous
islands. We were gratified, as usual, with the
sight of animals. The land on the West side
is very irregular, but has the appearance of
being a good beaver country; indeed we saw
some of those animals in the river. Wood is
in great plenty, and several rivulets added
their streams to the main river. A goose
was the only article of provision which we

procured to day. Smoke was seen, but at a great distance before us.

Wednesday, 15. The rain prevented us from continuing our route till past six in the morning, when our course was South-West by West three quarters of a mile; at which time we passed a river on the left, West by South two miles and an half. The bank was steep, and the current strong. The last course continued one mile and an half, West-South-West two miles, where a river flowed in from the right, West by South one mile and an half, West-North-West one mile, and West by North two miles. Here the land takes the form of an high ridge, and cut our course, which was West for three miles, at right angles. We now completed the voyage of this day.

In the preceding night the water rose upwards of two inches, and had risen in this proportion since our departure. The wind, which was West-South-West, blew very hard throughout the day, and with the strength of the current, greatly impeded our progress. The river, in this part of it, is full of islands; and the land, on the South or left side, is thick with wood. Several rivulets also fall in from that quarter. At the entrance of the last river which we passed, there was a quantity of wood, which had been cut down by axes, and some by the beaver. This fall, however, was not made, in the opinion of my people, by any of the Indians with whom we were acquainted.

The land to the right is of a very irregular elevation and appearance, composed in some places of clay, and rocky cliffs, and others exhibiting stratas of red, green, and yellow colours. Some parts, indeed, offer a beautiful scenery, in some degree similar to that which we passed on the second day of our voyage, and equally enlivened with the elk and the buffalo, who were feeding in great numbers, and unmolested by the hunter. In an island which we passed, there was a large quantity of white birch, whose bark might be employed in the construction of canoes.

Thursday, 16. The weather being clear, we reimbarked at four in the morning, and proceeded West by North three miles. Here the land again appeared as if it run across our course, and a considerable river discharged itself by various streams. According to the Rocky Mountain Indian, it is called the Sinew River. This spot would be an excellent situation for a fort or factory, as there is plenty of wood, and every reason to believe that the country abounds in beaver. As for the other animals, they are in evident abundance, as in every direction the elk and the buffalo are seen in possession of the hills and the plains. Our course continued West-North-West three miles and an half, North-West one mile and an half, South-West by West two miles; (the latitude was by observation 56. 16. 54.) North-West by North half a mile, West-North-West three quarters of a mile; a small river appearing on the right, North-West one mile and an half, West by North half a mile, West by South one mile and an half, West one mile; and at seven we formed our encampment.

Mr. Mackay, and one of the young men, killed two elks, and mortally wounded a buffalo, but we only took a part of the flesh of the former. The land above the spot where we encamped, spreads into an extensive plain, and stretches on to a very high ridge, which, in some parts, presents a face of rock, but is principally covered with verdure, and varied with the poplar and white birch tree. The country is so crowded with animals as to have the appearance, in some places, of a stall-yard, from the state of the ground, and the quantity of dung which is scattered over it. The soil is black and light. We this day saw two grisly and hideous bears.

Friday, 17. It froze during the night, and the air was sharp in the morning, when we continued our course West-North-West three

miles and an half, South-West by South two
miles and an half, South-West by West
one mile and an half, West three quarters of
a mile, West-South-West one mile and a
quarter, and South-West by South one mile
and an half. At two in the afternoon the
rocky mountains appeared in sight, with
their summits covered with snow, bearing
South-West by South: they formed a very
agreeable object to every person in the
canoe, as we attained the view of them much
sooner than we expected. A small river was
seen on our right, and we continued our
progress South-West by South six miles,
when we landed at seven, which was our
usual hour of encampment.

Mr. Mackay, who was walking along the
side of the river, discharged his piece at a
buffalo, when it burst near the muzzle, but
without any mischievous consequences. On
the high grounds, which were on the opposite
side of the river, we saw a buffalo tearing up
and down with great fury, but could not
discern the cause of his impetuous motions;
my hunters conjectured that he had been
wounded with an arrow by some of the
natives. We ascended several rapids in the
course of the day, and saw one bear.

Saturday, 18. It again froze very hard
during the night, and at four in the morning

we continued our voyage, but we had not proceeded two hundred yards, before an accident happened to the canoe, which did not, however, employ more than three quarters of an hour to complete the repair. We then steered South by West one mile and three quarters, South-West by South three miles, South-West by West one mile and a quarter, West by South three quarters of a mile, South-West half a mile, West by South one mile, South by West one mile and an half, South-South-West, where there is a small run of water from the right, three miles and an half, when the canoe struck on the stump of a tree, and unfortunately where the banks were so steep that there was no place to unload, except a small spot, on which we contrived to dispose the lading in the bow, which lightened the canoe so as to raise the broken part of it above the surface of the water: by which contrivance we reached a convenient situation. It required, however, two hours to complete the repair, when the weather became dark and cloudy, with thunder, lightning, and rain; we, however, continued the last course half a mile, and at six in the evening we were compelled by the rain to land for the night.

About noon we had landed on an island where there were eight lodges of last year.

The natives had prepared bark here for five canoes, and there is a road along the hills where they had passed. Branches were cut and broken along it; and they had also stripped off the bark of the trees, to get the interior rind, which forms a part of their food.

The current was very strong through the whole of the day, and the coming up along some of the banks was rendered very dangerous, from the continual falling of large stones from the upper parts of them. This place appears to be a particular pass for animals across the river, as there are paths leading to it on both sides, every ten yards.

In the course of the day we saw a ground hog, and two cormorants. The earth also appeared in several places to have been turned up by the bears, in search of roots.

Sunday, 19. It rained very hard in the early part of the night, but the weather became clear towards the morning, when we embarked at our usual hour. As the current threatened to be very strong, Mr. Mackay, the two hunters, and myself, went on shore, in order to lighten the canoe, and ascended the hills, which are covered with cypress, and but little encumbered with underwood. We found a beaten path, and before we had walked a mile fell in with an herd of buffaloes, with their young ones; but I would not suffer the Indians to fire on them, from an apprehension that the report of their fowling pieces would alarm the natives that might be in the neighbourhood; for we were at this time so near the mountains, as to justify our expectation of seeing some of them. We, however, sent our dog after the herd, and a calf was soon secured by him. While the young men were skinning the animal, we heard two reports of fire-arms from the canoe, which we answered, as it was a signal for my return: we then heard another, and immediately hastened down the hill, with our veal, through a very close wood. There we met one of the men, who informed us that the canoe was at a small distance below, at the foot of a very strong rapid, and that as several waterfalls appeared up the river, we should be obliged to unload and carry. I accordingly hastened to the canoe, and was greatly displeased that so much time had been lost, as I had given previous directions that the river should be followed as long as it was practicable. The last Indians whom we saw had informed us that at the first mountain there was a considerable succession of rapids, cascades, and falls, which they never attempted to ascend; and where they always passed over land the

length of a day's march. My men imagined
that the carrying place was at a small distance below us, as a path appeared to ascend
an hill, where there were several lodges, of
the last year's construction. The account
which had been given me of the rapids, was
perfectly correct: though by crossing to the
other side, I must acknowledge with some
risk, in such an heavy-laden canoe, the river
appeared to me to be practicable, as far as
we could see: the traverse, therefore, was
attempted, and proved successful. We now
towed the canoe along an island, and proceeded without any considerable difficulty
till we reached the extremity of it, when the
line could be no longer employed; and in
endeavouring to clear the point of the island,
the canoe was driven with such violence on
a stony shore, as to receive considerable
injury. We now employed every exertion in
our power to repair the breach that had been
made, as well as to dry such articles of our
loading as more immediately required it: we
then transported the whole across the point,
when we reloaded, and continued our course
about three quarters of a mile. We could now
proceed no further on this side of the water,
and the traverse was rendered extremely
dangerous, not only from the strength of the
current, but by the cascades just below us,

which, if we had got among them, would have involved us and the canoe in one common destruction. We had no other alternative than to return by the same course we came, or to hazard the traverse, the river on this side being bounded by a range of steep, over-hanging rocks, beneath which the current was driven on with resistless impetuosity from the cascades. Here are several islands of solid rock, covered with a small portion of verdure, which have been worn away by the constant force of the current, and occasionally, as I presume, of ice, at the water's edge, so as to be reduced in that part to one fourth the extent of the upper surface; presenting, as it were, so many large tables, each of which was supported by a pedestal of a more circumscribed projection. They are very elevated for such a situation, and afford an asylum for geese, which were at this time breeding on them. By crossing from one to the other of these islands, we came at length to the main traverse, on which we ventured, and were successful in our passage. Mr. Mackay, and the Indians, who observed our manœuvres from the top of a rock, were in continual alarm for our safety, with which their own, indeed, may be said to have been nearly connected: however, the dangers that we encountered were very much augmented by the heavy loading of the canoe.

When we had effected our passage, the current on the West side was almost equally violent with that from whence we had just escaped, but the craggy bank being somewhat lower, we were enabled, with a line of sixty fathoms, to tow the canoe, till we came to the foot of the most rapid cascade we had hitherto seen. Here we unloaded, and carried every thing over a rocky point of an hundred and twenty paces. When the canoe was reloaded, I, with those of my people who were not immediately employed, ascended the bank, which was there, and indeed, as far as we could see it, composed of clay, stone, and a yellow gravel. My present situation was so elevated, that the men, who were coming up a strong point could not hear me, though I called to them with the utmost strength of my voice, to lighten the canoe of part of its lading. And here I could not but reflect, with infinite anxiety, on the hazard of my enterprize: one false step of those who were attached to the line, or the breaking of the line itself, would have at once consigned the canoe, and every thing it contained, to instant destruction: it, however, ascended the rapid in perfect security, but new dangers immediately presented themselves, for stones, both small and great, were continually rolling from the bank, so as to render the situation of those who were dragging the canoe beneath it extremely perilous; besides, they were at every step in danger, from the steepness of the ground, of falling into the water: nor was my solicitude diminished by my being necessarily removed at times from the sight of them.

In our passage though the woods, we came to an inclosure, which had been formed by the natives for the purpose of setting snares for the elk, and of which we could not discover the extent. After we had travelled for some hours through the forest, which consisted of the spruce, birch, and the largest poplars I had ever seen, we sunk down upon the river, where the bank is low, and near the foot of a mountain; between which, and an high ridge, the river flows in a channel of about one hundred yards broad; though, at a small distance below, it rushes on between perpendicular rocks, where it is not much more than half that breadth. Here I remained, in great anxiety, expecting the arrival of the canoe, and after some time I sent Mr. Mackay with one of the Indians down the river in search of it, and with the other I went up it to examine what we might expect in that quarter. In about a mile and a half I came to a part where the river washes the feet of lofty precipices, and presented, in the form of rapids and cascades, a succession of difficulties to our navigation. As the canoe did not come in sight we returned, and from the place where I had separated with Mr. Mackay, we saw the men carrying it over a small rocky point. We met them at the entrance of the narrow channel already mentioned; their difficulties had been great indeed, and the canoe had been broken, but they had persevered with success, and having passed the carrying-place, we proceeded with the line as far as I had already been, when we crossed over and encamped on the opposite beach; but there was no wood on this side of the water, as the adjacent country had been entirely overrun by fire. We saw several elks feeding on the edge of the opposite precipice, which was upwards of three hundred feet in height.

Our course to-day was about South-South-West two miles and an half, South-West half a mile, South-West by South one mile and an half, South by West half a mile, South-West half a mile, and West one mile and an half. There was a shower of hail, and some rain from flying clouds. I now dispatched a man with an Indian to visit the rapids above, when the latter soon left him to pursue a beaver, which was seen in the shallow water on the inside of a stony island; and though Mr. Mackay, and the other Indian joined him, the animal at length escaped from their pursuit. Several others were seen in the course of the day, which I by no means expected, as the banks are almost every where so much elevated above the channel of the river. Just as the obscurity of the night drew on, the man returned with an account that it would be impracticable to pass several points, as well as the super-impending promontories.

Monday, 20. The weather was clear with a sharp air, and we renewed our voyage at a quarter past four, on a course South-West by West three quarters of a mile. We now, with infinite difficulty passed along the foot of a rock, which, fortunately, was not an hard stone, so that we were enabled to cut steps in it for the distance of twenty feet; from which, at the hazard of my life, I leaped on a small rock below, where I received those who followed me on my shoulders. In this manner four of us passed and dragged up the canoe, in which attempt we broke her. Very luckily, a dry tree had fallen from the rock above us, without which we could not have made a fire, as no wood was to be procured within a mile of the place. When the canoe

was repaired, we continued towing it along
the rocks to the next point, when we embarked, as we could not at present make any
further use of the line, but got along the
rocks of a round high island of stone, till we
came to a small sandy bay. As we had already damaged the canoe, and had every
reason to think that she soon would risk
much greater injury, it became necessary
for us to supply ourselves with bark, as our
provision of that material article was almost
exhausted; two men were accordingly sent
to procure it, who soon returned with the
necessary store.

Mr. Mackay, and the Indians who had
been on shore, since we broke the canoe,
were prevented from coming to us by the
rugged and impassable state of the ground.
We, therefore, again resumed our course
with the assistance of poles, with which we
pushed onwards till we came beneath a precipice, where we could not find any bottom;
so that we were again obliged to have re-
course to the line, the management of which
was rendered not only difficult but dangerous, as the men employed in towing were
under the necessity of passing on the outside
of trees that grew on the edge of the precipice. We, however, surmounted this difficulty, as we had done many others, and the

people who had been walking over land now joined us. They also had met with their obstacles in passing the mountain.

It now became necessary for us to make a traverse, where the water was so rapid, that some of the people stripped themselves to their shirts that they might be the better prepared for swimming, in case any accident happened to the canoe, which they seriously apprehended; but we succeeded in our attempt without any other inconvenience, except that of taking in water. We now came to a cascade, when it was thought necessary to take out part of the lading. At noon we stopped to take an altitude, opposite to a small river that flowed in from the left: while I was thus engaged, the men went on shore to fasten the canoe, but as the current was not very strong, they had been negligent in performing this office; it proved, however, sufficiently powerful to sheer her off, and if it had not happened that one of the men, from absolute fatigue had remained and held the end of the line, we should have been deprived of every means of prosecuting our voyage, as well as of present subsistence. But notwithstanding the state of my mind on such an alarming circumstance, and an intervening cloud that interrupted me, the altitude which I took has been since proved to be tolerably correct, and gave 56. North latitude. Our last course was South-South-West two miles and a quarter.

We now continued our toilsome and perilous progress with the line West by North, and as we proceeded the rapidity of the current increased, so that in the distance of two miles we were obliged to unload four times, and carry every thing but the canoe: indeed, in many places, it was with the utmost difficulty that we could prevent her from being dashed to pieces against the rocks by the violence of the eddies. At five we had proceeded to where the river was one continued rapid. Here we again took every thing out of the canoe, in order to tow her up with the line, though the rocks were so shelving as greatly to increase the toil and hazard of that operation. At length, however, the agitation of the water was so great, that a wave striking on the bow of the canoe broke the line, and filled us with inexpressible dismay, as it appeared impossible that the vessel could escape from being dashed to pieces, and those who were in her from perishing. Another wave, however, more propitious than the former, drove her out of the tumbling water, so that the men were enabled to bring her ashore, and though she had been carried over rocks by these swells which left them naked a moment after, the canoe had received no material injury. The men were, however, in such a state from their late alarm, that it would not only have been unavailing but imprudent to have proposed any further progress at present, particularly as the river above us, as far as we could see, was one white sheet of foaming water.

Chapter 4

May, 1793.

THAT the discouragements, difficulties, and dangers, which had hitherto attended the progress of our enterprize, should have excited a wish in several of those who were engaged in it to discontinue the pursuit, might be naturally expected; and indeed it began to be muttered on all sides that there was no alternative but to return.

Instead of paying any attention to these murmurs, I desired those who had uttered

them to exert themselves in gaining an ascent of the hill, and encamp there for the
night. In the mean time I set off with one
of the Indians, and though I continued my
examination of the river almost as long as
there was any light to assist me, I could see
no end of the rapids and cascades: I was,
therefore, perfectly satisfied, that it would
be impracticable to proceed any further by
water. We returned from this reconnoitring
excursion very much fatigued, with our shoes
worn out and wounded feet; when I found
that, by felling trees on the declivity of
the first hill, my people had contrived to
ascend it.

From the place where I had taken the
altitude at noon, to the place where we made
our landing, the river is not more than fifty
yards wide, and flows between stupendous
rocks, from whence huge fragments sometimes tumble down, and falling from such an
height, dash into small stones, with sharp
points, and form the beach between the
rocky projections. Along the face of some of
these precipices, there appears a stratum of
a bituminous substance which resembles
coal; though while some of the pieces of it
appeared to be excellent fuel, others resisted,
for a considerable time, the action of fire,
and did not emit the least flame. The whole

of this day's course would have been altogether impracticable, if the water had been
higher, which must be the case at certain
seasons. We saw also several encampments
of the Knisteneaux along the river, which
must have been formed by them on their war
excursions: a decided proof of the savage,
bloody-thirsty disposition of that people;
as nothing less than such a spirit could
impel them to encounter the difficulties
of this almost inaccessible country, whose
natives are equally unoffending and de-
fenceless.

Mr. Mackay informed me, that in passing
over the mountains, he observed several
chasms in the earth that emitted heat and
smoke, which diffused a strong sulphureous
stench. I should certainly have visited this
phænomenon, if I had been sufficiently qualified as a naturalist, to have offered scientific
conjectures or observations thereon.

Tuesday, 21. It rained in the morning, and
did not cease till about eight, and as the
men had been very fatigued and disheart-
ened, I suffered them to continue their rest
till that hour. Such was the state of the
river, as I have already observed, that no
alternative was left us; nor did any means of
proceeding present themselves to us, but the
passage of the mountain over which we were

to carry the canoe as well as the baggage. As this was a very alarming enterprize, I dispatched Mr. Mackay with three men and the two Indians to proceed in a straight course from the top of the mountain, and to keep the line of the river till they should find it navigable. If it should be their opinion, that there was no practicable passage in that direction, two of them were instructed to return in order to make their report; while the others were to go in search of the Indian carrying-place. While they were engaged in this excursion, the people who remained with me were employed in gumming the canoe, and making handles for the axes. At noon I got an altitude, which made our latitude 56. o. 8. At three o'clock had time, when my watch was slow 1. 31. 32. apparent time.

At sun-set, Mr. Mackay returned with one of the men, and in about two hours was followed by the others. They had penetrated thick woods, ascended hills and sunk into vallies, till they got beyond the rapids, which, according to their calculation, was a distance of three leagues. The two parties returned by different routes, but they both agreed, that with all its difficulties, and they were of a very alarming nature, the outward course was that which must be preferred. Unpromising, however, as the account of

their expedition appeared, it did not sink
them into a state of discouragement; and a
kettle of wild rice, sweetened with sugar,
which had been prepared for their return,
with their usual regale of rum, soon renewed
that courage which disdained all obstacles
that threatened our progress: and they went
to rest, with a full determination to surmount them on the morrow. I sat up, in
the hope of getting an observation of Jupiter
and his first satellite, but the cloudy weather
prevented my obtaining it.

Wednesday, 22. At break of day we entered
on the extraordinary journey which was to
occupy the remaining part of it. The men
began, without delay, to cut a road up the
mountain, and as the trees were but of small
growth, I ordered them to fell those which
they found convenient, in such a manner,
that they might fall parallel with the road,
but, at the same time, not separate them
entirely from the stumps, so that they might
form a kind of railing on either side. The
baggage was now brought from the water-
side to our encampment. This was likewise
from the steep shelving of the rocks, a very
perilous undertaking, as one false step of
any of the people employed in it, would have
been instantly followed by falling headlong
into the water. When this important object

was attained, the whole of the party proceeded with no small degree of apprehension, to fetch the canoe, which, in a short time, was also brought to the encampment; and, as soon as we had recovered from our fatigue, we advanced with it up the mountain, having the line doubled and fastened successively as we went on to the stumps; while a man at the end of it, hauled it round a tree, holding it on and shifting it as we proceeded; so that we may be said, with strict truth, to have warped the canoe up the mountain: indeed by a general and most laborious exertion, we got every thing to the summit by two in the afternoon. At noon, the latitude was 56. 0. 47 North. At five, I sent the men to cut the road onwards, which they effected for about a mile, when they returned.

The weather was cloudy at intervals, with showers and thunder. At about ten, I observed an emersion of Jupiter's second satellite; time by the achrometer 8. 32. 20. by which I found the longitude to be 120. 29. 30. West from Greenwich.

Thursday, 23. The weather was clear at four this morning, when the men began to carry. I joined Mr. Mackay, and the two Indians in the labour of cutting a road. The ground continued rising gently till noon, when it began to decline; but though on such an elevated situation, we could see but little, as mountains of a still higher elevation and covered with snow,.were seen far above us in every direction. In the afternoon the ground became very uneven; hills and deep defiles alternately presented themselves to us. Our progress, however, exceeded my expectation, and it was not till four in the afternoon that the carriers overtook us. At five, in a state of fatigue that may be more readily conceived than expressed, we encamped near a rivulet or spring that issued from beneath a large mass of ice and snow.

Our toilsome journey of this day I compute at about three miles; along the first of which the land is covered with plenty of wood, consisting of large trees, encumbered with little underwood, through which it was by no means difficult to open a road, by following a well-beaten elk path: for the two succeeding miles we found the country overspread with the trunks of trees, laid low by fire some years ago; among which large copses had sprung up of a close growth, and intermixed with briars, so as to render the passage through them painful and tedious. The soil in the woods is light and of a dusky colour; that in the burned country is a mixture of sand and clay with small stones. The trees are spruce, red-pine, cypress, poplar, white birch, willow, alder, arrow-wood, red-wood, liard, service-tree, bois-picant, etc. I never saw any of the last kind before. It rises to about nine feet in height, grows in joints without branches, and is tufted at the extremity. The stem is of an equal size from the bottom to the top, and does not exceed an inch in diameter; it is covered with small prickles, which caught our trowsers, and working through them, sometimes found their way to the flesh. The shrubs are, the gooseberry, the currant, and several kinds of briars.

Friday, 24. We continued our very laborious journey, which led us down some steep hills, and through a wood of tall pines. After much toil and trouble in bearing the canoe through the difficult passages which we encountered, at four in the afternoon we arrived at the river, some hundred yards above the rapids or falls, with all our baggage. I compute the distance of this day's progress to be about four miles; indeed I should have measured the whole of the way, if I had not been obliged to engage personally in the labour of making the road. But after all, the Indian carrying way, whatever may be its length, and I think it cannot exceed ten miles, will always be found more safe and expeditious than the passage which our toil and perseverance formed and surmounted.

Those of my people who visited this place on the 21st, were of opinion that the water had risen very much since that time. About two hundred yards below us the stream rushed with an astonishing but silent velocity, between perpendicular rocks, which are not more than thirty-five yards asunder: when the water is high, it runs over those rocks, in a channel three times that breadth, where it is bounded by far more elevated precipices. In the former are deep round holes, some of which are full of water, while others are empty, in whose bottom are small round stones, as smooth as marble. Some of these natural cylinders would contain two hundred gallons. At a small distance below the first of these rocks, the channel widens in a kind of zig-zag progression; and it was really awful to behold with what infinite force the water drives against the rocks on one side, and with what impetuous strength it is repelled to the other: it then falls back, as it were, into a more strait but rugged passage, over which it is tossed in high, foaming, half-formed billows, as far as the eye could follow it.

The young men informed me that this was the place where their relations had told me that I should meet with a fall equal to that of Niagara: to exculpate them, however, from their apparent misinformation, they declared that their friends were not accustomed to utter falsehoods, and that the fall had probably been destroyed by the force of the water. It is, however, very evident that those people had not been here, or did not adhere to the truth. By the number of trees which appeared to have been felled with axes, we discovered that the Knisteneaux, or some tribes who are known to employ that instrument, had passed this way. We passed through a snare enclosure, but saw no animals, though the country was very much intersected by their tracks.

Saturday, 25. It rained throughout the night, and till twelve this day; while the business of preparing great and small poles, and putting the canoe in order, etc. caused us to remain here till five in the afternoon. I now attached a knife, with a steel, flint, beads, and other trifling articles to a pole, which I erected, and left as a token of amity to the natives. When I was making this arrangement, one of my attendants, whom I have already described under the title of the Cancre, added to my assortment a small round piece of green wood, chewed at one end in the form of a brush, which the Indians

use to pick the marrow out of bones. This he
informed me was an emblem of a country
abounding in animals. The water had risen
during our stay here one foot and an half
perpendicular height.

We now embarked, and our course was
North-West one mile and three quarters.
There were mountains on all sides of us,
which were covered with snow: one in particular, on the South side of the river, rose to a
great height. We continued to proceed West
three quarters of a mile, North-West one
mile, and West-South-West a quarter of a
mile, when we encamped for the night. The
Cancre killed a small elk.

Sunday, 26. The weather was clear and
sharp, and between three and four in the
morning we renewed our voyage, our first
course being West by South three miles and
an half, when the men complained of the
cold in their fingers, as they were obliged to
push on the canoe with the poles. Here a
small river flowed in from the North. We now
continued to steer West-South-West a quarter of a mile, West-North-West a mile and
an half, and West two miles, when we found
ourselves on a parallel with a chain of mountains on both sides the river, running South
and North. The river, both yesterday and
the early part of to-day, was from four to

eight hundred yards wide, and full of islands, but was at this time diminished to about two hundred yards broad, and free from islands, with a smooth but strong current. Our next course was South-West two miles, when we encountered a rapid, and saw an encampment of the Knisteneaux. We now proceeded North-West by West one mile, among islands, South-West by West three quarters of a mile, South-South-East one mile, veered to South-West through islands three miles and an half, and South by East half a mile. Here a river poured in on the left, which was the most considerable that we had seen since we had passed the mountain. At seven in the evening we landed and encamped.

Though the sun had shone upon us throughout the day, the air was so cold that the men, though actively employed, could not resist it without the aid of their blanket coats. This circumstance might in some degree be expected from the surrounding mountains, which were covered with ice and snow; but as they are not so high as to produce the extreme cold which we suffered, it must be more particularly attributed to the high situation of the country itself, rather than to the local elevation of the mountains, the greatest height of which does not exceed fifteen hundred feet; though in general they do not rise to half that altitude. But, as I had not been able to take an exact measurement, I do not presume upon the accuracy of my conjecture. Towards the bottom of these heights, which were clear of snow, the trees were putting forth their leaves, while those in their middle region still retained all the characteristics of winter, and on their upper parts there was little or no wood.

Monday, 27.* The weather was clear, and we continued our voyage at the usual hour, when we successively found several rapids and points to impede our progress. At noon our latitude was 56. 5. 54. North. The Indians killed a stag; and one of the men who went to fetch it was very much endangered by the rolling down of a large stone from the heights above him.

Tuesday, 28. The day was very cloudy. The mountains on both sides of the river seemed to have sunk, in their elevation, during the voyage of yesterday. To-day they

*From this day, to the 4th of June the courses of my voyage are omitted, as I lost the book that contained them. I was in the habit of sometimes indulging myself with a short doze in the canoe, and I imagine that the branches of the trees brushed my book from me, when I was in such a situation, which renders the account of these few days less distinct than usual.

resumed their former altitude, and run so close on either side of the channel, that all view was excluded of every thing but themselves. This part of the current was not broken by islands; but in the afternoon we approached some cascades, which obliged us to carry our canoe and its lading for several hundred yards. Here we observed an encampment of the natives, though some time had elapsed since it had been inhabited. The greater part of the day was divided between heavy showers and small rain; and we took our station on the shore about six in the evening, about three miles above the last rapid.

Wednesday, 29. The rain was so violent throughout the whole of this day, that we did not venture to proceed. As we had almost expended the contents of a rum-keg, and this being a day which allowed of no active employment, I amused myself with the experiment of enclosing a letter in it, and dispatching it down the stream, to take its fate. I accordingly introduced a written account of all our hardships, etc. carefully enclosed in bark, into the small barrel by the bung-hole, which being carefully secured, I consigned this epistolatory cargo to the mercy of the current.

Thursday, 30. We were alarmed this morning at break of day, by the continual barking of our dog, who never ceased from running backwards and forwards in the rear of our situation: when, however, the day advanced, we discovered the cause of our alarm to proceed from a wolf, who was parading a ridge a few yards behind us, and had been most probably allured by the scent of our small portion of fresh meat. The weather was cloudy, but it did not prevent us from renewing our progress at a very early hour. A considerable river appeared from the left, and we continued our course till seven in the evening, when we landed at night where there was an Indian encampment.

Friday, 31. The morning was clear and cold, and the current very powerful. On crossing the mouth of a river that flowed in from the right of us, we were very much endangered; indeed all the rivers which I have lately seen, appear to overflow their natural limits, as it may be supposed, from the melting of the mountain snow. The water is almost white, the bed of the river being of lime-stone. The mountains are one solid mass of the same materials, but without the least shade of trees, or decoration of foliage. At nine the men were so cold that we landed, in order to kindle a fire, which was considered as a very uncommon circumstance at this season; a small quantity of rum, however, served as an adequate substitute;

and the current being so smooth as to admit of the use of paddles, I encouraged them to proceed without any further delay. In a short time an extensive view opened upon us, displaying a beautiful sheet of water, that was heightened by the calmness of the weather, and a splendid sun. Here the mountains, which were covered with wood, opened on either side, so that we entertained the hope of soon leaving them behind us. When we had got to the termination of this prospect, the river was barred with rocks, forming cascades and small islands. To proceed onwards, we were under the necessity of clearing a narrow passage of the drift wood, on the left shore. Here the view convinced us that our late hopes were without foundation, as there appeared a ridge or chain of mountains, running South and North as far as the eye could reach.

On advancing two or three miles, we arrived at the fork,[1] one branch running about West-North-West, and the other South-South-East. If I had been governed by my own judgment, I should have taken the former, as it appeared to me to be the most likely to bring us nearest to the part where I wished to fall on the Pacific Ocean, but the

[1] The junction of the Finlay and the Parsnip rivers; the latter, the party was now to ascend.—Ed.

old man whom I have already mentioned as
having been frequently on war expeditions
in this country, had warned me not, on any
account, to follow it, as it was soon lost in
various branches among the mountains, and
that there was no great river that ran in any
direction near it; but by following the latter,
he said, we should arrive at a carrying-place
to another large river, that did not exceed a
day's march, where the inhabitants build
houses, and live upon islands. There was so
much apparent truth in the old man's narrative, that I determined to be governed by
it; for I did not entertain the least doubt, if
I could get into the other river, that I should
reach the ocean.

I accordingly ordered my steersman to
proceed at once to the East branch,[2] which
appeared to be more rapid than the other,
though it did not possess an equal breadth.
These circumstances disposed my men and
Indians, the latter in particular being very
tired of the voyage, to express their wishes
that I should take the Western branch,
especially when they perceived the difficulty
of stemming the current, in the direction on
which I had determined. Indeed the rush of
water was so powerful, that we were the
greatest part of the afternoon in getting two

[2] That is, the northward-flowing Parsnip River.—ED.

or three miles—a very tardy and mortifying progress, and which, with the voyage, was openly execrated by many of those who were engaged in it: and the inexpressible toil these people had endured, as well as the dangers they had encountered, required some degree of consideration; I therefore employed those arguments which were the best calculated to calm their immediate discontents, as well as to encourage their future hopes, though, at the same time I delivered my sentiments in such a manner as to convince them that I was determined to proceed.

On the 1st of June we embarked at sunrise, and towards noon the current began to slacken; we then put to shore, in order to gum the canoe, when a meridian altitude gave me 55. 42. 16. North latitude. We then continued our course, and towards the evening the current began to recover its former strength. Mr. Mackay and the Indians had already disembarked, to walk and lighten the boat. At sun-set we encamped on a point, being the first dry land which had been found on this side the river, that was fit for our purpose, since our people went on shore. In the morning we passed a large rapid river, that flowed in from the right.

In no part of the North-West did I see so much beaver-work, within an equal distance,

as in the course of this day. In some places
they had cut down several acres of large
poplars; and we saw also a great number of
these active and sagacious animals. The time
which these wonderful creatures allot for
their labours, whether in erecting their curious habitations, or providing food, is the
whole of the interval between the setting and
the rising sun.

Towards the dusky part of the evening we
heard several discharges from the fowling
pieces of our people, which we answered, to
inform them of our situation; and some time
after it was dark, they arrived in an equal
state of fatigue and alarm: they were also
obliged to swim across a channel in order
to get to us, as we were situated on an island,
though we were ignorant of the circumstance, till they came to inform us. One of the
Indians was positive that he heard the discharge of fire-arms above our encampment;
and on comparing the number of our discharges with theirs, there appeared to be
some foundation for his alarm, as we imagined
that we had heard two reports more than
they acknowledged; and, in their turn, they
declared that they had heard twice the number of those which we knew had proceeded
from us. The Indians were therefore certain,
that the Knisteneaux must be in our vicinity,

on a war expedition, and consequently, if they were numerous, we should have had no reason to expect the least mercy from them in this distant country. Though I did not believe that circumstance, or that any of the natives could be in possession of fire-arms, I thought it right, at all events, we should be prepared. Our fusees were, therefore, primed and loaded, and having extinguished our fire, each of us took his station at the foot of a tree, where we passed an uneasy and restless night.

The succeeding morning being clear and pleasant, we proceeded at an early hour against a rapid current, intersected by islands. About eight we passed two large trees, whose roots having been undermined by the current, had recently fallen into the river; and, in my opinion, the crash of their fall had occasioned the noise which caused our late alarm. In this manner the water ravages the islands in these rivers, and by driving down great quantities of wood, forms the foundations of others. The men were so oppressed with fatigue, that it was necessary they should encamp at six in the afternoon. We, therefore, landed on a sandy island, which is a very uncommon object, as the greater part of the islands consist of a bottom of round stones and gravel, covered from three to ten feet with mud and old drift-wood. Beaver-work was as frequently seen as on the preceding day.

On the 3d of June we renewed our voyage with the rising sun. At noon I obtained a meridian altitude, which gave 55. 22. 3. North latitude. I also took time, and the watch was slow 1. 30. 14. apparent time. According to my calculation, this place is about twenty-five miles South-East of the fork.*

* I shall now proceed with my usual regularity, which, as I have already mentioned, has been, for some days, suspended, from the loss of my book of observation.

Chapter 5

Continue our voyage. Heavy fog. The water rises. Succession of courses. Progressive account of this branch. Leave the canoe to proceed, and ascend an hill to reconnoitre. Climb a tree to extend my view of the country. Return to the river. The canoe not arrived. Go in search of it. Extreme heat, musquitoes, &c. Increasing anxiety respecting the canoe. It at length appears. Violent storm. Circumstances of our progress. Forced to haul the canoe up the stream by the branches of trees. Succession of courses. Wild parsnips along the river. Expect to meet with natives. Courses continued. Fall in with some natives. Our intercourse with them. Account of their dress, arms, utensils, and manners, &c. New discouragements and difficulties present themselves.

June, 1793.

TUESDAY, 4. We embarked this morning at four in a very heavy fog. The water had been continually rising, and, in many places, overflowed its banks. The current also was so strong, that our progress was very tedious, and required the most laborious exertions. Our course was this day, South-South-East one mile, South-South-West half a mile, South-East three quarters of a mile, North-East by East three quarters of a mile, South-East half a mile, South-East by South one mile, South-South-East one mile three quarters, South-East by South half a mile, East by South a quarter of a mile, South-East three quarters of a mile, North-East by East half a mile, East by North a quarter of a mile, South-East half a mile, South-East by South a quarter of a mile, South-East by East half a mile, North-East by East half a mile, North-North-East three quarters of a mile, to South by East one mile and an half. We could not find a place fit for an encampment, till nine at night, when we landed on a bank of gravel, of which little more appeared above water than the spot we occupied.

Wednesday, *5*. This morning we found our canoe and baggage in the water, which had continued rising during the night. We then gummed the canoe, as we arrived at too late an hour to perform that operation on the preceding evening. This necessary business being completed, we traversed to the North shore, where I disembarked with Mr. Mackay, and the hunters, in order to ascend an adjacent mountain, with the hope of obtaining a view of the interior part of the country. I directed my people to proceed with all possible diligence, and that, if they met with any accident, or found my return necessary, they should fire two guns. They also understood, that when they should hear the same signal from me, they were to answer, and wait for me, if I were behind them.

When we had ascended to the summit of the hill, we found that it extended onwards in an even, level country; so that, encumbered as we were, with the thick wood, no distant view could be obtained; I therefore climbed a very lofty tree, from whose top I discerned on the right a ridge of mountains covered with snow, bearing about North-West; from thence another ridge of high land, whereon no snow was visible, stretched towards the South; between which and the snowy hills on the East side, there appeared to be an opening, which we determined to be the course of the river.

Having obtained all the satisfaction that the nature of the place would admit, we proceeded forward to overtake the canoe, and after a warm walk came down upon the river, when we discharged our pieces twice, but received no answering signal. I was of opinion, that the canoe was before us, while the Indians entertained an opposite notion. I, however, crossed another point of land, and came again to the waterside about ten. Here we had a long view of the river, which circumstance excited in my mind, some doubts of my former sentiments. We repeated our signals, but without any return;

and as every moment now increased my anxiety, I left Mr. Mackay and one of the Indians at this spot to make a large fire, and send branches adrift down the current as notices of our situation, if the canoe was behind us; and proceeded with the other Indian across a very long point, where the river makes a considerable bend, in order that I might be satisfied if the canoe was a-head. Having been accustomed, for the last fortnight to very cold weather, I found the heat of this day almost insupportable, as our way lay over a dry sand, which was relieved by no shade, but such as a few scattered cypresses could afford us. About twelve we arrived once more at the river, and the discharge of our pieces was as unsuccessful as it had hitherto been. The water rushed before us with uncommon velocity; and we also tried the experiment of sending fresh branches down it. To add to the disagreeableness of our situation, the gnats and musquitoes appeared in swarms to torment us. When we returned to our companions, we found that they had not been contented with remaining in the position where I had left them, but had been three or four miles down the river, but were come back to their station, without having made any discovery of the people on the water.

Various very unpleasing conjectures at
once perplexed and distressed us: the Indians, who are inclined to magnify evils of
any and every kind, had at once consigned
the canoe and every one on board it to the
bottom; and were already settling a plan to
return upon a raft, as well as calculating the
number of nights that would be required to
reach their home. As for myself, it will be
easily believed, that my mind was in a state
of extreme agitation; and the imprudence of
my conduct in leaving the people, in such a
situation of danger and toilsome exertion,
added a very painful mortification to the
severe apprehensions I already suffered: it
was an act of indiscretion which might have
put an end to the voyage that I had so much
at heart, and compelled me at length to submit to the scheme which my hunters had already formed for our return.

At half past six in the evening, Mr.
Mackay and the Cancre set off to proceed
down the river, as far as they could before
the night came on, and to continue their
journey in the morning to the place where we
had encamped the preceding evening. I also
proposed to make my excursion upwards;
and, if we both failed of success in meeting
the canoe, it was agreed that we should return to the place where we now separated.

In this situation we had wherewithal to drink in plenty, but with solid food we were totally unprovided. We had not seen even a partridge throughout the day, and the tracks of rein-deer that we had discovered, were of an old date. We were, however, preparing to make a bed of the branches of trees, where we should have had no other canopy than that afforded us by the heavens, when we heard a shot, and soon after another, which was the notice agreed upon, if Mr. Mackay and the Indian should see the canoe: that fortunate circumstance was also confirmed by a return of the signal from the people. I was, however, so fatigued from the heat and exercise of the day, as well as incommoded from drinking so much cold water, that I did not wish to remove till the following morning; but the Indian made such bitter complaints of the cold and hunger which he suffered, that I complied with his solicitations to depart; and it was almost dark when we reached the canoe, barefooted, and drenched with rain. But these inconveniences affected me very little, when I saw myself once more surrounded with my people. They informed me, that the canoe had been broken; and that they had this day experienced much greater toil and hardships than on any former occasion. I thought it prudent to affect a belief of every representation that they made, and even to comfort each of them with a consolatory dram: for, however difficult the passage might have been, it was too short to have occupied the whole day, if they had not relaxed in their exertions. The rain was accompanied with thunder and lightning.

It appeared from the various encampments which we had seen, and from several paddles we had found, that the natives frequent this part of the country at the latter end of the summer and the fall. The course to day was nearly East-South-East two miles and an half, South by West one mile, South-South-East one mile and an half, East two miles, and South-East by South one mile.

Thursday, 6. At half past four this morning we continued our voyage, our courses being South-East by South one mile, East by South three quarters of a mile, South-East by East two miles. The whole of this distance we proceeded by hauling the canoe from branch to branch. The current was so strong, that it was impossible to stem it with the paddles; the depth was too great to receive any assistance from the poles, and the bank of the river was so closely lined with willows and other trees, that it was impossible to employ the line. As it was past twelve before we could find a place that would allow of our landing, I could not get a meridian altitude. We occupied the rest of the day in repairing the canoe, drying our clothes, and making paddles and poles to replace those which had been broken or lost.

Friday, 7. The morning was clear and calm; and since we had been at this station the water had risen two inches; so that the current became still stronger; and its velocity had already been so great as to justify our despair in getting up it, if we had not been so long accustomed to surmount it. I last night observed an emersion of Jupiter's first satellite, but inadvertently went to bed, without committing the exact time to writing: if my memory is correct, it was 8. 18. 10. by the time-piece. The canoe, which had been little better than a wreck, being now repaired, we proceeded East two miles and a quarter, South-South-East half a mile, South-East a quarter of a mile, when we landed to take an altitude for time. We continued our route at South-East by East three quarters of a mile, and landed again to determine the latitude, which is 55. 2. 51. To this I add, 2. 45. Southing, which will make the place of taking altitude for time 55. 5. 36. with which I find that my time-piece was slow 1. 32. 23. apparent time; and made the longitude obtained 122. 35. 50. West of Greenwich.

From this place we proceeded East by South four miles and an half, East-South-East one mile and an half, in which space there falls in a small river from the East; East half a mile, South-East a mile and an half, East a quarter of a mile, and encamped at seven o'clock. Mr. Mackay and the hunters walked the greatest part of the day, and in the course of their excursion killed a porcupine.* Here we found the bed of a very large bear quite fresh. During the day several Indian encampments were seen, which were of a late erection. The current had also lost some of its impetuosity during the greater part of the day.

Saturday, 8. It rained and thundered through the night, and at four in the morning we again encountered the current. Our course was East a quarter of a mile, round to South by East along a very high white sandy bank on the East shore, three quarters of a mile, South-South-East a quarter of a mile, South-South-West a quarter of a mile,

---

*We had been obliged to indulge our hunters with sitting idle in the canoe, lest their being compelled to share in the labour of navigating it should disgust and drive them from us. We, therefore, employed them as much as possible on shore, as well to procure provisions as to lighten the canoe.

105

South-South-East one mile and a quarter, South-East two miles, with a slack current; South-East by East two miles and a quarter, East a quarter of a mile, South-South-East a quarter of a mile, South-East by South four miles and an half, South-East one mile and an half, South-South-West half a mile, East-North-East half a mile, East-South-East a quarter of a mile, South-East by South one mile, South-East by East half a mile, East by South three quarters of a mile, when the mountains were in full view in this direction, and Eastward. For the three last days we could only see them at short intervals and long distances; but till then, they were continually in sight on either side, from our entrance into the fork. Those to the left were at no great distance from us.

For the last two days we had been anxiously looking out for the carrying-place, but could not discover it, and our only hope was in such information as we should be able to procure from the natives. All that remained for us to do, was to push forwards till the river should be no longer navigable: it had now, indeed, overflowed its banks, so that it was eight at night before we could discover a place to encamp. Having found plenty of wild parsnips, we gathered the tops, and boiled them with pemmican for our supper.

Sunday, 9. The rain of this morning terminated in an heavy mist at half past five, when we embarked and steered South-East one mile and an half, when it veered North-North-East half a mile, South-East three quarters of a mile, East by South three quarters of a mile, East-South-East a quarter of a mile, South-South-East a quarter of a mile, South-East by East one mile, North-East by East half a mile, South-East by East half a mile, South-East by South three quarters of a mile, South-East three quarters of a mile, East by South half a mile, South-East by East half a mile, East-North-East three quarters of a mile, when it veered to South-South-East half a mile, then back to East (when a blue mountain, clear of snow, appeared a-head) one mile and an half; North-East by East half a mile, East by North one mile, when it veered to South-East half a mile, then on to North-West three quarters of a mile, and back to North-East by East half a mile, South by West a quarter of a mile, North-East by East to North-North-East half a mile, South-South-East a quarter of a mile, and East by North half a mile: here we perceived a smell of fire; and in a short time heard people in the woods, as if in a state of great confusion, which was occasioned, as we afterwards

understood, by their discovery of us. At the
same time this unexpected circumstance
produced some little discomposure among
ourselves, as our arms were not in a state of
preparation, and we were as yet unable to
ascertain the number of the party. I considered, that if there were but few it would
be needless to pursue them, as it would not
be probable that we should overtake them
in these thick woods; and if they were numerous, it would be an act of great imprudence to make the attempt, at least during
their present alarm. I therefore ordered my
people to strike off to the opposite side, that
we might see if any of them had sufficient
courage to remain; but, before we were half
over the river, which, in this part, is not
more than an hundred yards wide, two men
appeared on a rising ground over against us,
brandishing their spears, displaying their
bows and arrows, and accompanying their
hostile gestures with loud vociferations. My
interpreter did not hesitate to assure them,
that they might dispel their apprehensions,
as we were white people, who meditated no
injury, but were, on the contrary, desirous of
demonstrating every mark of kindness and
friendship. They did not, however, seem
disposed to confide in our declarations, and
actually threatened, if we came over before

they were more fully satisfied of our peaceable intentions, that they would discharge their arrows at us. This was a decided kind of conduct which I did not expect; at the same time I readily complied with their proposition, and after some time had passed in hearing and answering their questions, they consented to our landing, though not without betraying very evident symptoms of fear and distrust. They, however, laid aside their weapons, and when I stepped forward and took each of them by the hand, one of them, but with a very tremulous action, drew his knife from his sleeve, and presented it to me as a mark of his submission to my will and pleasure. On our first hearing the noise of these people in the woods, we displayed our flag, which was now shewn to them as a token of friendship. They examined us, and every thing about us, with a minute and suspicious attention. They had heard, indeed, of white men, but this was the first time that they had ever seen an human being of a complexion different from their own. The party had been here but a few hours; nor had they yet erected their sheds; and, except the two men now with us, they had all fled, leaving their little property behind them. To those which had given us such a proof of their confidence, we paid the most conciliating attentions in our power. One of them I sent to recall his people, and the other, for very obvious reasons, we kept with us. In the mean time the canoe was unloaded, the necessary baggage carried up the hill, and the tents pitched.

Here I determined to remain till the Indians became so familiarized with us, as to give all the intelligence which we imagined might be obtained from them. In fact, it had been my intention to land where I might most probably discover the carrying-place, which was our more immediate object, and undertake marches of two or three days, in different directions, in search of another river. If unsuccessful in this attempt, it was my purpose to continue my progress up the present river, as far as it was navigable, and if we did not meet with natives to instruct us in our further progress, I had determined to return to the fork, and take the other branch, with the hope of better fortune.

It was about three in the afternoon when we landed, and at five the whole party of Indians were assembled. It consisted only of three men, three women, and seven or eight boys and girls. With their scratched legs, bleeding feet, and dishevelled hair, as in the hurry of their flight they had left their shoes and leggins behind them, they displayed a most wretched appearance: they were consoled, however, with beads, and other trifles, which seemed to please them; they had pemmican also given them to eat, which was not unwelcome, and in our opinion, at least, superior to their own provision, which consisted entirely of dried fish.

When I thought that they were sufficiently composed, I sent for the men to my tent, to gain such information respecting the country as I concluded it was in their power to afford me. But my expectations were by no means satisfied: they said that they were not acquainted with any river to the Westward, but that there was one from whence they were just arrived, over a carrying-place of eleven days march, which they represented as being a branch only of the river before us. Their iron-work they obtained from the people who inhabit the bank of that river, and an adjacent lake, in exchange for beaver skins, and dressed moose skins. They represented the latter as travelling, during a moon, to get to the country of other tribes, who live in houses, with whom they traffic for the same commodities; and that these also extend their journies in the same manner to the sea coast, or, to use their expression, the Stinking Lake, where they trade with people like us, that come there in vessels as big as islands. They added, that the people to the Westward, as they have been told, are very numerous. Those who inhabit the other branch they stated as consisting of about forty families, while they themselves did not amount to more than a fourth of that number; and were almost continually compelled to remain in their strong holds, where they sometimes perished with cold and hunger, to secure themselves from their enemies, who never failed to attack them whenever an opportunity presented itself.

This account of the country, from a people who I had every reason to suppose were well acquainted with every part of it, threatened to disconcert the project on which my heart was set, and in which my whole mind was occupied. It occurred to me, however, that from fear, or other motives, they might be tardy in their communication; I therefore assured them that, if they would direct me to the river which I described to them, I would come in large vessels, like those that their neighbours had described, to the mouth of it, and bring them arms and ammunition in exchange for the produce of their country; so that they might be able to defend themselves against their enemies, and no longer remain in that abject, distressed,

and fugitive state in which they then lived. I
added also, that in the mean time, if they
would, on my return, accompany me below the mountains, to a country which was
very abundant in animals, I would furnish
them, and their companions, with every thing
they might want; and make peace between
them and the Beaver Indians. But all these
promises did not appear to advance the object of my inquiries, and they still persisted
in their ignorance of any such river as I
had mentioned, that discharged itself into
the sea.

In this state of perplexity and disappointment, various projects presented themselves
to my mind, which were no sooner formed
than they were discovered to be impracticable, and were consequently abandoned.
At one time I thought of leaving the canoe,
and every thing it contained, to go over land,
and pursue that chain of connexion by which
these people obtain their iron-work; but a
very brief course of reflection convinced me
that it would be impossible for us to carry
provisions for our support through any considerable part of such a journey, as well as
presents, to secure us a kind reception among
the natives, and ammunition for the service
of the hunters, and to defend ourselves
against any act of hostility. At another time

my solicitude for the success of the expedition incited a wish to remain with the natives, and go to the sea by the way they had described; but the accomplishment of such a journey, even if no accident should interpose, would have required a portion of time which it was not in my power to bestow. In my present state of information, to proceed further up the river was considered as a fruitless waste of toilsome exertion; and to return unsuccessful, after all our labour, sufferings, and dangers, was an idea too painful to indulge. Besides, I could not yet abandon the hope that the Indians might not yet be sufficiently composed and confident, to disclose their real knowledge of the country freely and fully to me. Nor was I altogether without my doubts respecting the fidelity of my interpreter, who being very much tired of the voyage, might be induced to withhold those communications which would induce me to continue it. I therefore continued my attentions to the natives, regaled them with such provisions as I had, indulged their children with a taste of sugar, and determined to suspend my conversation with them till the following morning. On my expressing a desire to partake of their fish, they brought me a few dried trout, well cured, that had been taken in the river which they lately left. One of the men also brought me five beaver skins, as a present.

Monday, 10. The solicitude that possessed my mind interrupted my repose; when the dawn appeared I had already quitted my bed, and was waiting with impatience for another conference with the natives. The sun, however, had risen before they left their leafy bowers, whither they had retired with their children, having most hospitably resigned their beds, and the partners of them, to the solicitations of my young men.

I now repeated my inquiries, but my perplexity was not removed by any favourable variation in their answers. About nine, however, one of them, still remaining at my fire, in conversation with the interpreters, I understood enough of his language to know that he mentioned something about a great river, at the same time pointing significantly up that which was before us. On my inquiring of the interpreter respecting that expression, I was informed that he knew of a large river that runs towards the midday sun, a branch of which flowed near the source of that which we were now navigating; and that there were only three small lakes, and as many carrying-places, leading to a small river, which discharges itself into the great river, but that the latter did not empty itself into the sea. The inhabitants, he said, built houses, lived on islands, and were a numerous and warlike people. I desired him to describe the road to the other river, by delineating it with a piece of coal, on a strip of bark, which he accomplished to my satisfaction. The opinion that the river did not discharge itself into the sea, I very confidently imputed to his ignorance of the country.

My hopes were now renewed, and an object presented itself which awakened my utmost impatience. To facilitate its attainment, one of the Indians was induced, by presents, to accompany me as a guide to the first inhabitants, which we might expect to meet on the small lakes in our way. I accordingly resolved to depart with all expedition, and while my people were making every necessary preparation, I employed myself in writing the following description of the natives around me:

They are low in stature, not exceeding five feet six or seven inches; and they are of that meagre appearance which might be expected in a people whose life is one succession of difficulties, in procuring subsistence. Their faces are round, with high cheek bones; and their eyes, which are small, are of a dark brown colour; the cartilage of their nose is perforated, but without any ornaments suspended from it; their hair is of a dingy black, hanging loose and in disorder over their shoulders, but irregularly cut in the front, so as not to obstruct the sight; their beards are eradicated, with the exception of a few straggling hairs, and their complexion is a swarthy yellow.

Their dress consists of robes made of the skins of the beaver, the ground hog, and the rein-deer, dressed in the hair, and of the moose-skin without it. All of them are ornamented with a fringe, while some of them have tassels hanging down the seams; those of the ground hog are decorated on the fur side with the tails of the animal, which they do not separate from them. Their garments they tie over the shoulders, and fasten them round the middle with a belt of green skin, which is as stiff as horn. Their leggins are long, and, if they were topped with a waist-band, might be called trowsers: they, as well as their shoes, are made of dressed moose, elk, or rein-deer skin. The organs of generation they leave uncovered.

The women differ little in their dress from the men, except in the addition of an apron, which is fastened round the waist, and hangs down to the knees. They are in general of a more lusty make than the other sex, and taller in proportion, but infinitely their inferiors in cleanliness. A black artificial stripe crosses the face beneath the eye, from ear to ear, which I first took for scabs, from the accumulation of dirt on it. Their hair, which is longer than that of the men, is divided from the forehead to the crown, and drawn back in long plaits behind the ears. They have also a few white beads, which they get where they procure their iron: they are from a line to an inch in length, and are worn in their ears, but are not of European manufacture. These, with bracelets made of horn and bone, compose all the ornaments which decorate their persons. Necklaces of the grisly or white bear's claws, are worn exclusively by the men.

Their arms consist of bows made of cedar, six feet in length, with a short iron spike at one end, and serve occasionally as a spear. Their arrows are well made, barbed, and pointed with iron, flint, stone, or bone; they are feathered, and from two to two feet and an half in length. They have two kinds of spears, but both are double edged, and of well polished iron; one of them is about twelve inches long, and two wide; the other about half the width, and two thirds of the length; the shafts of the first are eight feet in length, and the latter six. They have also spears made of bone. Their knives consist of pieces of iron, shaped and handled by themselves. Their axes are something like our adze, and they use them in the same manner as we employ that instrument. They were, indeed, furnished with iron in a manner that I could not have supposed, and plainly proved to me that their communication with those, who communicate with the inhabitants of the sea coast, cannot be very difficult, and from their ample provision of iron weapons, the means of procuring it must be of a more distant origin than I had at first conjectured.

They have snares made of green skin, which they cut to the size of sturgeon twine, and twist a certain number of them together; and though when completed they do not exceed the thickness of a cod-line, their strength is sufficient to hold a moose deer: they are from one and an half to two fathoms in length. Their nets and fishing lines are made of willow-bark and nettles; those made of the latter are finer and smoother than if made with hempen thread. Their hooks are small bones, fixed in pieces of wood split for that purpose, and tied round with fine watape, which has been particularly described in the former voyage. Their kettles are also made of watape, which

is so closely woven that they never leak, and
they heat water in them, by putting red-hot
stones into it. There is one kind of them,
made of spruce-bark, which they hang over
the fire, but at such a distance as to receive
the heat without being within reach of the
blaze; a very tedious operation. They have
various dishes of wood and bark; spoons of
horn and wood, and buckets; bags of leather
and net-work, and baskets of bark, some of
which hold their fishing-tackle, while others
are contrived to be carried on the back. They
have a brown kind of earth in great abundance, with which they rub their clothes, not
only for ornament but utility, as it prevents
the leather from becoming hard after it has
been wetted. They have spruce bark in great
plenty, with which they make their canoes,
an operation that does not require any great
portion of skill or ingenuity, and is managed
in the following manner.—The bark is taken
off the tree the whole length of the intended
canoe, which is commonly about eighteen
feet, and is sewed with watape at both ends;
two laths are then laid, and fixed along the
edge of the bark which forms the gunwale;
in these are fixed the bars, and against them
bear the ribs or timbers, that are cut to the
length to which the bark can be stretched;
and, to give additional strength, strips of

wood are laid between them: to make the whole water-tight, gum is abundantly employed. These vessels carry from two to five people. Canoes of a similar construction were used by the Beaver Indians within these few years, but they now very generally employ those made of the bark of the birch tree, which are by far more durable. Their paddles are about six feet long, and about one foot is occupied by the blade, which is in the shape of an heart.

Previous to our departure, the natives had caught a couple of trout, of about six pounds weight, which they brought me, and I paid them with beads. They likewise gave me a net, made of nettles, the skin of a moose-deer, dressed, and a white horn in the shape of a spoon, which resembles the horn of the buffalo of the Copper-Mine River; but their description of the animal to which it belongs does not answer to that. My young men also got two quivers of excellent arrows, a collar of white bear's claws, of a great length, horn bracelets, and other articles, for which they received an ample remuneration.

Chapter 6

Continue the voyage. State of the river. Succession of courses. Sentiment of the guide. Conical mountain. Continuation of courses. Leave the main branch. Enter another. Description of it. Saw beaver. Enter a lake. Arrive at the upper source of the Unjigah, or Peace River. Land, and cross to a second lake. Local circumstances. Proceed to a third lake. Enter a river. Encounter various difficulties. In danger of being lost. The circumstances of that situation described. Alarm and dissatisfaction among the people. They are at length composed. The canoe repaired. Roads cut through woods. Pass morasses. The guide deserts. After a succession of difficulties, dangers, and toilsome marches, we arrive at the great river.

June, 1793.

MONDAY, 10. At ten we were ready to embark. I then took leave of the Indians, but encouraged them to expect us in two moons, and expressed an hope that I should find them on the road with any of their relations whom they might meet. I also returned the beaver skins to the man who had presented them to me, desiring him to take care of them till I came back, when I would purchase them of him. Our guide expressed much less concern about the undertaking in which he had engaged, than his companions, who appeared to be affected with great solicitude for his safety.

We now pushed off the canoe from the bank, and proceeded East half a mile, when a river flowed in from the left, about half as large as that which we were navigating. We continued the same course three quarters of a mile, when we missed two of our fowling pieces, which had been forgotten, and I sent their owners back for them, who were absent on this errand upwards of an hour. We now proceeded North-East by East half a mile, North-East by North three quarters of a mile, when the current slackened: there was a verdant spot on the left, where, from the remains of some Indian timber-work, it appeared, that the natives have frequently encamped. Our next course was East one mile, and we saw a ridge of mountains covered with snow to the South-East. The land on our right was low and marshy for three or four miles, when it rose into a range of heights that extended to the mountains. We proceeded East-South-East a mile and an half, South-East by East one mile, East by South three quarters of a mile, South-East by East one mile, East by South half a mile, North-East by East one mile, South-East half a mile, East-North-East a mile and a quarter, South-South-East half a mile,

North-North-East a mile and an half: here a river flowed in from the left, which was about one-fourth part as large as that which received its tributary waters. We then continued East by South half a mile, to the foot of the mountain on the South of the above river. The course now veered short, South-West by West three quarters of a mile, East by South a quarter of a mile, South half a mile, South-East by South half a mile, South-West a quarter of a mile, East by South a quarter of a mile, veered to West-North-West a quarter of a mile, South-West one eighth of a mile, East South-East one quarter of a mile, East one sixth of a mile, South-South-West one twelfth of a mile, East South-East one eighth of a mile, North-East by East one third of a mile, East by North one twelfth of a mile, North-East by East one third of a mile, East one sixteenth of a mile, South-East one twelfth of a mile, North-East by East one twelfth of a mile, East one eighth of a mile, and East-South-East half a mile, when we landed at seven o'clock and encamped. During the greatest part of the distance we came to-day, the river runs close under the mountains on the left.

Tuesday, 11. The morning was clear and cold. On my interpreter's encouraging the guide to dispel all apprehension, to maintain his fidelity to me, and not to desert in the night, "How is it possible for me," he replied, "to leave the lodge of the Great Spirit!—When he tells me that he has no further occasion for me, I will then return to my children." As we proceeded, however, he soon lost, and with good reason, his exalted notions of me.

At four we continued our voyage, steering East by South a mile and an half, East-South-East half a mile. A river appeared on the left, at the foot of a mountain which, from its conical form, my young Indian called the Beaver Lodge Mountain. Having proceeded South-South-East half a mile, another river appeared from the right. We now came in a line with the beginning of the mountains we saw yesterday: others of the same kind ran parallel with them on the left side of the river, which was reduced to the breadth of fifteen yards, and with a moderate current.

We now steered East-North-East one eighth of a mile, South-East by South one eighth of a mile, East-South-East one sixth of a mile, South-West one eighth of a mile, East-South-East one eighth of a mile, South-South-East one sixth of a mile, North-East by East one twelfth of a mile, East-South-East half a mile, South-West by West one

third of a mile, South-South-East one eighth
of a mile, South-South-West one quarter of a
mile, North-East one sixth of a mile, South
by West one fourth of a mile, East three
quarters of a mile, and North-East one quarter of a mile. Here the mountain on the left
appeared to be composed of a succession of
round hills, covered with wood almost to
their summits, which were white with snow,
and crowned with withered trees. We now
steered East, in a line with the high lands on
the right five miles; North one twelfth of a
mile, North-East by North one eighth of a
mile, South by East one sixteenth of a mile,
North-East by North one fourth of a mile,
where another river fell in from the right;
North-East by East one sixth of a mile, East
two miles and an half, South one twelfth of a
mile, North-East half a mile, South-East
one third of a mile, East one mile and a quarter, South-South-West one sixteenth of a
mile, North-East by East half a mile, East
one mile and three quarters, South and
South-West by West half a mile, North-East
half a mile, South one third of a mile, North-
East by North one sixth of a mile, East by
South one fourth of a mile, South one eighth
of a mile, South-East three quarters of a
mile. The canoe had taken in so much water,
that it was necessary for us to land here, in

order to stop the leakage, which occasioned
the delay of an hour and a quarter, North-
East a quarter of a mile, East-North-East a
quarter of a mile, South-East by South a sixteenth of a mile, East by South a twelfth of
a mile, North-East one sixth of a mile, East-
South-East one sixteenth of a mile, South-
West half a mile, North-East a quarter of
a mile, East by South half a mile, South-
South-East one twelfth of a mile, East half
a mile, North-East by North a quarter of a
mile, South-South-East a quarter of a mile,
North-East by North one twelfth of a mile,
where a small river flowed in from the left,
South-East by East one twelfth of a mile,
South by East a quarter of a mile, South-
East one eighth of a mile, East one twelfth
of a mile, North-East by North a quarter of
a mile, South half a mile, South-East by
South one eighth of a mile, North-East one
fourth of a mile, South-East by East, and
South-East by South one third of a mile,
East-South-East, and North-North-East one
third of a mile, and South by West, East and
East-North-East one eighth of a mile.

Here we quitted the main branch, which,
according to the information of our guide,
terminates at a short distance, where it is
supplied by the snow which covers the mountains. In the same direction is a valley which

appears to be of very great depth, and is full of snow, that rises nearly to the height of the land, and forms a reservoir of itself sufficient to furnish a river, whenever there is a moderate degree of heat. The branch which we left was not, at this time, more than ten yards broad, while that which we entered was still less. Here the current was very trifling, and the channel so meandering, that we sometimes found it difficult to work the canoe forward. The straight course from this to the entrance of a small lake or pond, is about East one mile. This entrance by the river into the lake was almost choked up by a quantity of drift-wood, which appeared to me to be an extraordinary circumstance; but I afterwards found that it falls down from the mountains. The water, however, was so high, that the country was entirely overflowed, and we passed with the canoe among the branches of trees. The principal wood along the banks is spruce, intermixed with a few white birch, growing on detached spots, the intervening spaces being covered with willow and alder. We advanced about a mile in the lake, and took up our station for the night at an old Indian encampment. Here we expected to meet with natives, but were disappointed; but our guide encouraged us with the hope of seeing some on the morrow. We saw beaver in the course of the afternoon, but did not discharge our pieces, from the fear of alarming the inhabitants; there were also swans in great numbers, with geese and ducks, which we did not disturb for the same reason. We observed also the tracks of moose-deer that had crossed the river; and wild parsnips grew here in abundance, which have been already mentioned as a grateful vegetable. Of birds, we saw blue jays, yellow birds, and one beautiful humming-bird: of the first and last, I had not seen any since I had been in the North-West.

Wednesday, 12. The weather was the same as yesterday, and we proceeded between three and four in the morning. We took up the net which we had set the preceding evening, when it contained a trout, one white fish, one carp, and three jub. The lake is about two miles in length, East by South, and from three to five hundred yards wide. This I consider as the highest and Southernmost source of the Unjigah, or Peace River, latitude, 54. 24. North, longitude 121. West of Greenwich, which, after a winding course through a vast extent of country, receiving many large rivers in its progress, and passing through the Slave Lake, empties itself into the Frozen Ocean, in 70. North latitude, and about 135 West longitude.

We landed and unloaded, where we found a beaten path leading over a low ridge of land of eight hundred and seventeen paces in length to another small lake. The distance between the two mountains at this place is about a quarter of a mile, rocky precipices presenting themselves on both sides. A few large spruce trees and liards were scattered over the carrying-place. There were also willows along the side of the water, with plenty of grass and weeds. The natives had left their old canoes here, with baskets hanging on the trees, which contained various articles. From the latter I took a net, some hooks, a goat's-horn, and a kind of wooden trap, in which, as our guide informed me, the ground-hog is taken. I left, however, in exchange, a knife, some fire-steels, beads, awls, etc. Here two streams tumble down the rocks from the right, and lose themselves in the lake which we had left; while two others fall from the opposite heights, and glide into the lake which we were approaching; this being the highest point of land dividing these waters,[1] and we are now going with the stream. This lake runs in the same course as the last, but

[1] That is, the waters draining, by way of Peace River, into the Arctic Ocean and those which find their way to the Pacific. The explorers had now reached a tributary of the, as yet, unknown Fraser River.—ED.

is rather narrower, and not more than half the length. We were obliged to clear away some floating drift-wood to get to the carrying-place, over which is a beaten path of only an hundred and seventy-five paces long. The lake empties itself by a small river, which, if the channel were not interrupted by large trees that had fallen across it, would have admitted of our canoe with all its lading: the impediment, indeed, might have been removed by two axe-men in a few hours. On the edge of the water, we observed a large quantity of thick, yellow, scum or froth, of an acrid taste and smell.

We embarked on this lake, which is in the same course, and about the same size as that which we had just left, and from whence we passed into a small river, that was so full of fallen wood, as to employ some time, and require some exertion, to force a passage. At the entrance, it afforded no more water than was just sufficient to bear the canoe; but it was soon increased by many small streams which came in broken rills down the rugged sides of the mountains, and were furnished, as I suppose, by the melting of the snow. These accessory streamlets had all the coldness of ice. Our course continued to be obstructed by banks of gravel, as well as trees which had fallen across the river. We were obliged to force our way through the one, and to cut through the other, at a great expence of time and trouble. In many places the current was also very rapid and meandering. At four in the afternoon, we stopped to unload and carry, and at five we entered a small round lake of about one third of a mile in diameter. From the last lake to this is, I think, in a straight line, East by South six miles, though it is twice that distance by the winding of the river. We again entered the river, which soon ran with great rapidity, and rushed impetuously over a bed of flat stones. At half past six we were stopped by two large trees that lay across the river, and it was with great difficulty that the canoe was prevented from driving against them. Here we unloaded and formed our encampment.

The weather was cloudy and raw, and as the circumstances of this day's voyage had compelled us to be frequently in the water, which was cold as ice, we were almost in a benumbed state. Some of the people who had gone ashore to lighten the canoe, experienced great difficulty in reaching us, from the rugged state of the country; it was, indeed, almost dark when they arrived. We had no sooner landed than I sent two men down the river to bring me some account of its circumstances, that I might form a judgment of the difficulties which might await us on the morrow; and they brought back a fearful detail of rapid currents, fallen trees, and large stones. At this place our guide manifested evident symptoms of discontent: he had been very much alarmed in going down some of the rapids with us, and expressed an anxiety to return. He shewed us a mountain, at no great distance, which he represented as being on the other side of a river, into which this empties itself.

Thursday, 13. At an early hour of this morning the men began to cut a road, in order to carry the canoe and lading beyond the rapid; and by seven they were ready. That business was soon effected, and the canoe relaced, to proceed with the current which ran with great rapidity. In order to lighten her, it was my intention to walk with some of the people; but those in the boat with great earnestness requested me to embark, declaring, at the same time, that, if they perished, I should perish with them. I did not then imagine in how short a period their apprehension would be justified. We accordingly pushed off, and had proceeded but a very short way when the canoe struck, and notwithstanding all our exertions, the violence of the current was so great as to drive her sideways down the river, and break her by the first bar, when I instantly jumped into the water, and the men followed my example; but before we could set her straight, or stop her, we came to deeper water, so that we were obliged to re-embark with the utmost precipitation. One of the men who was not sufficiently active, was left to get on shore in the best manner in his power. We had hardly regained our situations when we drove against a rock which shattered the stern of the canoe in such a manner, that it held only by the gunwales, so that the steersman could no longer keep his place. The violence of this stroke drove us to the opposite side of the river, which is but narrow, when the bow met with the same fate as the stern. At this moment the foreman seized on some branches of a small tree in the hope of bringing up the canoe, but such was their elasticity that, in a manner not easily described, he was jerked on shore in an instant, and with a degree of violence that threatened his destruction. But we had no time to turn from our own situation to inquire what had befallen him; for, in a few moments, we came across a cascade which broke several large holes in the bottom of the canoe, and started all the bars, except one behind the scooping seat. If this accident, however, had not happened, the vessel must have been irretrievably overset. The wreck becoming flat on the water, we all jumped out, while the steersman, who had been compelled to abandon his place, and had not recovered from his fright, called out to his companions to save themselves. My peremptory commands superseded the effects of his fear, and they all held fast to the wreck; to which fortunate resolution we owed our safety, as we should otherwise have been dashed against the rocks by the force of the water, or driven over the cascades. In this condition we were forced several hundred yards, and every yard on the verge of destruction; but, at length, we most fortunately arrived in shallow water and a small eddy, where we were enabled to make a stand, from the weight of the canoe resting on the stones, rather than from any exertions of our exhausted strength. For though our efforts were short, they were pushed to the utmost, as life or death depended on them.

This alarming scene, with all its terrors and dangers, occupied only a few minutes; and in the present suspension of it, we called to the people on shore to come to our assistance, and they immediately obeyed the summons. The foreman however, was the first with us; he had escaped unhurt from the extraordinary jerk with which he was thrown out of the boat, and just as we were beginning to take our effects out of the water, he appeared to give his assistance. The Indians, when they saw our deplorable situation, instead of making the least effort to help us, sat down and gave vent to their tears. I was on the outside of the canoe, where I remained till every thing was got on shore, in a state of great pain from the extreme cold of the water; so that at length, it was with difficulty I could stand, from the benumbed state of my limbs.

The loss was considerable and important, for it consisted of our whole stock of balls, and some of our furniture; but these considerations were forgotten in the impressions of our miraculous escape. Our first inquiry was after the absent man, whom in the first moment of danger, we had left to get on shore, and in a short time his appearance removed our anxiety. We had, however, sustained no personal injury of consequence, and my bruises seemed to be in the greater proportion.

All the different articles were now spread out to dry. The powder had fortunately received no damage, and all my instruments had escaped. Indeed, when my people began to recover from their alarm, and to enjoy a sense of safety, some of them, if not all, were by no means sorry for our late misfortune, from the hope that it must put a period to our voyage, particularly as we were without a canoe, and all the bullets sunk in the river. It did not, indeed, seem possible to them that we could proceed under these circumstances. I listened, however, to the observations that were made on the occasion without replying to them, till their panic was dispelled, and they had got themselves warm and comfortable, with an hearty meal, and rum enough to raise their spirits.

I then addressed them, by recommending them all to be thankful for their late very narrow escape. I also stated, that the navigation was not impracticable in itself, but from our ignorance of its course; and that our late experience would enable us to pursue our voyage with greater security. I brought to their recollection, that I did not deceive them, and that they were made acquainted with the difficulties and dangers they must expect to encounter, before they engaged to accompany me. I also urged the honour of conquering disasters, and the disgrace that would attend them on their return home, without having attained the object of the expedition. Nor did I fail to mention the courage and resolution which was the peculiar boast of the North men;

and that I depended on them, at that moment, for the maintenance of their character. I quieted their apprehension as to the loss of the bullets, by bringing to their recollection that we still had shot from which they might be manufactured. I at the same time acknowledged the difficulty of restoring the wreck of the canoe, but confided in our skill and exertion to put it in such a state as would carry us on to where we might procure bark, and build a new one. In short, my harangue produced the desired effect, and a very general assent appeared to go wherever I should lead the way.

Various opinions were offered in the present posture of affairs, and it was rather a general wish that the wreck should be abandoned, and all the lading carried to the river, which our guide informed us was at no great distance, and in the vicinity of woods where he believed there was plenty of bark. This project seemed not to promise that certainty to which I looked in my present operations; besides, I had my doubts respecting the views of my guide, and consequently could not confide in the representation he made to me. I therefore dispatched two of the men at nine in the morning, with one of the young Indians, for I did not venture to trust the guide out of my sight, in search of bark, and to endeavour, if it were possible, in the course of the day, to penetrate to the great river, into which that before us discharges itself in the direction which the guide had communicated. I now joined my people in order to repair, as well as circumstances would admit, our wreck of a canoe, and I began to set them the example.

At noon I had an altitude, which gave 54. 23. North latitude. At four in the afternoon I took time, with the hope that in the night I might obtain an observation of Jupiter, and his satellites, but I had not a sufficient horizon, from the propinquity of the mountains. The result of my calculation for time was 1. 38. 28. slow apparent time.

It now grew late, and the people who had been sent on the excursion already mentioned, were not yet returned; about ten o'clock, however, I heard a man halloo, and I very gladly returned the signal. In a short time our young Indian arrived with a small roll of indifferent bark: he was oppressed with fatigue and hunger, and his clothes torn to rags: he had parted with the other two men at sun-set, who had walked the whole day, in a dreadful country, without procuring any good bark, or being able to get to the large river. His account of the river, on whose banks we were, could not be

more unfavourable or discouraging; it had
appeared to him to be little more than a succession of falls and rapids, with occasional
interruptions of fallen trees.

Our guide became so dissatisfied and trou-
bled in mind, that we could not obtain from
him any regular account of the country before us. All we could collect from him was,
that the river into which this empties itself
is but a branch of a large river, the great
fork being at no great distance from the con-
fluence of this; and that he knew of no lake,
or large body of still water, in the vicinity of
these rivers. To this account of the country,
he added some strange, fanciful, but terrify-
ing descriptions of the natives, similar to
those which were mentioned in the former
voyage.

We had an escape this day, which I must
add to the many instances of good fortune
which I experienced in this perilous expedition. The powder had been spread out, to
the amount of eighty pounds weight, to receive the air; and, in this situation, one of
the men carelessly and composedly walked
across it with a lighted pipe in his mouth,
but without any ill consequence resulting
from such an act of criminal negligence. I
need not add that one spark might have put
a period to all my anxiety and ambition.

I observed several trees and plants on the banks of this river, which I had not seen to the North of the latitude 52. such as the cedar, maple, hemlock, &c. At this time the water rose fast, and passed on with the rapidity of an arrow shot from a bow.

Friday, 14. The weather was fine, clear, and warm, and at an early hour of the morning we resumed our repair of the canoe. At half past seven our two men returned hungry and cold, not having tasted food, or enjoyed the least repose for twenty-four hours, with their clothes torn into tatters, and their skin lacerated, in passing through the woods. Their account was the same as that brought by the Indian, with this exception, that they had reason to think they saw the river, or branch which our guide had mentioned; but they were of opinion that from the frequent obstructions in this river, we should have to carry the whole way to it, through a dreadful country, where much time and labour would be required to open a passage through it.

Discouraging as these accounts were, they did not, however, interrupt for a moment the task in which we were engaged, of repairing the canoe; and this work we contrived to complete by the conclusion of the day. The bark which was brought by the Indian, with some pieces of oilcloth, and plenty of gum, enabled us to put our shattered vessel in a condition to answer our present purposes. The guide, who has been mentioned as manifesting continual signs of dissatisfaction, now assumed an air of contentment, which I attributed to a smoke that was visible in the direction of the river; as he naturally expected, if we should fall in with any natives, which was now very probable, from such a circumstance, that he should be released from a service which he had found so irksome and full of danger. I had an observation at noon, which made our latitude 54. 23. 43. North. I also took time, and found it slow apparent time 1. 38. 44.

Saturday, 15. The weather continued the same as the preceding day, and according to the directions which I had previously given, my people began at a very early hour to open a road, through which we might carry a part of our lading; as I was fearful of risquing the whole of it in the canoe, in its present weak state, and in a part of the river which is full of shoals and rapids. Four men were employed to conduct her, lightened as she was of twelve packages. They passed several dangerous places, and met with various obstructions, the current of the river being frequently stopped by rafts of drift wood, and fallen trees, so that after fourteen hours hard labour we had not made more than three miles. Our course was South-East by East, and as we had not met with any accident, the men appeared to feel a renewed courage to continue their voyage. In the morning, however, one of the crew, whose name was Beauchamp, peremptorily refused to embark in the canoe. This being the first example of absolute disobedience which had yet appeared during the course of our expedition, I should not have passed it over without taking some very severe means to prevent a repetition of it; but as he had the general character of a simple fellow, among his companions, and had been frightened out of what little sense he possessed, by our late dangers, I rather preferred to consider him as unworthy of accompanying us, and to represent him as an object of ridicule and contempt for his pusillanimous behaviour; though, in fact, he was a very useful, active, and laborious man.

At the close of the day we assembled round a blazing fire; and the whole party, being enlivened with the usual beverage which I supplied on these occasions, forgot their fatigues and apprehensions; nor did they fail to anticipate the pleasure they should enjoy in getting clear of their present difficulties, and gliding onwards with a strong and steady stream, which our guide had described as the characteristic of the large river we soon expected to enter.

Sunday, 16. The fine weather continued, and we began our work, as we had done the preceding day; some were occupied in opening a road, others were carrying, and the rest employed in conducting the canoe. I was of the first party, and soon discovered that we had encamped about half a mile above several falls, over which we could not attempt to run the canoe, lightened even as she was. This circumstance rendered it necessary that the road should be made sufficiently wide to admit the canoe to pass; a tedious and toilsome work. In running her down a rapid above the falls, an hole was broken in her bottom, which occasioned a considerable delay, as we were destitute of the materials necessary for her effectual reparation. On my being informed of this misfortune, I returned, and ordered Mr. Mackay, with two Indians, to quit their occupation in making the road, and endeavour to penetrate to the great river, according to the direction which the guide had communicated, without paying any attention to the course of the river before us.

When the people had repaired the canoe in the best manner they were able, we conducted her to the head of the falls; she was then unloaded and taken out of the water, when we carried her for a considerable distance through a low, swampy country. I appointed four men to this laborious office, which they executed at the peril of their lives, for the canoe was now become so heavy, from the additional quantity of bark and gum necessary to patch her up, that two men could not carry her more than an hundred yards, without being relieved; and as their way lay through deep mud, which was rendered more difficult by the roots and prostrate trunks of trees, they were every moment in danger of falling; and beneath such a weight, one false step might have been attended with fatal consequences. The other two men and myself followed as fast as we could, with the lading. Thus did we toil till seven o'clock in the evening, to get to the termination of the road that had been made in the morning. Here Mr. Mackay and the Indian joined us, after having been at the river, which they represented as rather large. They had also observed, that the lower part of the river before us was so full of fallen wood, that the attempt to clear a passage through it, would be an unavailing labour. The country through which they had passed was morass, and almost impenetrable wood.

In passing over one of the embarras, our dog, which was following them, fell in, and it was with very great difficulty that he was saved, as the current had carried him under the drift. They brought with them two geese, which had been shot in the course of their expedition. To add to our perplexities and embarrassments, we were persecuted by musquitoes and sand-flies, through the whole of the day.

The extent of our journey was not more than two miles South-East; and so much fatigue and pain had been suffered in the course of it, that my people, as might be expected, looked forward to a continuance of it with discouragement and dismay. I was, indeed, informed that murmurs prevailed among them, of which, however, I took no notice. When we were assembled together for the night, I gave each of them a dram, and in a short time they retired to the repose which they so much required. We could discover the termination of the mountains at a considerable distance on either side of us, which, according to my conjecture, marked the course of the great river. On the mountains to the East there were several fires, as their smokes were very visible to us. Excessive heat prevailed throughout the day.

Monday, 17. Having sat up till twelve last night, which had been my constant practice

since we had taken our present guide, I
awoke Mr. Mackay to watch him in turn. I
then laid down to rest, and at three I was
awakened to be informed that he had deserted. Mr. Mackay, with whom I was displeased on this occasion, and the Cancre, accompanied by the dog, went in search of
him, but he had made his escape: a design
which he had for some time meditated,
though I had done every thing in my power
to induce him to remain with me.

This misfortune did not produce any relaxation in our exertions. At an early hour of
the morning we were all employed in cutting
a passage of three quarters of a mile, through
which we carried our canoe and cargo, when
we put her into the water with her lading,
but in a very short time were stopped by the
drift-wood, and were obliged to land and
carry. In short, we pursued our alternate
journies, by land and water, till noon, when
we could proceed no further, from the various small unnavigable channels into which
the river branched in every direction; and no
other mode of getting forward now remained
for us, but by cutting a road across a neck
of land. I accordingly dispatched two men
to ascertain the exact distance, and we employed the interval of their absence in unloading and getting the canoe out of the

water. It was eight in the evening when we arrived at the bank of the great river. This journey was three quarters of a mile East-North-East, through a continued swamp, where, in many places, we waded up to the middle of our thighs. Our course in the small river was about South-East by East three miles. At length we enjoyed, after all our toil and anxiety, the inexpressible satisfaction of finding ourselves on the bank of a navigable river,[2] on the West side of the first great range of mountains.

[2] The North fork of the Fraser, now first discovered by white men, unless at its mouth, on the Pacific.—ED.

Chapter 7

Rainy night. Proceed on the great river. Circumstances of it. Account of courses. Come to rapids. Observe several smokes. See a flight of white ducks. Pass over a carrying-place with the canoe, &c. The difficulties of that passage. Abundance of wild onions. Re-embark on the river. See some of the natives. They desert their camp and fly into the woods. Courses continued. Kill a red deer, &c. Circumstances of the river. Arrive at an Indian habitation. Description of it. Account of a curious machine to catch fish. Land to procure bark for the purpose of constructing a new canoe. Conceal a quantity of pemmican for provision on our return. Succession of courses. Meet with some of the natives. Our inter-course with them. Their information respecting the river, and the country. Description of those people.

June, 1793.

TUESDAY, 18. It rained throughout the night and till seven in the morning; nor was I sorry that the weather gave me an excuse for indulging my people with that additional rest, which their fatigues, during the last three days, rendered so comfortable to them. Before eight, however, we were on the water, and driven on by a strong current, when we steered East-South-East half a mile, South-West by South half a mile, South-South-East half a mile, South-West half a mile, went round to North-West half a mile, backed South-South-East three quarters of a mile, South-South-West half a mile, South by East a quarter of a mile, and South-West by South three quarters of a mile. Here the water had fallen considerably, so that several mud and sand-banks were visible. There was also an hill ahead, West-South-West.

The weather was so hazy that we could not see across the river, which is here about two hundred yards wide. We now proceeded South by West one third of a mile, when we saw a considerable quantity of beaver work along the banks, North-North-West half a mile, South-West by West one mile and an half, South-South-West one third of a mile, West by South one third of a mile, South by East half a mile. Mountains rose on the left, immediately above the river, whose summits were covered with snow; South-West half a mile, South a quarter of a mile, South-East one third of a mile, South-South-West half a mile. Here are several islands, we then veered to West by South a third of a mile, South-South-East a sixth of a mile. On the right, the land is high, rocky, and covered with wood, West-South-West one mile, a small river running in from the South-East, South-West half a mile, South three quarters of a mile, South-West half a mile, South by West half a mile. Here a rocky point protrudes from the left, and narrows the river to an hundred yards; South-East half a mile, East by South one eighth of a mile. The current now was very strong, but perfectly safe, South-East by South an eighth of a mile, West by North one third of a mile, South by West a twelfth of a mile, South-West one fourth of a mile. Here the high land terminates on one side of the river, while rocks rise to a considerable height immediately above the other, and the channel widens to an hundred and fifty yards, West by South one mile. The river now narrows again between rocks of a moderate height, North-North-East an eighth of a mile, veered to South-West an eighth of a mile, South and South-West half a mile. The country appeared to be low, as far as I could judge of it from the canoe, as the view is confined by woods at the distance of about an hundred yards from the banks. Our course continued West by North two miles, North half a mile, North-West a quarter of a mile, South-West two miles, North-West three quarters of a mile; when a ridge of high land appeared in this direction, West one mile. A small river flowed in from the North, South a quarter of a mile, North-West half a mile,

South-South-West two miles and an half,
South-East three quarters of a mile; a rivulet
lost itself in the main stream, West-North-
West half a mile. Here the current slackened,
and we proceeded South-South-West three
quarters of a mile, South-West three quarters of a mile, South by East three quarters
of a mile, South-East by East one mile,
when it veered gradually to West North-
West half a mile; the river being full of
islands. We proceeded due North, with little
current, the river presenting a beautiful
sheet of water for a mile and an half, South-
West by West one mile, West-North-West
one mile, when it veered round to South-
East one mile, West by North one mile,
South-East one mile, West by North three
quarters of a mile, South one eighth of a
mile, when we came to an Indian cabin of
late erection. Here was the great fork, of
which our guide had informed us, and it
appeared to be the largest branch from
the South-East. It is about half a mile in
breadth, and assumes the form of a lake.
The current was very slack, and we got into
the middle of the channel, when we steered
West, and sounded in sixteen feet water.
A ridge of high land now stretched on, as
it were, across our present direction: this
course was three miles. We then proceeded

West-South-West two miles, and sounded in twenty-four feet water. Here the river narrowed and the current increased. We then continued our course North-North-West three quarters of a mile, a small river falling in from the North-East. It now veered to South by West one mile and a quarter, West-South-West four miles and an half, West by North one mile and a quarter, North-West by West one mile, West a mile and a quarter: the land was high on both sides, and the river narrowed to an hundred and fifty, or two hundred yards; North-West three quarters of a mile, South-West by South two miles and an half: here its breadth again increased; South by West one mile, West-South-West half a mile, South-West by South three miles, South-South-East one mile, with a small river running in from the left, South with a strong current one mile, then East three quarters of a mile, South-West one mile, South-South-East a mile and an half; the four last distances being a continual rapid; South-West by West one mile, East-North-East a mile and an half, East-South-East one mile, where a small river flowed in on the right; South-West by South two miles and an half, when another small river appeared from the same quarter; South by East half a mile, and South-West by West one mile and a quarter: here we landed for the night. When we had passed the last river we observed smoke rising from it, as if produced by fires that had been fresh lighted; I therefore concluded that there were natives on its banks; but I was unwilling to fatigue my people, by pulling back against the current in order to go in search of them.

This river appeared, from its high watermark, to have fallen no more than one foot, while the smaller branch, from a similar measurement, had sunk two feet and an half. On our entering it, we saw a flock of ducks which were entirely white, except the bill and part of the wings. The weather was cold and raw throughout the day, and the wind South-West. We saw smoke rising in columns from many parts of the woods, and I should have been more anxious to see the natives, if there had been any person with me who could have introduced me to them; but as that object could not be then attained without considerable loss of time, I determined to pursue the navigation while it continued to be so favourable, and to wait till my return, if no very convenient opportunity offered in the mean time, to engage in an intercourse with them.

Wednesday, 19. The morning was foggy, and at three we were on the water. At half past that hour, our course was East by South three quarters of a mile, a small river flowing in from the right. We then proceeded South by East half a mile, and South-South-West a mile and an half. During the last distance, clouds of thick smoke rose from the woods, that darkened the atmosphere, accompanied with a strong odour of the gum of cypress and the spruce-fir. Our courses continued to be South-West a mile and a quarter, North-West by West three quarters of a mile, South-South-East a mile and a quarter, East three quarters of a mile, South-West one mile, West by South three quarters of a mile, South-East by South three quarters of a mile, South by West half a mile, West by South three quarters of a mile, South by West two miles and an half. In the last course there was an island, and it appeared to me, that the main channel of the river had formerly been on the other side of it. The banks were here composed of high white cliffs, crowned with pinnacles in very grotesque shapes. We continued to steer South-East by South a mile and an half, South by East half a mile, East one mile and a quarter, South-East by East one mile, South by East three quarters of a mile, South-East by East one mile, South-South-East half a mile, East one mile and a quarter, South by

East half a mile, East a mile and an half,
South-South-East three miles, and South-
West three quarters of a mile. In the last
course the rocks contracted in such a manner on both sides of the river, as to afford
the appearance of the upper part of a fall or
cataract. Under this apprehension we landed
on the left shore, where we found a kind of
foot-path, imperfectly traced, through which
we conjectured that the natives occasionally
passed with their canoes and baggage. On examining the course of the river, however,
there did not appear to be any fall as we expected; but the rapids were of a considerable
length and impassable for a light canoe. We
had therefore no alternative but to widen
the road so as to admit the passage of our
canoe, which was now carried with great
difficulty; as from her frequent repairs, and
not always of the usual materials, her weight
was such, that she cracked and broke on the
shoulders of the men who bore her. The labour and fatigue of this undertaking, from
eight till twelve, beggars all description,
when we at length conquered this afflicting
passage, of about half a mile, over a rocky
and most rugged hill. Our course was South-
South-West. Here I took a meridian altitude
which gave me 53. 42. 20. North latitude. We,
however, lost some time to put our canoe in

a condition to carry us onwards. Our course was South a quarter of a mile to the next carrying-place; which was nothing more than a rocky point about twice the length of the canoe. From the extremity of this point to the rocky and almost perpendicular bank that rose on the opposite shore, is not more than forty or fifty yards. The great body of water, at the same time tumbling in successive cascades along the first carrying-place, rolls through this narrow passage in a very turbid current, and full of whirlpools. On the banks of the river there was great plenty of wild onions, which when mixed up with our pemmican was a great improvement of it; though they produced a physical effect on our appetites, which was rather inconvenient to the state of our provisions.

Here we embarked, and steered South-East by East three quarters of a mile. We now saw a smoke on the shore; but before we could reach land the natives had deserted their camp, which appeared to be erected for no more than two families. My two Indians were instantly dispatched in search of them, and, by following their tracks, they soon overtook them; but their language was mutually unintelligible; and all attempts to produce a friendly communication were fruitless. They no sooner perceived my young

men than they prepared their bows and
arrows, and made signs for them not to
advance; and they thought it prudent to de-
sist from proceeding, though not before the
natives had discharged five arrows at them,
which, however, they avoided, by means of
the trees. When they returned with this account, I very much regretted that I had not
accompanied them; and as these people
could not be at any very great distance, I
took Mr. Mackay, and one of the Indians
with me in order to overtake them; but they
had got so far that it would have been imprudent in me to have followed them. My
Indians, who, I believe, were terrified at the
manner in which these natives received
them, informed me, that, besides their bows,
arrows, and spears, they were armed with
long knives, and that they accompanied
their strange antics with menacing actions
and loud shoutings. On my return, I found
my people indulging their curiosity in examining the bags and baskets which the natives had left behind them. Some of them
contained their fishing tackle, such as nets,
lines, &c. others of a smaller size were filled
with a red earth, with which they paint
themselves. In several of the bags there
were also sundry articles of which we did
not know the use. I prevented my men from

taking any of them; and for a few articles of mere curiosity, which I took myself, I left such things in exchange as would be much more useful to their owners.

At four we left this place, proceeding with the stream South-East three quarters of a mile, East-South-East one mile, South three quarters of a mile, South-South-West one mile, South by East three quarters of a mile, South-South-East one mile, South-South-West two miles, South-South-East three miles and a quarter, East by North one mile, South-South-East one mile and a quarter, with a rapid, South-South-West three quarters of a mile, South one mile and an half, South-East one mile and a quarter, South three quarters of a mile, and South-South-East one mile and an half. At half past seven we landed for the night, where a small river flowed in from the right. The weather was showery, accompanied with several loud claps of thunder. The banks were overshadowed by lofty firs, and wide-spreading cedars.

Thursday, *20*. The morning was foggy, and at half past four we proceeded with a South wind, South-East by East two miles, South-South-East two miles and an half, and South-South-West two miles. The fog was so thick, that we could not see the length of our

canoe, which rendered our progress dangerous, as we might have come suddenly upon a
cascade or violent rapid. Our next course
was West-North-West two miles and an
half, which comprehended a rapid. Being
close in with the left bank of the river, we
perceived two red deer at the very edge of
the water: we killed one of them, and
wounded the other, which was very small.
We now landed, and the Indians followed the
wounded animal, which they soon caught,
and would have shot another in the woods,
if our dog, who followed them, had not disturbed it. From the number of their tracks
it appeared that they abounded in this country. They are not so large as the elk of the
Peace River, but are the real red deer, which
I never saw in the North, though I have been
told that they are to be found in great numbers in the plains along the Red, or Assini-
boin River. The bark had been stripped off
many of the spruce trees, and carried away,
as I presumed, by the natives, for the purpose of covering their cabins. We now got
the venison on board, and continued our
voyage South-West one mile, South a mile
and an half, and West one mile. Here the
country changed its appearance; the banks
were but of a moderate height, from whence
the ground continued gradually rising to. a

considerable distance, covered with poplars
and cypresses, but without any kind of underwood. There are also several low points
which the river, that is here about three hundred yards in breadth, sometimes overflows,
and are shaded with the liard, the soft birch,
the spruce, and the willow. For some distance before we came to this part of the
river, our view was confined within very
rugged, irregular, and lofty banks, which
were varied with the poplar, different kinds
of spruce fir, small birch trees, cedars, alders,
and several species of the willow. Our next
course was South-West by West six miles,
when we landed at a deserted house, which
was the only Indian habitation of this kind
that I had seen on this side of Michilima-
kina. It was about thirty feet long and
twenty wide, with three doors, three feet
high by one foot and an half in breadth.
From this and other circumstances, it appears to have been constructed for three
families. There were also three fire-places, at
equal distances from each other; and the
beds were on either side of them. Behind the
beds was a narrow space, in the form of a
manger, and somewhat elevated, which was
appropriated to the purpose of keeping fish.
The wall of the house, which was five feet
in height, was formed of very strait spruce

timbers, brought close together, and laid into each other at the corners. The roof was supported by a ridge pole, resting on two upright forks of about ten feet high; that and the wall support a certain number of spars, which are covered with spruce bark; and the whole attached and secured by the fibres of the cedar. One of the gable ends is closed with split boards; the other with poles. Large rods are also fixed across the upper part of the building, where fish may hang and dry. To give the walls additional strength, upright posts are fixed in the ground, at equal distances, both within and without, of the same height as the wall, and firmly attached with bark fibres. Openings appear also between the logs in the wall, for the purpose, as I conjectured, of discharging their arrows at a besieging enemy; they would be needless for the purpose of giving light, which is sufficiently afforded by fissures between the logs of the building, so that it appeared to be constructed merely for a summer habitation. There was nothing further to attract our attention in or about the house, except a large machine, which must have rendered the taking off the roof absolutely necessary, in order to have introduced it. It was of a cylindrical form, fifteen feet long, and four feet and an half in diameter; one end was square, like the head of a cask, and a conical machine was fixed inwards to the other end, of similar dimensions: at the extremity of which was an opening of about seven inches diameter. This machine was certainly contrived to set in the river, to catch large fish; and very well adapted to that purpose; as when they are once in, it must be impossible for them to get out, unless they should have strength sufficient to break through it. It was made of long pieces of split wood, rounded to the size of a small finger, and placed at the distance of an inch asunder, on six hoops; to this was added a kind of boot of the same materials, into which it may be supposed that the fish are driven, when they are to be taken out. The house was left in such apparent order as to mark the design of its owners to return thither. It answered in every particular the description given us by our late guide, except that it was not situated on an island.

We left this place, and steered South by East one mile and a quarter when we passed where there had been another house, of which the ridge-pole and supporters alone remained: the ice had probably carried away the body of it. The bank was at this time covered with water, and a small river flowed in on the left. On a point we observed

an erection that had the appearance of a
tomb; it was in an oblong form, covered, and
very neatly walled with bark. A pole was
fixed near it, to which, at the height of ten
or twelve feet, a piece of bark was attached,
which was probably a memorial, or symbol
of distinction. Our next course was South by
West two miles and an half, when we saw an
house on an island, South-East by East one
mile and three quarters, in which we observed another island, with an house upon it.
A river also flowed from the right, and the
land was high and rocky, and wooded with
the epinette.

Our canoe was now become so crazy, that
it was a matter of absolute necessity to construct another; and as from the appearance
of the country there was reason to expect
that bark was to be found, we landed at
eight, with the hope of procuring it. I accordingly dispatched four men with that
commission, and at twelve they returned
with a sufficient quantity to make the bottom of a canoe of five fathoms in length, and
four feet and an half in height. At noon I had
an observation, which gave me 53. 17. 28.
North latitude.

We now continued our voyage South-East
by South one mile and an half, East-South-
East one mile, East-North-East half a mile,

South-East two miles, South-East by South one mile, South-East six miles, and East-North-East. Here the river narrows between steep rocks, and a rapid succeeded, which was so violent that we did not venture to run it. I therefore ordered the loading to be taken out of the canoe, but she was now become so heavy that the men preferred running the rapid to the carrying her overland. Though I did not altogether approve of their proposition, I was unwilling to oppose it. Four of them undertook this hazardous expedition, and I hastened to the foot of the rapid with great anxiety, to wait the event, which turned out as I expected. The water was so strong, that although they kept clear of the rocks, the canoe filled, and in this state they drove half way down the rapid, but fortunately she did not overset; and having got her into an eddy, they emptied her, and in an half-drowned condition arrived safe on shore. The carrying-place is about half a mile over, with an Indian path across it. Mr. Mackay, and the hunters, saw some deer on an island above the rapid; and had that discovery been made before the departure of the canoe, there is little doubt but we should have added a considerable quantity of venison to our stock of provisions. Our vessel was in such a wretched condition, as I have already observed, that it occasioned a delay of three hours to put her in a condition to proceed. At length we continued our former course, East-North-East a mile and an half, when we passed an extensive Indian encampment; East-South-East one mile, where a small river appeared on the left; South-East by South one mile and three quarters, East by South half a mile, East by North one mile, and saw another house on an island; South half a mile, West three quarters of a mile, South-West half a mile, where the cliffs of white and red clay appeared like the ruins of ancient castles. Our canoe now veered gradually to East-North-East one mile and an half, when we landed in a storm of rain and thunder, where we perceived the remains of Indian houses. It was impossible to determine the wind in any part of the day, as it came a-head in all our directions.

Friday, 21. As I was very sensible of the difficulty of procuring provisions in this country, I thought it prudent to guard against any possibility of distress of that kind on our return; I therefore ordered ninety pounds weight of pemmican to be buried in an hole, sufficiently deep to admit of a fire over it without doing any injury to our hidden treasure, and which would, at the same time, secure it from the natives of the country, or the wild animals of the woods.

The morning was very cloudy, and at four o'clock we renewed our voyage, steering South by East one mile and a quarter, East-South-East half a mile, South by East one mile and an half, East half a mile, South-East two miles, where a large river flowed in from the left, and a smaller one from the right. We then continued South by West three quarters of a mile, East by South a mile and an half, South three quarters of a mile, South-East by East one mile, South by East half a mile, South-East three quarters of a mile, South-East by South half a mile, South-East by East half a mile, the cliffs of blue and yellow clay, displaying the same grotesque shapes as those which we passed yesterday, South-South-East a mile and an half, South by East two miles. The latitude by observation was 52. 47. 51. North.

Here we perceived a small new canoe, that had been drawn up to the edge of the woods, and soon after another appeared, with one man in it, which came out of a small river. He no sooner saw us than he gave the whoop, to alarm his friends, who immediately appeared on the bank, armed with bows and arrows, and spears. They were thinly habited, and displayed the most outrageous antics. Though they were certainly in a state of great apprehension, they manifested by their gestures that they were resolved to attack us, if we should venture to land. I therefore ordered the men to stop the way of the canoe, and even to check her drifting with the current, as it would have been extreme folly to have approached these savages before their fury had in some degree subsided. My interpreters, who understood their language, informed me that they threatened us with instant death if we drew nigh the shore; and they followed the menace by discharging a volley of arrows, some of which fell short of the canoe, and others passed over it, so that they fortunately did us no injury. As we had been carried by the current below the spot where the Indians were, I ordered my people to paddle to the opposite side of the river, without the least appearance of confusion, so that they brought me abreast of them. My interpreters, while we were within hearing, had done every thing in their power to pacify them, but in vain. We also observed that they had sent off a canoe with two men, down the river, as we concluded, to communicate their alarm, and procure assistance. This circumstance determined me to leave no means untried that might engage us in a friendly intercourse with them, before they acquired additional security and confidence, by the arrival of their relations and neighbours, to whom their situation would be shortly notified.

I therefore formed the following adventurous project, which was happily crowned with success. I left the canoe, and walked by myself along the beach, in order to induce some of the natives to come to me, which I imagined they might be disposed to do, when they saw me alone, without any apparent possibility of receiving assistance from my people, and would consequently imagine that a communication with me was not a service of danger. At the same time, in order to possess the utmost security of which my situation was susceptible, I directed one of the Indians to slip into the woods, with my gun and his own, and to conceal himself from their discovery; he also had orders to keep as near me as possible, without being seen; and if any of the natives should venture across, and attempt to shoot me from the water, it was his instructions to lay him low; at the same time he was particularly enjoined not to fire till I had discharged one or both of the pistols that I carried in my belt. If, however, any of them were to land, and approach my person, he was immediately to

169

join me. In the mean time my other interpreter assured them that we entertained the
most friendly disposition, which I confirmed
by such signals as I conceived would be comprehended by them. I had not, indeed, been
long at my station, and my Indian in am-
bush behind me, when two of the natives
came off in a canoe, but stopped when they
had got within an hundred yards of me. I
made signs for them to land, and as an inducement, displayed looking glasses, beads,
and other alluring trinkets. At length, but
with every mark of extreme apprehension,
they approached the shore, stern foremost,
but would not venture to land. I now made
them a present of some beads, with which
they were going to push off, when I renewed
my entreaties, and, after some time, prevailed on them to come ashore, and sit down
by me. My hunter now thought it right to
join me, and created some alarm in my new
acquaintance. It was, however, soon removed, and I had the satisfaction to find
that he, and these people perfectly understood each other. I instructed him to say
every thing that might tend to sooth their
fears and win their confidence. I expressed
my wish to conduct them to our canoe, but
they declined my offer; and when they observed some of my people coming towards

us, they requested me to let them return; and I was so well satisfied with the progress I had made in my intercourse with them, that I did not hesitate a moment in complying with their desire. During their short stay, they observed us, and every thing about us, with a mixture of admiration and astonishment. We could plainly distinguish that their friends received them with great joy on their return, and that the articles which they carried back with them were examined with a general and eager curiosity; they also appeared to hold a consultation, which lasted about a quarter of an hour, and the result was, an invitation to come over to them, which was cheerfully accepted. Nevertheless, on our landing, they betrayed evident signs of confusion, which arose, probably from the quickness of our movements, as the prospect of a friendly communication had so cheered the spirits of my people, that they paddled across the river with the utmost expedition. The two men, however, who had been with us, appeared, very naturally, to possess the greatest share of courage on the occasion, and were ready to receive us on our landing; but our demeanor soon dispelled all their apprehensions, and the most familiar communication took place between us. When I had secured their confidence, by the distribution of trinkets among them, and treated the children with sugar, I instructed my interpreters to collect every necessary information in their power to afford me.

According to their account, this river, whose course is very extensive, runs towards the mid-day sun; and that at its mouth, as they had been informed, white people were building houses. They represented its current to be uniformly strong, and that in three places it was altogether impassable, from the falls and rapids, which poured along between perpendicular rocks that were much higher, and more rugged, than any we had yet seen, and would not admit of any passage over them. But besides the dangers and difficulties of the navigation, they added, that we should have to encounter the inhabitants of the country, who were very numerous. They also represented their immediate neighbours as a very malignant race, who lived in large subterraneous recesses: and when they were made to understand that it was our design to proceed to the sea, they dissuaded us from prosecuting our intention, as we should certainly become a sacrifice to the savage spirit of the natives. These people they described as possessing iron, arms, and utensils, which they procured from their neighbours to the Westward, and were obtained by a commercial progress from people like ourselves, who brought them in great canoes.

Such an account of our situation, exaggerated as it might be in some points, and erroneous· in others, was sufficiently alarming, and awakened very painful reflections; nevertheless it did not operate on my mind so as to produce any change in my original determination. My first object, therefore, was to persuade two of these people to accompany me, that they might secure for us a favourable reception from their neighbours. To this proposition they assented, but expressed some degree of dissatisfaction at the immediate departure, for which we were making preparation; but when we were ready to enter the canoe, a small one was seen doubling the point below, with three men in it. We thought it prudent to wait for their arrival, and they proved to be some of their relations, who had received the alarm from the messengers, which I have already mentioned as having been sent down the river for that purpose, and who had passed on, as we were afterwards informed, to extend the notice of our arrival. Though these people saw us in the midst of their friends, they displayed the most menacing actions, and hostile postures. At length, however, this wild,

savage spirit appeared to subside, and they
were persuaded to land. One of them, who
was a middle aged person, whose agitations
had been less frequent than those of his companions, and who was treated with particular
respect by them all, inquired who we were,
whence we came, whither we were going, and
what was the motive of our coming into that
country. When his friends had satisfied him
as far as they were able, respecting us, he
instantly advised us to delay our departure
for that night, as their relations below, having been by this time alarmed by the messengers, who had been sent for that purpose,
would certainly oppose our passage, notwithstanding I had two of their own people
with me. He added, that they would all of
them be here by sun-set, when they would be
convinced, as he was, that we were good
people, and meditated no ill designs against
them.

Such were the reasons which this Indian
urged in favour of our remaining till the next
morning; and they were too well founded for
me to hesitate in complying with them; besides, by prolonging my stay till the next
morning, it was probable that I might obtain
some important intelligence respecting the
country through which I was to pass, and
the people who inhabited it. I accordingly

ordered the canoe to be unloaded, taken out of the water, and gummed. My tent was also pitched, and the natives were now become so familiar, that I was obliged to let them know my wish to be alone and undisturbed.

My first application to the native whom I have already particularly mentioned, was to obtain from him such a plan of the river as he should be enabled to give me; and he complied with this request with a degree of readiness and intelligence that evidently proved it was by no means a new business to him. In order to acquire the best information he could communicate, I assured him, if I found his account correct, that I should either return myself, or send others to them, with such articles as they appeared to want: particularly arms and ammunition, with which they would be able to prevent their enemies from invading them. I obtained, however, no addition to what I already knew, but that the country below us, as far as he was acquainted with it, abounded in animals, and that the river produced plenty of fish.

Our canoe was now become so weak, leaky, and unmanageable, that it became a matter of absolute necessity to construct a new one; and I had been informed, that if we delayed that important work till we got further down the river, we should not be able to procure bark. I therefore dispatched two of my people, with an Indian, in search of that necessary material. The weather was so cloudy that I could not get an observation.*

I passed the rest of the day in conversing with these people: they consisted of seven families, containing eighteen men; they were clad in leather, and had some beaver and rabbit-skin blankets. They had not been long arrived in this part of the country, where they proposed to pass the summer, to catch fish for their winter provision: for this purpose they were preparing machines similar to that which we found in the first Indian house we saw and described. The fish which they take in them are large, and only visit this part of the river at certain seasons. These people differ very little, if at all, either in their appearance, language, or manners, from the Rocky-Mountain Indians. The men whom I sent in search of bark, returned with a certain quantity of it, but of a very indifferent kind. We were not gratified with the arrival of any of the natives whom we expected from a lower part of the river.

* The observation, already mentioned, I got on my return.

Chapter 8

Renew our voyage, accompanied by two of the natives. Account of courses. State of the river. Arrive at a subterranean house. See several natives. Brief description of them. Account of our conference with them. Saw other natives. Description of them. Their conduct, &c. The account which they gave of the country. The narrative of a female prisoner. The perplexities of my situation. Specimen of the language of two tribes. Change the plan of my journey. Return up the river. Succession of dangers and difficulties. Land on an island to build another canoe.

June, 1793.

SATURDAY, 22. At six in the morning we proceeded on our voyage, with two of the Indians, one of them in a small pointed canoe, made after the fashion of the Esquimaux, and the other in our own. This precaution was necessary in a two-fold point of view, as the small canoe could be sent ahead to speak to any of the natives that might be seen down the river, and, thus divided, it would not be easy for them both to make their escape. Mr. Mackay also embarked with the Indian, which seemed to afford him great satisfaction, and he was thereby enabled to keep us company with diminution of labour.

Our courses were South-South-East a mile and an half, South-East half a mile, South by East four miles and an half, South-East by South half a mile, South by West half a mile, South-East by East one mile, South-South-West a mile and an half, South by East one mile and a quarter. The country, on the right, presented a very beautiful appearance: it rose at first rather abruptly to the height of twenty-five feet, when the precipice was succeeded by an inclined plain to the foot of another steep; which was followed by another extent of gently-rising ground: these objects, which were shaded with groves of fir, presenting themselves alternately to a considerable distance.

We now landed near an house, the roof of which alone appeared above ground; but it was deserted by its inhabitants who had been alarmed at our approach. We observed several men in the second steep, who displayed the same postures and menacing actions as those which we have so lately described. Our conductors went to them immediately on an embassy of friendship, and, after a very vociferous discourse, one of them was persuaded to come to us, but presented a very ferocious aspect: the rest, who were seven in number, soon followed his example. They held their bows and arrows in their hands, and appeared in their garments, which were fastened round the neck, but left the right arm free for action. A cord fastened a blanket or leather covering under the right armpit, so that it hung upon the left shoulder, and might be occasionally employed as a target, that would turn an arrow which was nearly spent. As soon as they had recovered from their apprehensions, ten women made their appearance, but without any children, whom, I imagine, they had sent to a greater distance, to be out of the reach of all possible danger. I distributed a few presents among them, and left my guides to explain to them the object of my journey, and the friendliness of my designs, with which they had themselves been made acquainted; their fears being at length removed, I gave them a specimen of the use to which we applied our fire-arms: at the same time, I calmed their astonishment, by the assurance, that, though we could at once destroy those who did us injury, we could equally protect those who shewed us kindness. Our stay here did not exceed half an hour, and we left these people with favourable impressions of us.

From this place we steered East by North half a mile, South by East three quarters of a mile, and South by West a mile and an half, when we landed again on seeing some of the natives on the high ground, whose appearance was more wild and ferocious than any whom we had yet seen. Indeed I was under some apprehension that our guides, who went to conciliate them to us, would have fallen a prey to their savage fury. At length, however, they were persuaded to entertain a more favourable opinion of us, and they approached us one after another, to the number of sixteen men, and several women, I shook hands with them all, and desired my interpreters to explain that salutation as a token of friendship. As this was not a place where we could remain with the necessary convenience, I proposed to proceed further, in search of a more commodious spot. They immediately invited us to pass the night at their lodges, which were at no great distance, and promised, at the same time, that they would, in the morning, send two men to introduce us to the next nation, who were very numerous, and ill-disposed towards strangers. As we were pushing from the shore, we were very much surprised at hearing a woman pronounce several words in the Knisteneaux language. She proved to be a Rocky-Mountain native, so that my interpreters perfectly understood her. She informed us that her country is at the forks of this river, and that

she had been taken prisoner by the Knisteneaux, who had carried her across the
mountains. After having passed the greatest
part of the summer with them, she had contrived to escape, before they had reached
their own country, and had re-crossed the
mountains, when she expected to meet her
own friends: but after suffering all the hardships incident to such a journey, she had
been taken by a war-party of the people
with whom she then was, who had driven her
relations from the river into the mountains.
She had since been detained by her present
husband, of whom she had no cause to complain; nevertheless she expressed a strong
desire to return to her own people. I presented her with several useful articles, and
desired her to come to me at the lodges,
which she readily engaged to do. We arrived
thither before the Indians, and landed, as
we had promised. It was now near twelve
at noon, but on attempting to take an altitude I found the angle too great for my
sextant.

The natives whom we had already seen,
and several others, soon joined us, with a
greater number of women than I had yet
seen; but I did not observe the female prisoner among them. There were thirty-five of
them, and my remaining store of presents

was not sufficient to enable me to be very
liberal to so many claimants. Among the
men I found four of the adjoining nation,
and a Rocky-Mountain Indian, who had
been with them for some time. As he was
understood by my interpreters, and was himself well acquainted with the language of the
strangers, I possessed the means of obtaining
every information respecting the country,
which it might be in their power to afford
me. For this purpose I selected an elderly
man, from the four strangers, whose countenance had prepossessed me in his favour.
I stated to these people, as I had already
done to those from whom I had hitherto derived information, the objects of my voyage,
and the very great advantages which they
would receive from my successful termination of it. They expressed themselves very
much satisfied at my communication, and
assured me that they would not deceive me
respecting the subject of my inquiry. An old
man also, who appeared to possess the character of a chief, declared his wish to see me
return to his land, and that his two young
daughters should then be at my disposal. I
now proceeded to request the native, whom I
had particularly selected, to commence his
information, by drawing a sketch of the
country upon a large piece of bark, and he

immediately entered on the work, frequently appealing to, and sometimes asking the advice of, those around him. He described the river as running to the East of South, receiving many rivers, and every six or eight leagues encumbered with falls and rapids, some of which were very dangerous, and six of them impracticable. The carrying-places he represented as of great length, and passing over hills and mountains. He depicted the lands of three other tribes, in succession, who spoke different languages. Beyond them he knew nothing either of the river or country, only that it was still a long way to the sea; and that, as he had heard, there was a lake, before they reached the water, which the natives did not drink. As far as his knowledge of the river extended, the country on either side was level, in many places without wood, and abounding in red deer, and some of a small fallow kind. Few of the natives, he said, would come to the banks for some time; but that at a certain season they would arrive there in great numbers, to fish. They now procured iron, brass, copper, and trinkets, from the Westward; but formerly these articles were obtained from the lower parts of the river, though in small quantities. A knife was produced which had been brought from that quarter. The blade was ten inches long, and an inch and an half broad, but with a very blunted edge. The handle was of horn. We understood that this instrument had been obtained from white men, long before they had heard that any came to the Westward. One very old man observed, that as long as he could remember, he was told of white people to the Southward; and that he had heard, though he did not vouch for the truth of the report, that one of them had made an attempt to come up the river, and was destroyed.

These people describe the distance across the country as very short to the Western ocean; and, according to my own idea, it cannot be above five or six degrees. If the assertion of Mr. Mears[1] be correct, it cannot be so far, as the inland sea which he mentions within Nootka, must come as far East as 126 West longitude. They assured us that the road was not difficult, as they avoided the mountains, keeping along the low lands between them, many parts of which are entirely free from wood. According to their account, this way is so often travelled by them, that their path is visible throughout the whole journey, which lies along small lakes and rivers. It occupied them, they said,

[1] John Meares, English navigator, who in 1789 had explored the north Pacific Coast.—ED.

no more than six nights, to go to where they meet the people who barter iron, brass, copper, beads, &c. with them, for dressed leather, and beaver, bear, lynx, fox, and marten skins. The iron is about eighteen inches of two-inch bar. To this they give an edge at one end, and fix it to an handle at right angles, which they employ as an axe. When the iron is worn down, they fabricate it into points for their arrows and spikes. Before they procured iron they employed bone and horn for those purposes. The copper and brass they convert into collars, arm-bands, bracelets, and other ornaments. They sometimes also point their arrows with those metals. They had been informed by those whom they meet to trade with, that the white people, from whom these articles are obtained, were building houses at the distance of three days, or two nights journey from the place where they met last fall. With this route they all appeared to be well acquainted.

I now requested that they would send for the female prisoner whom I saw yesterday, but I received only vague and evasive answers: they probably apprehended, that it was our design to take her from them. I was, however, very much disappointed at being prevented from having an interview with her, as she might have given me a correct account of the country beyond the forks of the river, as well as of the pass, through the mountains, from them.

My people had listened with great attention to the relation which had been given me, and it seemed to be their opinion, that it would be absolute madness to attempt a passage through so many savage and barbarous nations. My situation may, indeed, be more easily conceived than expressed: I had no more than thirty days provision remaining, exclusive of such supplies as I might obtain from the natives, and the toil of our hunters, which, however, was so precarious as to be matter of little dependence: besides, our ammunition would soon be exhausted, particularly our ball, of which we had not more than an hundred and fifty, and about thirty pounds weight of shot, which, indeed, might be converted into bullets, though with great waste.

The more I heard of the river, the more I was convinced it could not empty itself into the ocean to the North of what is called the River of the West, so that with its windings, the distance must be very great.[2] Such being

[2] The "River of the West" was the Columbia, on whose upper waters Mackenzie mistakenly supposed himself to be.—ED.

the discouraging circumstances of my situation, which were now heightened by the discontents of my people, I could not but be alarmed at the idea of attempting to get to the discharge of such a rapid river, especially when I reflected on the tardy progress of my return up it, even if I should meet with no obstruction from the natives; a circumstance not very probable, from the numbers of them which would then be on the river; and whom I could have no opportunity of conciliating in my passage down, for the reasons which have been already mentioned. At all events, I must give up every expectation of returning this season to Athabasca. Such were my reflections at this period; but instead of continuing to indulge them, I determined to proceed with resolution, and set future events at defiance. At the same time I suffered myself to nourish the hope that I might be able to penetrate with more safety, and in a shorter period, to the ocean by the inland, western communication.

To carry this project into execution I must have returned a considerable distance up the river, which would necessarily be attended with a very serious inconvenience, if I passed over every other; as in a voyage of this kind, a retrograde motion could not fail to cool the ardour, slacken the zeal, and weaken the confidence of those, who have no greater inducement in the undertaking, than to follow the conductor of it. Such was the state of my mind at this period, and such the circumstances by which it was distressed and distracted.

To the people who had given me the foregoing information, I presented some beads, which they preferred to any other articles in my possession, and I recompensed in the same manner two of them who communicated to me the following vocabulary in the languages of the Nagailer and Atnah tribes.

	The Nagailer, or Carrier-Indians.	The Atnah, or Chin-Indians.
Eye,	Nah,	Thloustin.
Hair,	Thigah,	Cahowdin.
Teeth,	Gough,	Chliough.
Nose,	Nenzeh,	Pisax.
Head,	Thie,	Scapacay.
Wood,	Dekin,	Shedzay.
Hand,	Lah,	Calietha.
Leg,	Kin,	Squacht.
Tongue,	Thoula,	Dewhasjisk.
Ear,	Zach,	Ithlinah.
Man,	Dinay,	Scuynlouch.
Woman,	Chiqoui,	Smosledgensk.
Beaver,	Zah,	Schugh.
Elk,	Yezey,	Oikoy-Beh.

	The Nagailer, or Carrier-Indians.	The Atnah, or Chin-Indians.
Dog,	Sleing,	Scacah.
Ground-hog,	Thidnu,	Squaiquais.
Iron,	Thlisitch,	Soucoumang.
Fire,	Coun,	Teuck.
Water,	Tou,	Shaweliquoih.
Stone,	Zeh,	Ishehoineah.
Bow,	Nettuny,	Isquoinah.
Arrow,	Igah,	Squaili.
Yes,	Nesi,	Amaig.
Plains,	Thoughoud,	Spilela.
Come here,	Andezei,	Thla-elyeh.

The Atnah language has no affinity to any with which I am acquainted; but the Nagailer differs very little from that spoken by the Beaver Indians, and is almost the same as that of the Chepewyans.

We had a thunder-storm with heavy rain; and in the evening when it had subsided, the Indians amused us with singing and dancing, in which they were joined by the young women. Four men now arrived whom we had not yet seen; they had left their families at some distance in the country, and expressed a desire that we should visit them there.

Sunday, 23. After a restless night, I called the Indians together, from whom I yesterday received the intelligence which has been already mentioned, in the hope that I might obtain some additional information. From their former account they did not make the least deviation; but they informed me further, that where they left this river, a small one from the Westward falls into it, which was navigable for their canoes during four days, and from thence they slept but two nights, to get to the people with whom they trade, and who have wooden canoes much larger than ours, in which they go down a river to the sea. They continued to inform me, that if I went that way we must leave our own canoe behind us; but they thought it probable that those people would furnish us with another. From thence they stated the distance to be only one day's voyage with the current to the lake whose water is nauseous, and where they had heard that great canoes came two winters ago, and that the people belonging to them, brought great quantities of goods and built houses.

At the commencement of this conversation, I was very much surprised by the following question from one of the Indians: "What," demanded he, "can be the reason that you are so particular and anxious in your inquiries of us respecting a knowledge of this country: do not you white men know every thing in the world?" This interrogatory was so very unexpected, that it occasioned some hesitation before I could answer it. At length, however, I replied, that we certainly were acquainted with the principal circumstances of every part of the world; that I knew where the sea is, and where I myself then was, but that I did not exactly understand what obstacles might interrupt me in getting to it; with which, he and his relations must be well acquainted, as they had so frequently surmounted them. Thus I fortunately preserved the impression in their minds, of the superiority of white people over themselves.

It was now, however, absolutely necessary that I should come to a final determination which route to take; and no long interval of reflection was employed, before I preferred to go over land: the comparative shortness and security of such a journey, were alone sufficient to determine me. I accordingly proposed to two of the Indians to accompany me, and one of them readily assented to my proposition.

I now called those of my people about me, who had not been present at my consultation with the natives; and after passing a warm eulogium on their fortitude, patience, and perseverance, I stated the difficulties that

threatened our continuing to navigate the
river, the length of time it would require,
and the scanty provision we had for such a
voyage: I then proceeded for the foregoing
reasons to propose a shorter route, by try-
ing the over-land road to the sea. At the
same time, as I knew from experience, the
difficulty of retaining guides, and as many
circumstances might occur to prevent our
progress in that direction, I declared my resolution not to attempt it, unless they would
engage, if we could not after all proceed over
land, to return with me, and continue our
voyage to the discharge of the waters, whatever the distance might be. At all events, I
declared, in the most solemn manner, that I
would not abandon my design of reaching
the sea, if I made the attempt alone, and
that I did not despair of returning in safety
to my friends.

This proposition met with the most zeal-
ous return, and they unanimously assured
me, that they were as willing now as they
had ever been, to abide by my resolutions,
whatever they might be, and to follow me
wherever I should go. I therefore requested
them to prepare for an immediate departure,
and at the same time gave notice to the
man who had engaged to be our guide, to
be in readiness to accompany us. When our

determination to return up the river was made known, several of the natives took a very abrupt departure; but to those who remained, I gave a few useful articles, explaining to them at the same time, the advantages that would result to them, if their relations conducted me to the sea, along such a road as they had described. I had already given a moose skin to some of the women for the purpose of making shoes, which were now brought us; they were well sewed but ill shaped, and a few beads were considered as a sufficient remuneration for the skill employed on them. Mr. Mackay, by my desire, engraved my name, and the date of the year on a tree.[3]

When we were ready to depart, our guide proposed, for the sake of expedition, to go over land to his lodge, that he might get there before us, to make some necessary preparation for his journey. I did not altogether relish his design, but was obliged to consent: I thought it prudent, however, to send Mr. Mackay, and the two Indians along with him. Our place of rendezvous, was the subterraneous house which we passed yesterday.

[3] The point at which the party abandoned the descent of the Fraser is marked by the present-day village of Alexandria, named in Mackenzie's honor.—Ed.

At ten in the morning we embarked, and went up the current much faster than I expected with such a crazy vessel as that which carried us. We met our people at the house as had been appointed; but the Indian still continued to prefer going on by land, and it would have been needless for me to oppose him. He proceeded, therefore, with his former companions, whom I desired to keep him in good humour by every reasonable gratification. They were also furnished with a few articles that might be of use if they should meet with strangers.

In a short time after we had left the house, I saw a wooden canoe coming down the river, with three natives in it, who, as soon as they perceived us, made for the shore, and hurried into the woods. On passing their vessel, we discovered it to be one of those which we had seen at the lodges. A severe gust of wind, with rain, came from the South-South-East. This we found to be a very prevalent wind in these parts. We soon passed another wooden canoe drawn stern foremost on the shore; a circumstance which we had not hitherto observed. The men worked very hard, and though I imagined we went a-head very fast, we could not reach the lodges, but landed for the night at nine, close to the encampment of two families of the natives whom we had formerly seen at the lodges. I immediately went and sat down with them, when they gave me some roasted fish; two of my men who followed me were gratified also with some of their provisions. The youngest of the two natives now quitted the shed, and did not return during the time I remained there. I endeavoured to explain to the other by signs, the cause of my sudden return, which he appeared to understand. In the mean time my tent was pitched, and on my going to it, I was rather surprised that he did not follow me, as he had been constantly with me during the day and night I had passed with his party on going down. We, however, went to rest in a state of perfect security; nor had we the least apprehension for the safety of our people who were gone by land.

Monday, 24. We were in our canoe by four this morning, and passed by the Indian hut, which appeared in a state of perfect tranquillity. We soon came in sight of the point where we first saw the natives, and at eight were much surprised and disappointed at seeing Mr. Mackay, and our two Indians coming alone from the ruins of an house that had been partly carried away by the ice and water, at a short distance below the place where we had appointed to meet. Nor was our surprise and apprehension diminished by the alarm which was painted in their countenances. When we had landed, they informed me that they had taken refuge in that place, with the determination to sell their lives, which they considered in the most imminent danger, as dear as possible. In a very short time after they had left us, they met a party of the Indians, whom we had known at this place, and were probably those whom we had seen to land from their canoe. They appeared to be in a state of extreme rage, and had their bows bent, with their arrows across them. The guide stopped to ask them some questions, which my people did not understand, and then set off with his utmost speed. Mr. Mackay, however, did not leave him till they were both exhausted with running. When the young man came up, he then said, that some treacherous design was meditated against them, as he was induced to believe from the declaration of the natives, who told him that they were going to do mischief, but refused to name the enemy. The guide then conducted them through very bad ways, as fast as they could run; and when he was desired to slacken his pace, he answered that they might follow him in any manner they pleased, but that he was impatient to get to his family, in order to prepare shoes, and other necessaries, for his journey. They did not, however, think it prudent to quit him, and he would not stop till ten at night. On passing a track that was but lately made, they began to be seriously alarmed, and on inquiring of the guide where they were, he pretended not to understand them. They then all laid down, exhausted with fatigue, and without any kind of covering: they were cold, wet, and hungry, but dared not light a fire, from the apprehension of an enemy. This comfortless spot they left at the dawn of day, and, on their arrival at the lodges, found them deserted; the property of the Indians being scattered about, as if abandoned for ever. The guide then made two or three trips into the woods, calling aloud, and bellowing like a madman. At length he set off in the same direction as they came, and had not since appeared. To heighten their misery, as they did not find us at the place appointed, they concluded that we were all destroyed, and had already formed their plan to take to the woods, and cross in as direct a line as they could proceed, to the waters of the Peace River, a scheme which could only be suggested by despair. They intended to have waited for us till noon, and if we did not appear by that time, to have entered without further delay on their desperate expedition.

This alarm among the natives was a very unexpected as well as perilous event, and my powers of conjecture were exhausted in searching for the cause of it. A general panic seized all around me, and any further prosecution of the voyage was now considered by them as altogether hopeless and impracticable. But without paying the least attention to their opinions or surmises, I ordered them to take every thing out of the canoe, except six packages: when that was done, I left four men to take care of the lading, and returned with the others to our camp of last night, where I hoped to find the two men, with their families, whom we had seen there, and to be able to bring them to lodge with us, when I should wait the issue of this mysterious business. This project, however, was disappointed, for these people had quitted their sheds in the silence of the night, and had not taken a single article of their little property with them.

These perplexing circumstances made a deep impression on my mind, not as to our immediate safety, for I entertained not the least apprehension of the Indians I had hitherto seen, even if their whole force should have been combined to attack us, but these untoward events seemed to threaten the prosecution of my journey; and I could not reflect on the possibility of such a disappointment but with sensations little short of agony. Whatever might have been the wavering disposition of the people on former occasions, they were now decided in their opinions as to the necessity of returning without delay; and when we came back to them, their cry was—"Let us reimbark, and be gone." This, however, was not my design, and in a more peremptory tone than I usually employed, they were ordered to unload the canoe, and take her out of the water. On examining our property, several articles appeared to be missing, which the Indians must have purloined; and among them were an axe, two knives, and the young men's bag of medicines. We now took a position that was the best calculated for defence, got our arms in complete order, filled each man's flask of powder, and distributed an hundred bullets, which were all that remained, while some were employed in melting down shot to make more. The weather was so cloudy that I had not an opportunity of taking an observation.

While we were employed in making these preparations, we saw an Indian in a canoe come down the river, and land at the huts, which he began to examine. On perceiving us he stood still, as if in a state of suspense, when I instantly dispatched one of my Indians towards him, but no persuasions could induce him to have confidence in us; he even threatened that he would hasten to join his friends, who would come and kill us. At the conclusion of this menace he disappeared. On the return of my young man, with this account of the interview, I pretended to discredit the whole, and attributed it to his own apprehensions and alarms. This, however, he denied, and asked with a look and tone of resentment, whether he had ever told me a lie? Though he was but a young man, he said, he had been on war excursions before he came with me, and that he should no longer consider me as a wise man, which he had hitherto done.

To add to our distresses we had not an ounce of gum for the reparation of the canoe, and not one of the men had sufficient courage to venture into the woods to collect it. In this perplexing situation I entertained the hope that in the course of the night some of the natives would return, to take away a part at least of the things which they had left behind them, as they had gone away without the covering necessary to defend them from the weather and the flies. I therefore ordered the canoe to be loaded, and dropped to an old house, one side of which, with its roof, had been carried away by the water; but the three remaining angles were sufficient to shelter us from the woods. I then ordered two strong piquets to be driven into the ground, to which the canoe was fastened, so that if we were hard pressed we had only to step on board and push off. We were under the necessity of making a smoke to keep off the swarms of flies, which would have otherwise tormented us; but we did not venture to excite a blaze, as it would have been a mark for the arrows of the enemy. Mr. Mackay and myself, with three men kept alternate watch, and allowed the Indians to do as they fancied. I took the first watch, and the others laid down in their clothes by us. I also placed a centinel at a small distance, who was relieved every hour. The weather was cloudy, with showers of rain.

Tuesday, 25. At one I called up the other watch, and laid down to a small portion of broken rest. At five I arose, and as the situation which we left yesterday was preferable to that which we then occupied, I determined to return to it. On our arrival Mr. Mackay informed me that the men had expressed their dissatisfaction to him in a very unreserved manner, and had in very strong terms declared their resolution to follow me no further in my proposed enterprize. I did not appear, however, to have received such communications from him, and continued to employ my whole thoughts in contriving means to bring about a reconciliation with the natives, which alone would enable me to procure guides, without whose assistance it would be impossible for me to proceed, when my darling project would end in disappointment.

At twelve we saw a man coming with the stream upon a raft, and he must have discovered us before we perceived him, as he was working very hard to get to the opposite shore, where he soon landed, and instantly fled into the woods. I now had a meridional altitude, which gave 60. 23. natural horizon, (the angle being more than the sextant could measure with the artificial horizon,) one mile and an half distant; and the eye five feet above the level of the water, gave 52. 47. 51. North latitude.

While I was thus employed, the men loaded the canoe without having received any orders from me, and as this was the first time they had ventured to act in such a decided manner, I naturally concluded, that they had preconcerted a plan for their return. I thought it prudent, however, to take no notice of this transaction, and to wait the issue of future circumstances. At this moment our Indians perceived a person in the edge of the woods above us, and they were immediately dispatched to discover who it was. After a short absence they returned with a young woman whom we had seen before: her language was not clearly comprehended by us, so that we could not learn from her, at least with any degree of certainty, the cause of this unfortunate alarm that had taken place among the natives. She told us that her errand was to fetch some things which she had left behind her; and one of the dogs whom we found here, appeared to acknowledge her as his mistress. We treated her with great kindness, gave her something to eat, and added a present of such articles as we thought might please her. On her expressing a wish to leave us, we readily consented to her departure, and indulged the hope that her reception would induce the natives to return in peace, and give us an opportunity to convince them, that we had no hostile designs whatever against them. On leaving us, she went up the river without taking a single article of her own, and the dog followed. The wind was changeable throughout the day, and there were several showers in the course of it.

Though a very apparent anxiety prevailed among the people for their departure, I appeared to be wholly inattentive to it, and at eight in the evening I ordered four men to step into the canoe, which had been loaded for several hours, and drop down to our guard-house, and my command was immediately obeyed: the rest of us proceeded there by land. When I was yet at a considerable distance from the house, and thought it impossible for an arrow to reach it, having a bow and quiver in my hand, I very imprudently let fly an arrow, when, to my astonishment and infinite alarm, I heard it strike a log of the house. The men who had just landed, imagined that they were attacked by an enemy from the woods. Their confusion was in proportion to their imaginary danger, and on my arrival I found that the arrow had passed within a foot of one of the men; though it had no point, the weapon, incredible as it may appear, had entered an hard, dry log of wood upwards of an inch. But this was not all: for the men readily availed themselves of this circumstance, to remark upon the danger of remaining in the power of a people possessed of such means of destruction. Mr. Mackay having the first watch, I laid myself down in my cloak.

Wednesday, 26. About midnight a rustling noise was heard in the woods which created a general alarm, and I was awakened to be informed of the circumstance, but heard nothing. At one I took my turn of the watch, and our dog continued unceasingly to run backwards and forwards along the skirts of the wood in a state of restless vigilance. At two in the morning the centinel informed me, that he saw something like an human figure creeping along on all-fours about fifty paces above us. After some time had passed in our search, I at length discovered that his information was true, and it appeared to me that a bear had occasioned the alarm; but when day appeared, it proved to be an old, grey-haired, blind man, who had been compelled to leave his hiding-place by extreme hunger, being too infirm to join in the flight of the natives to whom he belonged. When I put my hand on this object of decaying nature, his alarm was so great, that I expected it would have thrown him into convulsions. I immediately led him to our fire which had been just lighted, and gave him something to eat, which he much wanted, as he had not tasted food for two days. When his hunger was satisfied, and he had got warm and composed, I requested him to acquaint me with the cause of that alarm which had taken place respecting us among his relations and friends, whose regard we appeared to have conciliated but a few days past. He replied, that very soon after we had left them, some

natives arrived from above, who informed
them that we were enemies; and our unexpected return, in direct contradiction to our
own declarations, confirmed them in that
opinion. They were now, he said, so scattered, that a considerable time would elapse,
before they could meet again. We gave him
the real history of our return, as well as of
the desertion of our guide, and, at the same
time, stated the impossibility of our proceeding, unless we procured a native to conduct
us. He replied, that if he had not lost his
sight, he would with the greatest readiness
have accompanied us on our journey. He
also confirmed the accounts which we had
received of the country, and the route to
the Westward. I did not neglect to employ
every argument in my power, that he might
be persuaded of our friendly disposition to
the inhabitants wheresoever we might meet
them.

At sun-rise we perceived a canoe with one
man in it on the opposite side of the river,
and at our request, the blind man called to
him to come to us, but he returned no answer, and continued his course as fast as he
could paddle down the current. He was considered as a spy by my men, and I was confirmed in that opinion, when I saw a wooden
canoe drifting with the stream close in to the

other shore, where it was more than probable that some of the natives might be concealed. It might, therefore, have been an useless enterprise, or perhaps fatal to the future success of our undertaking, if we had pursued these people, as they might, through fear, have employed their arms against us, and provoked us to retaliate.

The old man informed me, that some of the natives whom I had seen here were gone up the river, and those whom I saw below had left their late station to gather a root in the plains, which, when dried, forms a considerable article in their winter stock of provisions. He had a woman, he said, with him, who used to see us walking along the small adjoining river, but when he called her he received no answer, so that she had probably fled to join her people. He informed me, also, that he expected a considerable number of his tribe to come on the upper part of the river to catch fish for their present support, and to cure them for their winter store; among whom he had a son and two brothers.

In consequence of these communications, I deemed it altogether unnecessary to lose any more time at this place, and I informed the old man that he must accompany me for the purpose of introducing us to his friends and relations, and that if we met with his son or brothers, I depended upon him to persuade them, or some of their party, to attend us as guides in our meditated expedition. He expressed his wish to be excused from this service, and in other circumstances we should not have insisted on it, but, situated as we were, we could not yield to his request.

At seven in the morning we left this place, which I named Deserter's River or Creek. Our blind guide was, however, so averse to continuing with us, that I was under the very disagreeable necessity of ordering the men to carry him into the canoe; and this was the first act during my voyage, that had the semblance of violent dealing. He continued to speak in a very loud tone, while he remained, according to his conjecture, near enough to the camp to be heard, but in a language that our interpreters did not understand. On asking him what he said, and why he did not speak in a language known to us, he replied, that the woman understood him better in that which he spoke, and he requested her, if she heard him, to come for him to the carrying-place, where he expected we should leave him.

At length our canoe was become so leaky, that it was absolutely unfit for service; and it was the unremitting employment of one person to keep her clear of water: we, therefore, inquired of the old man where we could conveniently obtain the articles necessary to build a new one; and we understood from him that, at some distance up the river, we should find plenty of bark and cedar.

At ten, being at the foot of a rapid, we saw a small canoe coming down with two men in it. We thought it would be impossible for them to escape, and therefore struck off from the shore with a design to intercept them, directing the old man at the same time to address them; but they no sooner perceived us, than they steered into the strength of the current, where I thought that they must inevitably perish; but their attention appeared to be engrossed by the situation of their canoe, and they escaped without making us the least reply.

About three in the afternoon we perceived a lodge at the entrance of a considerable river on the right, as well as the tracks of people in the mud at the mouth of a small river on the left. As they appeared to be fresh, we landed, and endeavoured to trace them, but without success. We then crossed over to the lodge, which was deserted, but all the usual furniture of such buildings remained untouched.

Throughout the whole of this day the men had been in a state of extreme ill-humour, and as they did not choose openly to vent it upon me, they disputed and quarrelled among themselves. About sun-set the canoe struck upon the stump of a tree, which broke a large hole in her bottom; a circumstance that gave them an opportunity to let loose their discontents without reserve. I left them as soon as we had landed, and ascended an elevated bank, in a state of mind which I scarce wish to recollect, and shall not attempt to describe. At this place there was a subterraneous house, where I determined to pass the night. The water had risen since we had passed down, and it was with the utmost exertion that we came up several points in the course of the day.

Thursday, *27*. We embarked at half past four, with very favourable weather, and at eight we landed, where there was an appearance of our being able to procure bark; we, however, obtained but a small quantity. At twelve we went on shore again, and collected as much as was necessary for our purpose. It now remained for us to fix on a proper place for building another canoe, as it was impossible to proceed with our old one, which was become an absolute wreck. At five in the afternoon we came to a spot well adapted to the business in which we were about to engage. It was on a small island not much encumbered with wood, though there was plenty of the spruce kind on the opposite land, which was only divided from us by a small channel. We now landed, but before the canoe was unloaded, and the tent pitched, a violent thunder-storm came on, accompanied with rain, which did not subside till the night had closed in upon us. Two of our men who had been in the woods for axe-handles, saw a deer, and one of them shot at it, but unluckily missed his aim. A net was also prepared and set in the eddy at the end of the island.

Chapter 9

Make preparations to build a canoe. Engage in that important work. It proceeds with great expedition. The guide who had deserted arrives with another Indian. He communicates agreeable intelligence. They take an opportunity to quit the island. Complete the canoe. Leave the island, which was now named the Canoe Island. Obliged to put the people on short allowance. Account of the navigation. Difficult ascent of a rapid. Fresh perplexities. Continue our voyage up the river. Meet the guide and some of his friends. Conceal some pemmican and other articles. Make preparations for proceeding over land. Endeavour to secure the canoe till our return. Proceed on our journey. Various circumstances of it.

June, 1793.

FRIDAY, 28. At a very early hour of the morning every man was employed in making preparations for building another canoe, and different parties went in search of wood, watape, and gum. At two in the afternoon they all returned successful, except the collectors of gum, and of that article it was feared we should not obtain here a sufficient supply for our immediate wants. After a necessary portion of time allotted for refreshment, each began his respective work.

I had an altitude at noon, which made us in 53. 2. 32. North latitude.

Saturday, 29. The weather continued to be fine. At five o'clock we renewed our labour, and the canoe was got in a state of considerable forwardness. The conductor of the work, though a good man, was remarkable for the tardiness of his operations, whatever they might be, and more disposed to eat than to be active; I, therefore, took this opportunity of unfolding my sentiments to him, and thereby discovering to all around me the real state of my mind, and the resolutions I had formed for my future conduct. After reproaching him for his general inactivity, but particularly on the present occasion, when our time was so precious, I mentioned the apparent want of economy both of himself and his companions, in the article of provisions. I informed him that I was not altogether a stranger to their late conversations, from whence I drew the conclusion that they wished to put an end to the voyage. If that were so, I expressed my wish that they would be explicit, and tell me at once of their determination to follow me no longer. I concluded, however, by assuring him, that whatever plan they had meditated to pursue, it was my fixed and unalterable determination to proceed, in spite of every difficulty that might oppose, or danger that should threaten me. The man was very much mortified at my addressing this remonstrance particularly to him; and replied, that he did not deserve my displeasure more than the rest of them. My object being answered, the conversation dropped, and the work went on.

About two in the afternoon one of the men perceived a canoe with two natives in it, coming along the inside of the island, but the water being shallow, it turned back, and we imagined that on perceiving us they had taken the alarm; but we were agreeably surprised on seeing them come up the outside of the island, when we recognised our guide, and one of the natives whom we had already seen. The former began immediately to apologize for his conduct, and assured me that since he had left me, his whole time had been employed in searching after his family, who had been seized with the general panic, that had been occasioned by the false reports of the people who had first fled from us. He said it was generally apprehended by the natives that we had been unfriendly to their relations above, who were expected upon the river in great numbers at this time; and that many of the Atnah or Chin nation, had come up the river to where we had been, in the hope of seeing us, and were very much displeased with him and his friends for having neglected to give them an early notice of our arrival there. He added, that the two men whom we had seen yesterday, or the day before, were just returned from their rendezvous, with the natives of the sea coast, and had brought a message from his brother-in-law, that he had a new axe for him, and not to forget to bring a moose-skin dressed in exchange, which he actually had in his canoe. He expected to meet him, he said, at the other end of the carrying-place.

This was as pleasing intelligence as we had reason to expect, and it is almost superfluous to observe that we stood in great need of it. I had a meridian altitude, which gave 53. 3. 7. North latitude. I also took time in the fore and afternoon, that gave a mean of 1. 37. 42. Achrometer slow apparent time, which, with an observed immersion of Jupiter's first satellite, made our longitude 122. 48. West of Greenwich.

The blind old man gave a very favourable account of us to his friends, and they all three were very merry together during the whole of the afternoon. That our guide, however, might not escape from us during the night, I determined to watch him.

Alexander Mackenzie

Sunday, 30. Our strangers conducted themselves with great good-humour throughout the day. According to their information we should find their friends above and below the carrying-place. They mentioned, also, that some of them were not of their tribe, but are allied to the people of the sea coast, who trade with the white men. I had a meridian altitude, that gave 53. 3. 17. North latitude.

July. Monday, 1. Last night I had the first watch, when one of my Indians proposed to sit up with me, as he understood, from the old man's conversation, that he intended, in the course of the night, to make his escape. Accordingly at eleven I extinguished my light, and sat quietly in my tent, from whence I could observe the motions of the natives. About twelve, though the night was rather dark, I observed the old man creeping on his hands and knees towards the water-side. We accordingly followed him very quietly to the canoe, and he would have gone away with it, if he had not been interrupted in his design. On upbraiding him for his treacherous conduct, when he had been treated with so much kindness by us, he denied the intention of which we accused him, and declared that his sole object was to assuage his thirst. At length, however, he acknowledged the truth, and when we brought him to the fire, his friends, who now awoke, on being informed of what had passed, reprobated his conduct, and asked him how he could expect that the white people would return to this country, if they experienced such ungrateful treatment. The guide said, for his part, he was not a woman, and would never run away through fear. But notwithstanding this courageous declaration, at one I awakened Mr. Mackay, related to him what had passed, and requested him not to indulge himself in sleep till I should rise. It was seven before I awoke, and on quitting my tent I was surprised at not seeing the guide and his companion, and my apprehensions were increased when I observed that the canoe was removed from its late situation. To my inquiries after them, some of the men very composedly answered that they were gone up the river, and had left the old man behind them. Mr. Mackay also told me, that while he was busily employed on the canoe, they had got to the point before he had observed their departure. The interpreter now informed me that at the dawn of day the guide had expressed his design, as soon as the sun was up, to go and wait for us, where he might find his friends. I hoped this might be true; but that my people should suffer them to

depart without giving me notice, was a circumstance that awakened very painful reflections in my breast. The weather was clear
in the forenoon. My observation this day
gave 53. 3. 32 North latitude.

At five in the afternoon our vessel was
completed, and ready for service. She proved
a stronger and better boat than the old one,
though had it not been for the gum obtained
from the latter, it would have been a matter
of great difficulty to have procured a suffi-
ciency of that article to have prevented her
from leaking. The remainder of the day was
employed by the people in cleaning and refreshing themselves, as they had enjoyed no
relaxation from their labour since we landed
on this spot.

The old man having manifested for various
and probably very fallacious reasons, a very
great aversion to accompany us any further,
it did not appear that there was any necessity to force his inclination. We now put our
arms in order, which was soon accomplished,
as they were at all times a general object of
attention.

Tuesday, 2. It rained throughout the night,
but at half past three we were ready to embark, when I offered to conduct the old man
where he had supposed we should meet his
friends, but he declined the proposition. I

therefore directed a few pounds of pemmican to be left with him, for his immediate support, and took leave of him and the place, which I named Canoe Island. During our stay there we had been most cruelly tormented by flies, particularly the sand-fly, which I am disposed to consider as the most tormenting insect of its size in nature. I was also compelled to put the people upon short allowance, and confine them to two meals a-day, a regulation peculiarly offensive to a Canadian voyageur. One of these meals was composed of the dried roes of fish, pounded, and boiled in water, thickened with a small quantity of flour, and fattened with a bit of grain. These articles, being brought to the consistency of an hasty pudding, produced a substantial and not unpleasant dish. The natives are very careful of the roes of fish, which they dry, and preserve in baskets made of bark. Those we used were found in the huts of the first people who fled from us. During our abode in Canoe Island, the water sunk three perpendicular feet. I now gave the men a dram each, which could not but be considered, at this time, as a very comfortable treat. They were, indeed, in high spirits, when they perceived the superior excellence of the new vessel, and reflected that it was the work of their own hands.

At eleven we arrived at the rapids, and the
foreman, who had not forgotten the fright
he suffered on coming down it, proposed that
the canoe and lading should be carried over
the mountain. I threatened him with taking
the office of foreman on myself, and suggested
the evident change there was in the appearance of the water since we passed it, which
upon examination had sunk four feet and an
half. As the water did not seem so strong on
the West side, I determined to cross over,
having first put Mr. Mackay, and our two
hunters, on shore, to try the woods for game.
We accordingly traversed, and got up close
along the rocks, to a considerable distance,
with the paddles, when we could proceed no
further without assistance from the line; and
to draw it across a perpendicular rock, for
the distance of fifty fathoms, appeared to be
an insurmountable obstacle. The general
opinion was to return, and carry on the other
side; I desired, however, two of the men to
take the line, which was seventy fathoms in
length, with a small roll of bark, and endeavour to climb up the rocks, from whence they
were to descend on the other side of that
which opposed our progress; they were then
to fasten the end of the line to the roll of
bark, which the current would bring to us;
this being effected, they would be able to

draw us up. This was an enterprise of difficulty and danger, but it was crowned with success; though to get to the water's edge above, the men were obliged to let themselves down with the line, run round a tree, from the summit of the rock. By a repetition of the same operation, we at length cleared the rapid, with the additional trouble of carrying the canoe, and unloading at two cascades. We were not more than two hours getting up this difficult part of the river, including the time employed in repairing an hole which had been broken in the canoe, by the negligence of the steersman.

Here we expected to meet with the natives, but there was not the least appearance of them, except that the guide, his companion, and two others, had apparently passed the carrying-place. We saw several fish leap out of the water, which appeared to be of the salmon kind. The old man, indeed, had informed us that this was the season when the large fish begin to come up the river. Our hunters returned, but had not seen the track of any animal. We now continued our journey; the current was not strong, but we met with frequent impediments from the fallen trees, which lay along the banks. We landed at eight in the evening; and suffered indescribable inconveniences from the flies.

Wednesday, 3. It had rained hard in the night, and there was some small rain in the morning. At four we entered our canoe, and at ten we came to a small river, which answered to the description of that whose course the natives said, they follow in their journies towards the sea coast; we therefore put into it, and endeavoured to discover if our guide had landed here; but there were no traces of him or of any others. My former perplexities were now renewed. If I passed this river, it was probable that I might miss the natives; and I had reason to suspect that my men would not consent to return thither. As for attempting the woods, without a guide, to introduce us to the first inhabitants, such a determination would be little short of absolute madness. At length, after much painful reflection, I resolved to come at once to a full explanation with my people, and I experienced a considerable relief from this resolution. Accordingly, after repeating the promise they had so lately made me, on our putting back up the river, I represented to them that this appeared to me to be the spot from which the natives took their departure for the sea coast, and added, withal, that I was determined to try it; for though our guide had left us, it was possible that, while we were making the necessary preparations, he or some others might appear, to relieve us from our present difficulties. I now found, to my great satisfaction, that they had not come to any fixed determination among themselves, as some of them immediately assented to undertake the woods with me. Others, however, suggested that it might be better to proceed a few leagues further up the river, in expectation of finding our guide, or procuring another, and that after all we might return hither. This plan I very readily agreed to adopt, but before I left this place, to which I gave the name of the West-Road River,[1] I sent some of the men into the woods, in different directions, and went some distance up the river myself, which I found to be navigable only for small canoes. Two of the men found a good beaten path, leading up an hill just behind us, which I imagined to be the great road.

At four in the afternoon we left this place, proceeding up the river; and had not been upon the water more than three quarters of an hour, when we saw two canoes coming with the stream. No sooner did the people in them perceive us than they landed, and we went on shore at the same place with them. They proved to be our guide, and six of his relations. He was covered with a

[1] Modern Blackwater River.—ED.

painted beaver robe, so that we scarcely knew him in his fine habiliment. He instantly desired us to acknowledge that he had not disappointed us, and declared, at the same time, that it was his constant intention to keep his word. I accordingly gave him a jacket, a pair of trowsers, and an handkerchief, as a reward for his honourable conduct. The strangers examined us with the most minute attention, and two of them, as I was now informed, belonged to the people whom we first saw, and who fled with so much alarm from us. They told me, also, that they were so terrified on that occasion, as not to approach their huts for two days; and that when they ventured thither, they found the greater part of their property destroyed, by the fire running in the ground. According to their account, they were of a different tribe, though I found no difference in their language from that of the Nagailas or Carriers. They are called Nascud Denee. Their lodges were at some distance, on a small lake, where they take fish, and if our guide had not gone for them there, we should not have seen an human being on the river. They informed me that the road by their habitation is the shortest, and they proposed that we should take it.

Thursday, 4. At an early hour this morning, and at the suggestion of our guide, we proceeded to the landing-place that leads to the strangers' lodges. Our great difficulty here was to procure a temporary separation from our company, in order to hide some articles we could not carry with us, and which it would have been imprudent to leave in the power of the natives. Accordingly Mr. Mackay, and one of our Indians embarked with them, and soon run out of our sight. At our first hiding-place we left a bag of pemmican, weighing ninety pounds, two bags of wild rice, and a gallon keg of gunpowder. Previous to our putting these articles in the ground, we rolled them up in oil cloth, and dressed leather. In the second hiding-place, and guarded with the same rollers, we hid two bags of Indian corn, or maize, and a bale of different articles of merchandise. When we had completed this important object, we proceeded till half past eight, when we landed at the entrance of a small rivulet, where our friends were waiting for us.

Here it was necessary that we should leave our canoe, and whatever we could not carry on our backs. In the first place, therefore, we prepared a stage, on which the canoe was placed bottom upwards, and shaded by a covering of small trees and branches, to keep her from the sun. We then built an oblong hollow square, ten feet by five, of green logs, wherein we placed every article it was necessary for us to leave here, and covered the whole with large pieces of timber.

While we were eagerly employed in this necessary business, our guide and his companions were so impatient to be gone, that we could not persuade the former to wait till we were prepared for our departure, and we had some difficulty in persuading another of the natives to remain, who had undertaken to conduct us where the guide had promised to wait our arrival.

At noon we were in a state of preparation to enter the woods, an undertaking of which I shall not here give any preliminary opinion, but leave those who read it to judge for themselves.

We carried on our backs four bags and an half of pemmican, weighing from eighty-five to ninety pounds each; a case with my instruments, a parcel of goods for presents, weighing ninety pounds, and a parcel containing ammunition of the same weight. Each of the Canadians had a burden of about ninety pounds, with a gun, and some ammunition. The Indians had about forty-five pounds weight of pemmican to carry, besides their gun, &c. with which they were very much dissatisfied, and if they had dared would have instantly left us. They had hitherto been very much indulged, but the moment was now arrived when indulgence was no longer practicable. My own load, and that of Mr. Mackay, consisted of twenty-two pounds of pemmican, some rice, a little sugar, &c. amounting in the whole to about seventy pounds each, besides our arms and ammunition. I had also the tube of my telescope swung across my shoulder, which was a troublesome addition to my burthen. It was determined that we should content ourselves with two meals a day, which were regulated without difficulty, as our provisions did not require the ceremony of cooking.

In this state of equipment we began our journey, as I have already mentioned, about twelve at noon, the commencement of which was a steep ascent of about a mile; it lay along a well-beaten path, but the country through which it led was rugged and ridgy, and full of wood. When we were in a state of extreme heat, from the toil of our journey, the rain came on, and continued till the evening, and even when it ceased the underwood continued its drippings upon us.

About half past six we arrived at an Indian camp of three fires, where we found our guide, and on his recommendation we determined to remain there for the night. The computed distance of this day's journey was about twelve geographical miles; the course about West.

At sun-set an elderly man and three other natives joined us from the Westward. The former bore a lance that very much resembled a serjeant's halberd. He had lately received it, by way of barter, from the natives of the Sea-Coast, who procured it from the white men. We should meet, he said, with many of his countrymen who had just returned from thence. According to his report, it did not require more than six days' journey, for people who are not heavily laden, to reach the country of those with whom they bartered their skins for iron, &c. and from thence it is not quite two days' march to the sea. They proposed to send two young men on before us, to notify to the different tribes that we were approaching, that they might not be surprised at our appearance, and be disposed to afford us a friendly reception. This was a measure which I could not but approve, and endeavoured by some small presents to prepossess our couriers in our favour.

These people live but poorly at this season, and I could procure no provision from them, but a few small, dried fish, as I think, of the carp kind. They had several European articles; and one of them had a strip of fur, which appeared to me to be of the sea otter. He obtained it from the natives of the coast, and exchanged it with me for some beads and a brass cross.

We retired to rest in as much security as if we had been long habituated to a confidence in our present associates: indeed, we had no alternative; for so great were the fatigues of the day in our mode of travelling, that we were in great need of rest at night.

Friday, 5. We had no sooner laid ourselves down to rest last night, than the natives began to sing, in a manner very different from what I had been accustomed to hear among savages. It was not accompanied either with dancing, drum, or rattle; but consisted of soft, plaintive tones, and a modulation that was rather agreeable: it had somewhat the air of church music. As the natives had requested me not to quit them at a very early hour in the morning, it was five before I desired that the young men, who were to proceed with us, should depart, when they prepared to set off: but, on calling to our guide to conduct us, he said, that he did not intend to accompany us any further, as the young men would answer our purpose as well as himself. I knew it would be in vain to remonstrate with him, and therefore submitted to his caprice without a reply. However, I thought proper to inform him, that one of my people had lost his dag, or poinard, and requested his assistance in the recovery of it. He asked me what I would give him to conjure it back again; and a knife was agreed to be the price of his necromantic exertions. Accordingly, all the dags and knives in the place were gathered together, and the natives formed a circle round them; the conjurer also remaining in the middle. When this part of the ceremony was arranged, he began to sing, the rest joining in the chorus; and after some time he produced the poinard which was stuck in the ground, and returned it to me.

At seven we were ready to depart; when I was surprised to hear our late guide propose, without any solicitation on our part, to resume his office; and he actually conducted us as far as a small lake, where we found an encampment of three families. The young men who had undertaken to conduct us were not well understood by my interpreters, who continued to be so displeased with their journey, that they performed this part of their duty with great reluctance. I endeavoured to persuade an elderly man of this encampment to accompany us to the next tribe, but no inducement of mine could prevail on him to comply with my wishes. I was, therefore, obliged to content myself with the guides I had already engaged, for whom we were obliged to wait some time, till they had provided shoes for their journey. I exchanged two halfpence here, one of his present Majesty, and the other of the State of Massachuset's Bay, coined in 1787. They hung as ornaments in children's ears.

My situation here was rendered rather unpleasant by the treatment which my hunters received from these people. The former, it appeared, were considered as belonging to a tribe who inhabit the mountains, and are the natural enemies of the latter. We had also been told by one of the natives, of a very stern aspect, that he had been stabbed by a relation of theirs, and pointed to a scar as the proof of it. I was, therefore, very glad to proceed on my journey.

Our guides conducted us along the lake through thick woods, and without any path, for about a mile and an half, when we lost sight of it. This piece of water is about three miles long and one broad. We then crossed a creek and entered upon a beaten track, through an open country, sprinkled with cypress trees. At twelve the sky became black, and an heavy gust with rain shortly followed, which continued for upwards of an hour. When we perceived the approaching storm, we fixed our thin, light oil-cloth to screen us from it. On renewing our march, as the bushes were very wet, I desired our guides, they having no burdens, to walk in front, and beat them as they went: this task they chose to decline, and accordingly I undertook it. Our road now lay along a lake, and across a creek that ran into it. The guides informed me, that this part of the country abounds in beaver: many traps were seen along the road which had been set for lynxes and martens. About a quarter of a mile from the place where we had been stopped by the rain, the ground was covered with hail, and as we advanced, the hailstones increased in size, some of them being as big as musket-balls. In this manner was the ground whitened for upwards of two miles. At five in the afternoon we arrived on the banks of another lake, when it again threatened rain; and we had already been sufficiently wetted in the course of the day, to look with complacency towards a repetition of it: we accordingly fixed our shed, the rain continuing with great violence through the remainder of the day: it was, therefore, determined, that we should stop here for the night.

In the course of the day we passed three winter huts; they consisted of low walls, with a ridge-pole, covered with the branches of the Canadian balsam-tree. One of my men had a violent pain in his knee, and I asked the guides to take a share of his burden, as they had nothing to carry but their beaver robes, and bows and arrows, but they could not be made to understand a word of my request.

Saturday, 6. At four this morning I arose from my bed, such as it was. As we must have been in a most unfortunate predicament, if our guides should have deserted us in the night, by way of security, I proposed to the youngest of them to sleep with me, and he readily consented. These people have no covering but their beaver garments, and that of my companion was a nest of vermin. I, however, spread it under us, and having laid down upon it, we covered ourselves with my camblet cloak. My companion's hair being greased with fish-oil, and his body smeared with red earth, my sense of smelling, as well as that of feeling, threatened to interrupt my rest; but these inconveniences yielded to my fatigue, and I passed a night of sound repose.

I took the lead in our march, as I had done yesterday, in order to clear the branches of the wet which continued to hang upon them. We proceeded with all possible expedition through a level country with but little underwood; the larger trees were of the fir kind. At half past eight we fell upon the road,

which we first intended to have taken from
the Great River, and must be shorter than
that which we had travelled. The West-road
river was also in sight, winding through a
valley. We had not met with any water since
our encampment of last night, and though
we were afflicted with violent thirst, the
river was at such a distance from us, and the
descent to it so long and steep, that we were
compelled to be satisfied with casting our
longing looks towards it. There appeared to
be more water in the river here, than at its
discharge. The Indian account, that it is
navigable for their canoes, is, I believe, perfectly correct.

Our guides now told us, that as the road
was very good and well traced, they would
proceed to inform the next tribe that we were
coming. This information was of a very unpleasant nature; as it would have been easy
for them to turn off the road at an hundred
yards from us, and, when we had passed
them, to return home. I proposed that one
of them should remain with us, while two
of my people should leave their loads behind
and accompany the other to the lodges. But
they would not stay to hear our persuasions,
and were soon out of sight.

I now desired the Cancre to leave his burden, take a small quantity of provision, with

his arms and blanket, and follow me. I also told my men to come on as fast as they could, and that I would wait for them as soon as I had formed an acquaintance with the natives of the country before us. We accordingly followed our guides with all the expedition in our power, but did not overtake them till we came to a family of natives, consisting of one man, two women, and six children, with whom we found them. These people betrayed no signs of fear at our appearance, and the man willingly conversed with my interpreter, to whom he made himself more intelligible, than our guides had been able to do. They, however, had informed him of the object of our journey. He pointed out to us one of his wives, who was a native of the sea coast, which was not a very great distance from us. This woman was more inclined to corpulency than any we had yet seen, was of low stature, with an oblong face, grey eyes, and a flattish nose. She was decorated with ornaments of various kinds, such as large blue beads, either pendant from her ears, encircling her neck, or braided in her hair: she also wore bracelets of brass, copper, and horn. Her garments consisted of a kind of tunic, which was covered with a robe of matted bark, fringed round the bottom with skin of the sea otter. None of the women whom I had seen since we crossed the mountain wore this kind of tunic; their blankets being merely girt round the waist. She had learned the language of her husband's tribe, and confirmed his account, that we were at no great distance from the sea. They were on their way, she said, to the great river to fish. Age seemed to be an object of great veneration among these people, for they carried an old woman by turns on their backs who was quite blind and infirm from the very advanced period of her life.

Our people having joined us and rested themselves, I requested our guides to proceed, when the elder of them told me that he should not go any further, but that these people would send a boy to accompany his brother, and I began to think myself rather fortunate, that we were not deserted by them all.

About noon we parted, and in two hours we came up with two men and their families: when we first saw. them they were sitting down, as if to rest themselves; but no sooner did they perceive us than they rose up and seized their arms. The boys who were behind us immediately ran forwards and spoke to them, when they laid by their arms and received us as friends. They had been eating green berries and dried fish. We had, indeed, scarcely joined them, when a woman and a boy came from the river with water, which they very hospitably gave us to drink. The people of this party had a very sickly appearance, which might have been the consequence of disease, or that indolence which is so natural to them, or of both. One of the women had a tattooed line along the chin, of the same length as her mouth.

The lads now informed me that they would go no further, but that these men would take their places; and they parted from their families with as little apparent concern, as if they were entire strangers to each other. One of them was very well understood by my interpreter, and had resided among the natives of the sea coast, whom he had left but a short time. According to his information, we were approaching a river, which was neither large nor long, but whose banks are inhabited; and that in the bay which the sea forms at the mouth of it, a great wooden canoe, with white people, arrives about the time when the leaves begin to grow: I presume in the early part of May.

After we parted with the last people, we came to an uneven, hilly, and swampy country, through which our way was impeded by a considerable number of fallen trees. At five in the afternoon we were over-taken by a heavy shower of rain and hail, and being at the same time very much fatigued, we encamped for the night near a small creek. Our course, till we came to the river, was about South-West ten miles, and then West, twelve or fourteen miles. I thought it prudent, by way of security, to submit to the same inconveniences I have already described, and shared the beaver robe of one of my guides during the night.

Sunday, *7*. I was so busily employed in collecting intelligence from our conductors, that I last night forgot to wind up my time-piece, and it was the only instance of such an act of negligence since I left Fort Chepewyan, on the 11th of last October. At five we quitted our station, and proceeded across two mountains, covered with spruce, poplar, white birch, and other trees. We then descended into a level country, where we found a good road, through woods of cypress. We then came to two small lakes, at the distance of about fourteen miles. Course about West. Through them the river passes, and our road kept in a parallel line with it on a range of elevated ground. On observing some people before us, our guides hastened to meet them, and, on their approach, one of them stepped forward with an axe in his hand. This party consisted only of a man, two women, and the same number of children. The eldest of the women, who probably was the man's mother, was engaged, when we joined them, in clearing a circular spot, of about five feet in diameter, of the weeds that infested it; nor did our arrival interrupt her employment, which was sacred to the memory of the dead. The spot to which her pious care was devoted, contained the grave of an husband, and a son, and whenever she passed this way, she always stopped to pay this tribute of affection.

As soon as we had taken our morning allowance, we set forwards, and about three we perceived more people before us. After some alarm we came up with them. They consisted of seven men, as many women, and several children. Here I was under the necessity of procuring another guide, and we continued our route on the same side of the river, till six in the evening, when we crossed it. It was knee deep, and about an hundred yards over. I wished now to stop for the night, as we were all of us very much fatigued, but our guide recommended us to proceed onwards to a family of his friends, at a small distance from thence, where we arrived at half past seven. He had gone forward, and procured us a welcome and quiet reception. There being a net hanging to dry, I requested the man to prepare and set it in the water, which he did with great expedition, and then presented me with a few small dried fish. Our course was South-West about twelve miles, part of which was an extensive swamp, that was seldom less than knee deep. In the course of the afternoon we had several showers of rain. I had attempted to take an altitude, but it was past meridian. The water of the river before the lodge was quite still, and expanded itself into the form of a small lake. In many other places, indeed, it had assumed the same form.

Monday, 8. It rained throughout the night, and it was seven in the morning before the weather would allow us to proceed. The guide brought me five small boiled fish, in a platter made of bark; some of them were of the carp kind, and the rest of a species for which I am not qualified to furnish a name. Having dried our clothes, we set off on our march about eight, and our guide very cheerfully continued to accompany us; but he was not altogether so intelligible as his predecessors in our service. We learned from him, however, that this lake, through which the river passes, extends to the foot of the mountain, and that he expected to meet nine men, of a tribe which inhabits the North side of the river.

In this part of our journey we were surprised with the appearance of several regular basons, some of them furnished with water, and the others empty; their slope from the edge to the bottom formed an angle of about forty-five degrees, and their perpendicular depth was about twelve feet. Those that contained water, discovered gravel near their edges, while the empty ones were covered with grass and herbs, among which we discovered mustard, and mint. There were also several places from whence the water appears to have retired, which are covered with the same soil and herbage.

We now proceeded along a very uneven country, the upper parts of which were covered with poplars, a little under-wood, and plenty of grass: the intervening vallies were watered with rivulets. From these circumstances, and the general appearance of vegetation, I could not account for the apparent absence of animals of every kind.

At two in the afternoon we arrived at the largest river that we had seen, since we left our canoe, and which forced its way between and over the huge stones that opposed its current.[2] Our course was about South-South-West sixteen miles along the river, which might here justify the title of a lake. The

[2]The party had again come upon the Blackwater River, whose general course they had been following since July 3.—ED.

road was good, and our next course, which was West by South, brought us onward ten miles, where we encamped, fatigued and wet, it having rained three parts of the day. This river abounds with fish, and must fall into the great river, further down than we had extended our voyage.

Tuesday, 9. A heavy and continued rain fell through great part of the night, and as we were in some measure exposed to it, time was required to dry our clothes; so that it was half past seven in the morning before we were ready to set out. As we found the country so destitute of game, and foreseeing the difficulty of procuring provisions for our return, I thought it prudent to conceal half a bag of pemmican: having sent off the Indians, and all my people except two, we buried it under the fire-place, as we had done on a former occasion. We soon overtook our party, and continued our route along the river or lake. About twelve I had an altitude, but it was inaccurate from the cloudiness of the weather. We continued our progress till five in the afternoon, when the water began to narrow, and in about half an hour we came to a ferry, where we found a small raft. At this time it began to thunder, and torrents of rain soon followed, which terminated our journey for the day. Our course was about South, twenty-one miles from the lake already mentioned. We now discovered the tops of mountains, covered with snow, over very high intermediate land. We killed a whitehead and a grey eagle, and three grey partridges; we saw also two otters in the river, and several beaver lodges along it. When the rain ceased, we caught a few small fish, and repaired the raft for the service of the ensuing day.

Wednesday, 10. At an early hour of this morning we prepared to cross the water. The traverse is about thirty yards, and it required five trips to get us all over. At a short distance below, a small river falls in, that comes from the direction in which we were proceeding. It is a rapid for about three hundred yards, when it expands into a lake, along which our road conducted us, and beneath a range of beautiful hills, covered with verdure. At half past eight we came to the termination of the lake, where there were two houses that occupied a most delightful situation, and as they contained their necessary furniture, it seemed probable that their owners intended shortly to return. Near them were several graves or tombs, to which the natives are particularly attentive, and never suffer any herbage to grow upon them. In about half an hour we reached a place where there were two temporary huts, that contained thirteen men, with whom we found our guide who had preceded us, in order to secure a good reception. The buildings were detached from each other, and conveniently placed for fishing in the lake. Their inhabitants called themselves Sloua-cuss-Dinais, which denomination, as far as my interpreter could explain it to me, I understood to mean Red-fish Men. They were much more cleanly, healthy, and agreeable in their appearance, than any of the natives whom we had passed; nevertheless, I have no doubt that they are the same people, from their name alone, which is of the Chepewyan language. My interpreters, however, understood very little of what they said, so that I did not expect much information from them. Some of them said it was a journey of four days to the sea, and others were of opinion that it was six; and there were among them who extended it to eight; but they all uniformly declared that they had been to the coast. They did not entertain the smallest apprehension of danger from us, and, when we discharged our pieces, expressed no sensation but that of astonishment, which, as may be supposed, was proportionably encreased when one of the hunters shot an eagle, at a considerable distance. At twelve I obtained an altitude, which made our latitude 53. 4. 32. North, being not so far South as I expected.

I now went, accompanied by one of my men, an interpreter, and the guide, to visit some huts at the distance of a mile. On our arrival the inhabitants presented us with a dish of boiled trout, of a small kind. The fish would have been excellent if it had not tasted of the kettle, which was made of the bark of the white spruce, and of the dried grass with which it was boiled. Besides this kind of trout, red and white carp and jub, are the only fish I saw as the produce of these waters.

These people appeared to live in a state of comparative comfort: they take a greater share in the labour of the women, than is common among the savage tribes, and are, as I was informed, content with one wife. Though this circumstance may proceed rather from the difficulty of procuring subsistence, than any habitual aversion to polygamy.

My present guide now informed me, that he could not proceed any further, and I accordingly engaged two of these people to succeed him in that office; but when they desired us to proceed on the beaten path without them, as they could not set off till the following day, I determined to stay that night, in order to accommodate myself to their convenience. I distributed some trifles among the wives and children of the men who were to be our future guides, and returned to my people. We came back by a different way, and passed by two buildings, erected between four trees, and about fifteen feet from the ground, which appeared to me to be intended as magazines for winter provisions. At four in the afternoon, we proceeded with considerable expedition, by the side of the lake, till six, when we came to the end of it: we then struck off through a much less beaten track, and at half past seven stopped for the night. Our course was about West-South-West thirteen miles, and West six miles.

Thursday, 11. I passed a most uncomfortable night: the first part of it I was tormented with flies, and in the latter deluged with rain. In the morning the weather cleared, and as soon as our clothes were dried, we proceeded through a morass. This part of the country had been laid waste by fire, and the fallen trees added to the pain and perplexity of our way. An high, rocky ridge stretched along our left. Though the rain returned, we continued our progress till noon, when our guides took to some trees for shelter. We then spread our oil-cloth, and, with some difficulty, made a fire. About two the rain ceased, when we continued our journey through the same kind of country which we had hitherto passed. At half past three we came in sight of a lake; the land, at the same time gradually rising to a range of mountains whose tops were covered with snow. We soon after observed two fresh tracks, which seemed to surprise our guides, but they supposed them to have been made by the inhabitants of the country who were come into this part of it to fish. At five in the afternoon we were so wet and cold, (for it had at intervals continued to rain,) that we were compelled to stop for the night. We passed seven rivulets and a creek in this day's journey. As I had hitherto regulated our course by the sun, I could not form an accurate judgment of this route, as we had not been favoured with a sight of it during the day; but I imagine it to have been nearly in the same direction as that of yesterday. Our distance could not have been less than fifteen miles.

Our conductors now began to complain of our mode of travelling, and mentioned their intention of leaving us; and my interpreters, who were equally dissatisfied, added to our perplexity by their conduct. Besides, these circumstances, and the apprehension that the distance from the sea might be greater than I had imagined, it became a matter of real necessity that we should begin to diminish the consumption of our provisions, and to subsist upon two-thirds of our allowance; a proposition which was as unwelcome to my people, as it was necessary to be put into immediate practice.

Friday, 12. At half past five this morning we proceeded on our journey, with cloudy weather, and when we came to the end of the lake several tracks were visible that led to the side of the water; from which circumstance I concluded, that some of the natives were fishing along the banks of it. This lake is not more than three miles long, and about one broad. We then passed four smaller lakes, the two first being on our right, and those which preceded on our left. A small river also flowed across our way from the right, and we passed it over a beaver-dam. A larger lake now appeared on our right, and the mountains on each side of us were covered with snow. We afterwards came to another lake on our right, and soon reached a river, which our guides informed us was the same that we had passed on a raft. They said it was navigable for canoes from the great river, except two rapids, one of which we had seen. At this place it is upwards of twenty yards across, and deep water. One of the guides swam over to fetch a raft which was on the opposite side; and having increased its dimensions, we crossed at two trips, except four of the men, who preferred swimming.

Here our conductors renewed their menace of leaving us, and I was obliged to give them several articles, and promise more, in order to induce them to continue till we could procure other natives to succeed them. At four in the afternoon we forded the same river, and being with the guides at some distance before the rest of the people, I sat down to wait for them, and no sooner did they arrive, than the former set off with so much speed, that my attempt to follow them proved unsuccessful. One of my Indians, however, who had no load, overtook them, when they excused themselves to him by declaring, that their sole motive for leaving us, was to prevent the people, whom they expected to find, from shooting their arrows at us. At seven o'clock, however, we were so fatigued, that we encamped without them: the mountains covered with snow now appeared to be directly before us. As we were collecting wood for our fire, we discovered a cross road, where it appeared that people had passed within seven or eight days. In short, our situation was such as to afford a just cause of alarm, and that of the people with me was of a nature to defy immediate alleviation. It was necessary, however, for me to attempt it; and I rested my principles of encouragement on a representation of our past perplexities and unexpected relief, and endeavoured to excite in them the hope of similar good fortune. I stated to them, that we could not be at a great distance from the sea, and that there were but few natives to pass, till we should arrive among those, who being accustomed to visit the sea coast, and, having seen white people, would be disposed to treat us with kindness. Such was the general tenor of the reasoning I employed on the occasion, and I was happy to find that it was not offered in vain.

The weather had been cloudy till three in the afternoon, when the sun appeared; but surrounded, as we were, with snow-clad mountains, the air became so cold, that the violence of our exercise, was not sufficient to produce a comfortable degree of warmth. Our course to-day was from West to South, and at least thirty-six miles. The land in general was very barren and stony, and lay in ridges, with cypress trees scattered over them. We passed several swamps, where we saw nothing to console us but a few tracks of deer.

Saturday, 13. The weather this morning was clear but cold, and our scanty covering was not sufficient to protect us from the severity of the night. About five, after we had warmed ourselves at a large fire, we proceeded on our dubious journey. In about an hour we came to the edge of a wood, when we perceived an house, situated on a green spot, and by the side of a small river. The smoke that issued from it informed us that it was inhabited. I immediately pushed forward toward this mansion, while my people were in such a state of alarm, that they followed me with the utmost reluctance. On looking back I perceived that we were in an Indian defile, of fifty yards in length. I, however, was close upon the house before the inhabitants perceived us, when the women and children uttered the most horrid shrieks, and the only man who appeared to be with them, escaped out of a back door, which I reached in time to prevent the women and children from following him. The man fled with all his speed into the wood, and I called in vain on my interpreters to speak to him, but they were so agitated with fear as to have lost the power of utterance. It is impossible to describe the distress and alarm of these poor people, who believing that they were attacked by enemies, expected an immediate massacre, which, among themselves, never fails to follow such an event.

Our prisoners consisted of three women, and seven children, which apparently composed three families. At length, however, by our demeanor, and our presents, we contrived to dissipate their apprehensions. One of the women then informed us, that their people, with several others had left that place three nights before, on a trading journey to a tribe whom she called Annah, which is the name the Chepewyans give to the Knisteneaux, at the distance of three days. She added also, that from the mountains before us, which were covered with snow, the sea was visible; and accompanied her information with a present of a couple of dried fish. We now expressed our desire that the man might be induced to return, and conduct us in the road to the sea. Indeed, it was not long before he discovered himself in the wood, when he was assured, both by the women and our interpreters, that we had no hostile design against him; but these assurances had no effect in quieting his apprehensions. I then attempted to go to him alone, and shewed him a knife, beads, &c. to induce him to come to me, but he, in return, made an hostile display of his bow and arrows; and, having for a time exhibited a variety of strange antics, again disappeared. However, he soon presented himself in another quarter, and after a succession of parleys between us, he engaged to come and accompany us.

While these negotiations were proceeding, I proposed to visit the fishing machines, to which the women readily consented, and I found in them twenty small fish, such as trout, carp, and jub, for which I gave her a large knife; a present that appeared to be equally unexpected and gratifying to her. Another man now came towards us, from an hill, talking aloud from the time he appeared till he reached us. The purport of his speech was, that he threw himself upon our mercy, and we might kill him, if it was our pleasure, but that from what he had heard, he looked rather for our friendship than our enmity. He was an elderly person, of a decent appearance, and I gave him some articles to conciliate him to us. The first man now followed with a lad along with him, both of whom were the sons of the old man, and, on his arrival, he gave me several half-dried fish, which I considered as a peace-offering. After some conversation with these people, respecting the country, and our future progress through it, we retired to rest, with sensations very different from those with which we had risen in the morning. The weather had been generally cloudy throughout the day, and when the sun was obscured, extremely cold for the season. At noon I obtained a meridian altitude, which gave 52. 58. 53. North latitude. I likewise took time in the afternoon.

Sunday, 14. This morning we had a bright sun, with an East wind. These people examined their fishing machines, when they found in them a great number of small fish, and we dressed as many of them as we could eat. Thus was our departure retarded until seven, when we proceeded on our journey, accompanied by the man and his two sons. As I did not want the younger, and should be obliged to feed him, I requested of his father to leave him, for the purpose of fishing for the women. He replied, that they were accustomed to fish for themselves, and that I need not be apprehensive of their encroaching upon my provisions, as they were used to sustain themselves in their journies on herbs, and the inner tegument of the bark of trees, for the stripping of which he had a thin piece of bone, then hanging by his side. The latter is of a glutinous quality, of a clammy, sweet taste, and is generally considered by the more interior Indians as a delicacy, rather than an article of common food. Our guide informed me that there is a short cut across the mountains, but as there was no trace of a road, and it would shorten our journey but one day, he should prefer the beaten way.

We accordingly proceeded along a lake, West five miles. We then crossed a small river, and passed through a swamp, about South-West, when we began gradually to ascend for some time till we gained the summit of an hill, where we had an extensive view to the South-East, from which direction a considerable river appeared to flow, at the distance of about three miles: it was represented to me as being navigable for canoes. The descent of this hill was more steep than its ascent, and was succeeded by another, whose top, though not so elevated as the last, afforded a view of the range of mountains, covered with snow, which, according to the intelligence of our guide, terminates in the ocean. We now left a small lake on our left, then crossed a creek running out of it, and at one in the afternoon came to an house, of the same construction and dimensions as have already been mentioned, but the materials were much better prepared and finished. The timber was squared on two sides, and the bark taken off the two others; the ridge pole was also shaped in the same manner, extending about eight or ten feet beyond the gable end, and supporting a shed

over the door: the end of it was carved into
the similitude of a snake's head. Several
hieroglyphics and figures of a similar workmanship, and painted with red earth, decorated the interior of the building. The inhabitants had left the house but a short time,
and there were several bags or bundles in it,
which I did not suffer to be disturbed. Near
it were two tombs, surrounded in a neat
manner with boards, and covered with bark.
Beside them several poles had been erected,
one of which was squared, and all of them
painted. From each of them were suspended
several rolls or parcels of bark, and our guide
gave the following account of them; which,
as far as we could judge from our imperfect
knowledge of the language, and the incidental errors of interpretation, appeared to
involve two different modes of treating their
dead; or it might be one and the same ceremony, which we did not distinctly comprehend: at all events, it is the practice of these
people to burn the bodies of their dead, except the larger bones, which are rolled up in
bark and suspended from poles, as I have
already described. According to the other
account, it appeared that they actually bury
their dead; and when another of the family dies, the remains of the person who was
last interred are taken from the grave and

burned, as has been already mentioned; so that the members of a family are thus successively buried and burned, to make room for each other; and one tomb proves sufficient for a family through succeeding generations. There is no house in this country without a tomb in its vicinity. Our last course extended about ten miles.

We continued our journey along the lake before the house, and, crossing a river that flowed out of it, came to a kind of bank, or weir, formed by the natives, for the purpose of placing their fishing machines, many of which, of different sizes, were lying on the side of the river. Our guide placed one of them, with the certain expectation that on his return he should find plenty of fish in it. We proceeded nine miles further, on a good road, West-South-West, when we came to a small lake: we then crossed a river that ran out of it, and our guides were in continual expectation of meeting with some of the natives. To this place our course was a mile and an half, in the same direction as the last. At nine at night we crossed a river on rafts, our last distance being about four miles South-East, on a winding road, through a swampy country, and along a succession of small lakes. We were now quite exhausted, and it was absolutely necessary for us to stop for the night.

The weather being clear throughout the day, we had no reason to complain of the cold. Our guides encouraged us with the hope that, in two days of similar exertion, we should arrive among the people of the other nation.

Monday, 15. At five this morning we were again in motion, and passing along a river, we at length forded it. This stream was not more than knee deep, about thirty yards over, and with a stony bottom. The old man went onward by himself, in the hope of falling in with the people, whom he expected to meet in the course of the day. At eleven we came up with him, and the natives whom he expected, consisting of five men, and part of their families. They received us with great kindness, and examined us with the most minute attention. They must, however, have been told that we were white, as our faces no longer indicated that distinguishing complexion. They called themselves Neguia Dinais, and were come in a different direction from us, but were now going the same way, to the Anah-yoe Tesse or River, and appeared to be very much satisfied with our having joined them. They presented us with some fish which they had just taken in the adjoining lake.

Here I expected that our guides, like their predecessors, would have quitted us, but, on

the contrary, they expressed themselves to
be so happy in our company, and that of
their friends, that they voluntarily, and with
great cheerfulness proceeded to pass another
night with us. Our new acquaintances were
people of a very pleasing aspect. The hair of
the women was tied in large loose knots over
the ears, and plaited with great neatness
from the division of the head, so as to be included in the knots. Some of them had
adorned their tresses with beads, with a very
pretty effect. The men were clothed in
leather, their hair was nicely combed, and
their complexion was fairer, or perhaps it
may be said, with more propriety, that they
were more cleanly, than any of the natives
whom we had yet seen. Their eyes, though
keen and sharp, are not of that dark colour,
so generally observable in the various tribes
of Indians; they were, on the contrary, of a
grey hue, with a tinge of red. There was one
man amongst them of at least six feet four
inches in height; his manners were affable,
and he had a more prepossessing appearance
than any Indian I had met with in my journey; he was about twenty-eight years of age,
and was treated with particular respect by
his party. Every man, woman, and child,
carried a proportionate burden, consisting of
beaver coating and parchment, as well as

skins of the otter, the marten, the bear, the lynx, and dressed moose-skins. The last they procure from the Rocky-Mountain Indians. According to their account, the people of the sea coast prefer them to any other article. Several of their relations and friends, they said, were already gone, as well provided as themselves, to barter with the people of the coast; who barter them in their turn, except the dressed leather, with white people who, as they had been informed, arrive there in large canoes.

Such an escort was the most fortunate circumstance that could happen in our favour. They told us, that as the women and children could not travel fast, we should be three days in getting to the end of our journey; which must be supposed to have been very agreeable information to people in our exhausted condition.

In about half an hour after we had joined our new acquaintance, the signal for moving onwards was given by the leader of the party, who vociferated the words, Huy, Huy, when his people joined him and continued a clamorous conversation. We passed along a winding road over hills, and through swampy vallies, from South to West. We then crossed a deep, narrow river, which discharges itself into a lake, on whose side we stopped at five in the afternoon, for the night, though we had reposed several times since twelve at noon; so that our mode of travelling had undergone a very agreeable change. I compute the distance of this day's journey at about twenty miles. In the middle of the day the weather was clear and sultry.

We all sat down on a very pleasant green spot, and were no sooner seated, than our guide and one of the party prepared to engage in play. They had each a bundle of about fifty small sticks, neatly polished, of the size of a quill, and five inches long: a certain number of these sticks had red lines round them; and as many of these as one of the players might find convenient were curiously rolled up in dry grass, and according to the judgment of his antagonist respecting their number and, marks, he lost or won. Our friend was apparently the loser, as he parted with his bow and arrows, and several articles which I had given him.

Tuesday, 16. The weather of this morning was the same as yesterday; but our fellow-travellers were in no hurry to proceed, and I was under the necessity of pressing them into greater expedition, by representing the almost exhausted state of our provisions. They, however, assured us, that after the next night's sleep we should arrive at the river where they were going, and that we should there get fish in great abundance. My young men, from an act of imprudence, deprived themselves last night of that rest which was so necessary to them. One of the strangers asking them several questions respecting us, and concerning their own country, one of them gave such answers as were not credited by the audience; whereupon he demanded, in a very angry tone, if they thought he was disposed to tell lies, like the Rocky-Mountain Indians; and one of that tribe happening to be of the party, a quarrel ensued, which might have been attended with the most serious consequences, if it had not been fortunately prevented by the interference of those who were not interested in the dispute.

Though our stock of provisions was getting so low, I determined nevertheless, to hide about twenty pounds of pemmican, by way of providing against our return. I therefore left two of the men behind, with directions to bury it, as usual, under the place where we had made our fire.

Our course was about West-South-West by the side of the lake, and in about two miles we came to the end of it. Here was a general halt, when my men overtook us. I was now informed, that some people of another tribe were sent for, who wished very much to see us, two of whom would accompany us over the mountains; that, as for themselves, they had changed their mind, and intended to follow a small river which issued out of the lake, and went in a direction very different from the line of our journey. This was a disappointment, which, though not uncommon to us, might have been followed by considerable inconveniences. It was my wish to continue with them whatever way they went; but neither my promises or entreaties would avail: these people were not to be turned from their purpose; and when I represented the low state of our provisions, one of them answered, that if we would stay with them all night, he would boil a kettle of fish-roes for us. Accordingly, without receiving any answer, he began to make preparation to fulfil his engagement. He took the roes out of a bag, and having bruised them between two stones, put them in water to soak. His wife then took an handful of dry grass in her hand, with which she squeezed them through her fingers; in the mean time her husband was employed in gathering wood to make a fire, for the purpose of heating stones. When she had finished her operation, she filled a watape kettle nearly full of water, and poured

the roes into it. When the stones were sufficiently heated, some of them were put into
the kettle, and others were thrown in from
time to time, till the water was in a state of
boiling; the woman also continued stirring
the contents of the kettle, till they were
brought to a thick consistency; the stones
were then taken out, and the whole was sea-
soned with about a pint of strong rancid oil.
The smell of this curious dish was sufficient to
sicken me without tasting it, but the hunger
of my people surmounted the nauseous meal.
When unadulterated by the stinking oil,
these boiled roes are not unpalatable food.

In the mean time four of the people who
had been expected, arrived, and, according
to the account given of them, were of two
tribes whom I had not yet known. After
some conversation, they proposed, that I
should continue my route by their houses;
but the old guide, who was now preparing to
leave us, informed me that it would lengthen
my journey; and by his advice I proposed to
them to conduct us along the road which had
been already marked out to us. This they
undertook without the least hesitation; and,
at the same time, pointed out to me the pass
in the mountain, bearing South by East by
compass. Here I had a meridian altitude, and
took time.

At four in the afternoon we parted with our late fellow-travellers in a very friendly manner, and immediately forded the river. The wild parsnip, which luxuriates on the borders of the lakes and rivers, is a favourite food of the natives: they roast the tops of this plant, in their tender state, over the fire, and taking off the outer rind, they are then a very palatable food.

We now entered the woods, and some time after arrived on the banks of another river that flowed from the mountain, which we also forded. The country soon after we left the river was swampy; and the fire having passed through it, the number of trees, which had fallen, added to the toil of our journey. In a short time we began to ascend, and continued ascending till nine at night. We walked upwards of fourteen miles, according to my computation, in the course of the day, though the straight line of distance might not be more than ten. Notwithstanding that we were surrounded by mountains covered with snow, we were very much tormented with musquitoes.

Wednesday, 17. Before the sun rose, our guides summoned us to proceed, when we descended into a beautiful valley, watered by a small river. At eight we came to the termination of it, where we saw a great number of moles, and began again to ascend. We

now perceived many ground-hogs, and heard
them whistle in every direction. The Indians
went in pursuit of them, and soon joined us
with a female and her litter, almost grown to
their full size. They stripped off their skins,
and gave the carcasses to my people. They
also pulled up a root, which appeared like a
bunch of white berries of the size of a pea;
its shape was that of a fig, while it had the
colour and taste of a potatoe.

We now gained the summit of the mountain, and found ourselves surrounded by
snow. But this circumstance is caused rather
by the quantity of snow drifted in the pass,
than the real height of the spot, as the surrounding mountains rise to a much higher
degree of elevation. The snow had become so
compact that our feet hardly made a perceptible impression on it. We observed, however, the tracks of an herd of small deer
which must have passed a short time before
us, and the Indians and my hunters went
immediately in pursuit of them. Our way
was now nearly level, without the least
snow, and not a tree to be seen in any part
of it. The grass is very short, and the soil a
reddish clay, intermixed with small stones.
The face of the hills, where they are not enlivened with verdure, appears, at a distance,
as if fire had passed over them. It now began

to hail, snow, and rain, nor could we find any shelter but the leeward side of an huge rock. The wind also rose into a tempest, and the weather was as distressing as any I had ever experienced. After an absence of an hour and an half, our hunters brought a small doe of the rein-deer species, which was all they had killed, though they fired twelve shots at a large herd of them. Their ill success they attributed to the weather. I proposed to leave half of the venison in the snow, but the men preferred carrying it, though their strength was very much exhausted. We had been so long shivering with cold in this situation that we were glad to renew our march. Here and there were scattered a few crowberry bushes and stinted willows; the former of which had not yet blossomed.

Before us appeared a stupendous mountain, whose snow-clad summit was lost in the clouds; between it and our immediate course, flowed the river to which we were going. The Indians informed us that it was at no great distance. As soon as we could gather a sufficient quantity of wood, we stopped to dress some of our venison; and it is almost superfluous to add, that we made an heartier meal than we had done for many a day before. To the comfort which I have just mentioned, I added that of taking off my beard, as well as

changing my linen, and my people followed
the humanising example. We then set forwards, and came to a large pond, on whose
bank we found a tomb, but lately made,
with a pole, as usual, erected beside it, on
which two figures of birds were painted, and
by them the guides distinguished the tribe
to which the deceased person belonged. One
of them, very unceremoniously, opened the
bark and shewed us the bones which it contained, while the other threw down the pole,
and having possessed himself of the feathers
that were tied to it, fixed them on his own
head. I therefore conjectured, that these fu-
neral memorials belonged to an individual of
a tribe at enmity with them.

We continued our route with a considerable degree of expedition, and as we proceeded the mountains appeared to withdraw
from us. The country between them soon
opened to our view, which apparently added
to their awful elevation. We continued to descend till we came to the brink of a precipice,
from whence our guides discovered the river
to us, and a village on its banks.[3] This precipice, or rather succession of precipices, is

[3] The village was at the junction of Burnt Bridge
Creek with the Bella Coola River. On his return
journey, Mackenzie gave to it the name "Friendly
Village." See *post*, 347.—ED.

covered with large timber, which consists of
the pine, the spruce, the hemlock, the birch,
and other trees. Our conductors informed us,
that it abounded in animals, which, from
their description, must be wild goats. In
about two hours we arrived at the bottom,
where there is a conflux of two rivers, that
issue from the mountains. We crossed the
one which was to the left. They are both
very rapid, and continue so till they unite
their currents, forming a stream of about
twelve yards in breadth. Here the timber
was also very large; but I could not learn
from our conductors why the most considerable hemlock trees were stripped of their
bark to the tops of them. I concluded, indeed, at that time that the inhabitants
tanned their leather with it. Here were also
the largest and loftiest elder and cedar trees
that I had ever seen. We were now sensible
of an entire change in the climate, and the
berries were quite ripe.

The sun was about to set, when our conductors left us to follow them as well as we
could. We were prevented, however, from
going far astray, for we were hemmed in on
both sides and behind by such a barrier as
nature never before presented to my view.
Our guides had the precaution to mark
the road for us, by breaking the branches of

trees as they passed. This small river must, at certain seasons, rise to an uncommon height and strength of current most probably on the melting of the snow; as we saw a large quantity of drift wood lying twelve feet above the immediate level of the river. This circumstance impeded our progress, and the protruding rocks frequently forced us to pass through the water. It was now dark, without the least appearance of houses, though it would be impossible to have seen them, if there had been any, at the distance of twenty yards, from the thickness of the woods. My men were anxious to stop for the night; indeed the fatigue they had suffered justified the proposal, and I left them to their choice; but as the anxiety of my mind impelled me forwards, they continued to follow me, till I found myself at the edge of the woods; and, notwithstanding the remonstrances that were made, I proceeded, feeling rather than seeing my way, till I arrived at an house, and soon discovered several fires, in small huts, with people busily employed in cooking their fish. I walked into one of them without the least ceremony, threw down my burden, and, after shaking hands with some of the people, sat down upon it. They received me without the least appearance of surprize, but soon made signs for me to go up to the large house, which was erected, on upright posts, at some distance from the ground. A broad piece of timber with steps cut in it, led to the scaffolding even with the floor, and by this curious kind of ladder I entered the house at one end; and having passed three fires, at equal distances in the middle of the building, I was received by several people, sitting upon a very wide board, at the upper end of it. I shook hands with them, and seated myself beside a man, the dignity of whose countenance induced me to give him that preference. I soon discovered one of my guides seated a little above me, with a neat mat spread before him, which I supposed to be the place of honour, and appropriated to strangers. In a short time my people arrived, and placed themselves near me, when the man by whom I sat, immediately rose, and fetched, from behind a plank of about four feet wide, a quantity of roasted salmon. He then directed a mat to be placed before me and Mr. Mackay, who was now sitting by me. When this ceremony was performed, he brought a salmon for each of us, and half an one to each of my men. The same plank served also as a screen for the beds, whither the women and children were already retired; but whether that circumstance took place on our arrival, or was the natural consequence of the late hour of the night, I did not discover. The signs of our protector seemed to denote, that we might sleep in the house, but as we did not understand him with a sufficient degree of certainty, I thought it prudent, from the fear of giving offence, to order the men to make a fire without, that we might sleep by it. When he observed our design, he placed boards for us that we might not take our repose on the bare ground, and ordered a fire to be prepared for us. We had not been long seated round it, when we received a large dish of salmon roes, pounded fine and beat up with water so as to have the appearance of a cream. Nor was it without some kind of seasoning that gave it a bitter taste. Another dish soon followed, the principal article of which was also salmon-roes, with a large proportion of gooseberries, and an herb that appeared to be sorrel. Its acidity rendered it more agreeable to my taste than the former preparation. Having been regaled with these delicacies, for such they were considered by that hospitable spirit which provided them, we laid ourselves down to rest with no other canopy than the sky; but I never enjoyed a more sound and refreshing rest, though I had a board for my bed, and a billet for my pillow.

Thursday, 18. At five this morning I awoke, and found that the natives had lighted a fire for us, and were sitting by it. My hospitable friend immediately brought me some berries and roasted salmon, and his companions soon followed his example. The former, which consisted among many others, of gooseberries, whirtleberries and raspberries, were the finest I ever saw or tasted, of their respective kinds. They also brought the dried roes of fish to eat with the berries.

Salmon is so abundant in this river, that these people have a constant and plentiful supply of that excellent fish. To take them with more facility, they had, with great labour, formed an embankment or weir across the river for the purpose of placing their fishing machines, which they disposed both above and below it. I expressed my wish to visit this extraordinary work, but these people are so superstitious, that they would not allow me a nearer examination than I could obtain by viewing it from the bank. The river is about fifty yards in breadth, and by observing a man fish with a dipping net, I judged it to be about ten feet deep at the foot of the fall. The weir is a work of great labour, and contrived with considerable ingenuity. It was near four feet above the level of the water, at the time I saw it, and nearly the height of the bank on which I stood to examine it. The stream is stopped nearly two thirds by it. It is constructed by fixing small trees in the bed of the river in a slanting position (which could be practicable only when the water is much lower than I saw it) with the thick part downwards; over these is laid a bed of gravel, on which is placed a range of lesser trees, and so on alternately till the work is brought to its proper height. Beneath it the machines are placed, into which the salmon fall when they attempt to leap over. On either side there is a large frame of timber-work six feet above the level of the upper water, in which passages are left for the salmon leading directly into the machines, which are taken up at pleasure. At the foot of the fall dipping nets are also successfully employed.

The water of this river is of the colour of asses milk, which I attributed in part to the limestone that in many places forms the bed of the river, but principally to the rivulets which fall from mountains of the same material.

These people indulge an extreme superstition respecting their fish, as it is apparently their only animal food. Flesh they never taste, and one of their dogs having picked and swallowed part of a bone which we had left, was beaten by his master till he disgorged it. One of my people also having thrown a bone of the deer into the river, a native, who had observed the circumstance, immediately dived and brought it up, and, having consigned it to the fire, instantly proceeded to wash his polluted hands.

As we were still at some distance from the sea, I made application to my friend to procure us a canoe or two, with people to conduct us thither. After he had made various excuses, I at length comprehended that his only objection was to the embarking venison in a canoe on their river, as the fish would instantly smell it and abandon them, so that he, his friends, and relations, must starve. I soon eased his apprehensions on that point, and desired to know what I must do with the venison that remained, when he told me to give it to one of the strangers whom he pointed out to me, as being of a tribe that eat flesh. I now requested him to furnish me with some fresh salmon in its raw state; but, instead of complying with my wish, he brought me a couple of them roasted, observing at the same time, that the current was very strong, and would bring us to the next village, where our wants would be abundantly supplied. In short, he requested that we would make haste to depart. This was rather unexpected after so much kindness and hospitality, but

our ignorance of the language prevented us
from being able to discover the cause.

At eight this morning, fifteen men armed,
the friends and relations of these people, arrived by land, in consequence of notice sent
them in the night, immediately after the appearance of our guides. They are more cor-
pulent and of a better appearance than the
inhabitants of the interior. Their language
totally different from any I had heard; the
Atnah or Chin tribe, as far as I can judge
from the very little I saw of that people,
bear the nearest resemblance to them. They
appear to be of a quiet and peaceable character, and never make any hostile incursions
into the lands of their neighbours.

Their dress consists of a single robe tied
over the shoulders, falling down behind, to
the heels, and before, a little below the knees,
with a deep fringe round the bottom. It is generally made of the bark of the cedar tree, which
they prepare as fine as hemp; though some of
these garments are interwoven with strips of
the sea-otter skin, which give them the appearance of a fur on one side. Others have
stripes of red and yellow threads fancifully
introduced toward the borders, which have a
very agreeable effect. The men have no other
covering than that which I have described,
and they unceremoniously lay it aside when

they find it convenient. In addition to this robe, the women wear a close fringe hanging down before them about two feet in length, and half as wide. When they sit down they draw this between their thighs. They wear their hair so short, that it requires little care or combing. The men have theirs in plaits, and being smeared with oil and red earth, instead of a comb they have a small stick hanging by a string from one of the locks, which they employ to alleviate any itching or irritation in the head. The colour of the eye is grey with a tinge of red. They have all high cheekbones, but the women are more remarkable for that feature than the men. Their houses, arms, and utensils I shall describe hereafter.

I presented my friend with several articles, and also distributed some among others of the natives who had been attentive to us. One of my guides had been very serviceable in procuring canoes for us to proceed on our expedition; he appeared also to be very desirous of giving these people a favourable impression of us; and I was very much concerned that he should leave me as he did, without giving me the least notice of his departure, or receiving the presents which I had prepared for him, and he so well deserved. At noon I had an observation which gave 52. 28. 11. North longitude.

Chapter 10

Continue our journey. Embark on a river. Come to a weir. Dexterity of the natives in passing it. Arrive at a village. Alarm occasioned among the natives. The subsequent favourable reception, accompanied with a banquet of ceremony. Circumstances of it. Description of a village, its houses, and places of devotion. Account of the customs, mode of living, and superstition of the inhabitants. Description of the chief's canoe. Leave the place, and proceed on our voyage.

July, 1793.

AT one in the afternoon we embarked, with our small baggage, in two canoes, accompanied by seven of the natives. The stream was rapid, and ran upwards of six miles an hour. We came to a weir, such as I have already described, where the natives landed us, and shot over it without taking a drop of water. They then received us on board again, and we continued our voyage, passing many canoes on the river, some with people in them, and others empty. We proceeded at a very great rate for about two hours and an half, when we were informed that we must land, as the village was only at a short distance. I had imagined that the Canadians who accompanied me were the most expert canoe-men in the world, but they are very inferior to these people, as they themselves acknowledged, in conducting those vessels.

Some of the Indians ran before us, to announce our approach, when we took our bundles and followed. We had walked along a well-beaten path, through a kind of coppice, when we were informed of the arrival of our couriers at the houses, by the loud and confused talking of the inhabitants. As we approached the edge of the wood, and were almost in sight of the houses, the Indians who were before me made signs for me to take the lead, and that they would follow. The noise and confusion of the natives now seemed to increase, and when we came in sight of the village, we saw them running from house to house, some armed with bows and arrows, others with spears, and many with axes, as if in a state of great alarm. This very unpleasant and unexpected circumstance, I attributed to our sudden arrival, and the very short notice of it which had been given them. At all events, I had but one line of conduct to pursue, which was to walk resolutely up to them, without manifesting any signs of apprehension at their hostile appearance. This resolution produced the desired effect, for as we approached the houses, the greater part of the people laid down their weapons, and came forward to meet us. I was, however, soon obliged to stop from the number of them that surrounded me. I shook hands, as usual with such as were the nearest to me, when an elderly man broke through the crowd, and took me in his arms; another then came, who turned him away without the least ceremony, and paid me the same compliment. The latter was followed by a young man, whom I understood to be his son. These embraces, which at first rather surprised me, I soon found to be marks of regard and friendship. The crowd pressed with so much violence and contention to get a view of us, that we could not move in any direction. An opening was at length made to allow a person to approach me, whom the old man made me understand was another of his sons. I instantly stepped forward to meet him, and presented my hand, whereupon he broke the string of a very handsome robe of sea-otter skin, which he had on, and covered me with it. This was as flattering a reception as I could possibly receive, especially as I considered him to be the eldest son of the chief. Indeed it appeared to me that we had been detained here for the purpose of giving him time to bring the robe with which he had presented me

The chief now made signs for us to follow him, and he conducted us through a narrow coppice, for several hundred yards, till we came to an house built on the ground, which was of larger dimensions, and formed of better materials than any I had hitherto seen; it was his residence. We were no sooner arrived there, than he directed mats to be spread before it, on which we were told to take our seats, when the men of the village, who came to indulge their curiosity, were ordered to keep behind us. In our front other mats were placed, where the chief and his counsellors took their seats. In the intervening space, mats, which were very clean, and of a much neater workmanship than those on which we sat were also spread, and a small roasted salmon placed before each of us. When we had satisfied ourselves with the fish, one of the people who came with us from the last village approached, with a kind of ladle in one hand, containing oil, and in the other something that resembled the inner rind of the cocoa-nut, but of a lighter colour; this he dipped in the oil, and, having eat it, indicated by his gestures how palatable he thought it. He then presented me with a small piece of it, which I chose to taste in its dry state, though the oil was free from any unpleasant smell. A square cake of this was next produced, when a man took it to the water near the house, and having thoroughly soaked it, he returned, and, after he had pulled it to pieces like oakum, put it into a well-made trough, about three feet long, nine inches wide, and five deep; he then plentifully sprinkled it with salmon oil, and manifested by his own example that we were to eat of it. I just tasted it, and found the oil perfectly sweet, without which the other ingredient would have been very insipid. The chief partook of it with great avidity, after it had received an additional quantity of oil. This dish is considered by these people as a great delicacy; and on examination, I discovered it to consist of the inner rind of the hemlock tree, taken off early in summer, and put into a frame, which shapes it into cakes of fifteen inches long, ten broad, and half an inch thick; and in this form I should suppose it may be preserved for a great length of time. This discovery satisfied me respecting the many hemlock trees which I had observed stripped of their bark.

In this situation we remained for upwards of three hours, and not one of the curious natives left us during all that time, except a party of ten or twelve of them, whom the chief ordered to go and catch fish, which they did in great abundance, with dipping nets, at the foot of the Weir.

At length we were relieved from the gazing crowd, and got a lodge erected, and covered in for our reception during the night. I now presented the young chief with a blanket, in return for the robe with which he had favoured me, and several other articles, that appeared to be very gratifying to him. I also presented some to his father, and amongst them was a pair of scissors, whose use I explained to him, for clipping his beard, which was of great length; and to that purpose he immediately applied them. My distribution of similar articles was also extended to others, who had been attentive to us. The communication, however, between us was awkward and inconvenient, for it was carried on entirely by signs, as there was not a person with me who was qualified for the office of an interpreter.

We were all of us very desirous to get some fresh salmon, that we might dress them in our own way, but could not by any means obtain that gratification, though there were thousands of that fish strung on cords, which were fastened to stakes in the river. They were even averse to our approaching the spot where they clean and prepare them for their own eating. They had, indeed, taken our kettle from us, lest we should employ it in getting water from the river; and they assigned as the reason for this precaution, that the salmon dislike the smell of iron. At the same time they supplied us with wooden boxes, which were capable of holding any fluid. Two of the men that went to fish, in a canoe capable of containing ten people, returned with a full lading of salmon, that weighed from six to forty pounds, though the far greater part of them were under twenty. They immediately strung the whole of them, as I have already mentioned, in the river.

I now made the tour of the village, which consisted of four elevated houses, and seven built on the ground, besides a considerable number of other buildings or sheds, which are used only as kitchens, and places for curing their fish. The former are constructed by fixing a certain number of posts in the earth, on some of which are laid, and to others are fastened, the supporters of the floor, at about twelve feet above the surface of the ground: their length is from an hundred to an hundred and twenty feet, and they are about forty feet in breadth. Along the centre are built three, four, or five hearths, for the twofold purpose of giving warmth, and dressing their fish. The whole length of the building on either side is divided by cedar planks, into partitions or apartments of seven feet square, in the front of which there are boards, about three feet wide, over which, though they are not immovably fixed, the inmates of these recesses generally pass, when they go to rest. The greater part of them are intended for that purpose, and such are covered with boards, at the height of the wall of the house, which is about seven or eight feet, and rest upon beams that stretch across the building. On those also are placed the chests which contain their provisions, utensils, and whatever they possess. The intermediate space is sufficient for domestic purposes. On poles that run along the beams, hang roasted fish, and the whole building is well covered with boards and bark, except within a few inches of the ridge pole; where open spaces are left on each side to let in light and emit the smoke. At the end of the house that fronts the river, is a narrow scaffolding, which is also ascended by a piece of timber, with steps cut in it; and at each corner of this erection there are openings, for the inhabitants to ease nature. As it does not appear to be a custom among them to remove these heaps of excremental filth, it may be supposed that the effluvia does not annoy them.

The houses which rest on the ground are built of the same materials, and on the same plan. A sloping stage that rises to a cross-piece of timber, supported by two forks, joins also to the main building, for those purposes which need not be repeated.

When we were surrounded by the natives on our arrival, I counted sixty-five men, and several of them may be supposed to have been absent; I cannot, therefore, calculate the inhabitants of this village at less than two hundred souls.

The people who accompanied us hither, from the other village, had given the chief a very particular account of every thing they knew concerning us: I was, therefore, requested to produce my astronomical instruments; nor could I have any objection to afford them this satisfaction, as they would necessarily add to our importance in their opinion.

Near the house of the chief I observed several oblong squares, of about twenty feet by eight. They were made of thick cedar boards, which were joined with so much neatness, that I at first thought they were one piece. They were painted with hieroglyphics, and figures of different animals, and with a degree of correctness that was not to be expected from such an uncultivated people. I could not learn the use of them, but they appeared to be calculated for occasional acts of devotion or sacrifice, which all these tribes perform at least twice in the year, at the spring and fall. I was confirmed in this opinion by a large building in the middle of the village, which I at first took for the half finished frame of an house. The ground-plot of it was fifty feet by forty-five; each end is formed by four stout posts, fixed perpendicularly in the ground. The corner ones are plain, and support a beam of the whole length, having three intermediate props on each side, but of a larger size, and eight or nine feet in height. The two centre posts, at each end, are two feet and an half in diameter, and carved into human figures, supporting two ridge poles on their heads, at twelve feet from the ground. The figures at the upper part of this square represent two persons, with their hands upon their knees, as if they supported the weight with pain and difficulty: the others opposite to them stand at their ease, with their hands resting on their hips. In the area of the building there were the remains of several fires. The posts, poles, and figures, were painted red and black; but the sculpture of these people is superior to their painting.

Friday, 19. Soon after I had retired to rest last night, the chief paid me a visit to insist on my going to his bed-companion, and taking my place himself; but, notwithstanding his repeated entreaties, I resisted this offering of his hospitality.

At an early hour this morning I was again visited by the chief, in company with his son. The former complained of a pain in his breast; to relieve his suffering, I gave him a few drops of Turlington's Balsam on a piece of sugar; and I was rather surprised to see him take it without the least hesitation. When he had taken my medicine, he requested me to follow him, and conducted me to a shed, where several people were assembled round a sick man, who was another of his sons. They immediately uncovered him, and shewed me a violent ulcer in the small of his back, in the foulest state that can be imagined. One of his knees was also afflicted in the same manner. This unhappy man was reduced to a skeleton, and, from his appearance, was drawing near to an end of his pains. They requested that I would touch him, and his father was very urgent with me to administer medicine; but he was in such a dangerous state, that I thought it prudent to yield no further to the importunities than to give the sick person a few drops of Turlington's balsam in some water. I therefore left them, but was soon called back by the loud lamentations of the women, and was rather apprehensive that some inconvenience might result from my compliance with the chief's request. On my return I found the native physicians busy in practising their skill and art on the patient. They blew on him, and then whistled; at times they pressed their extended fingers, with all their strength on his stomach; they also put their fore fingers doubled into his mouth, and spouted water from their own with great violence into his face. To support these operations the wretched sufferer was held up in a sitting posture; and when they were concluded, he was laid down and covered with a new robe made of the skins of the lynx. I had observed that his belly and breast were covered with scars, and I understood that they were caused by a custom prevalent among them, of applying pieces of lighted touch wood to their flesh, in order to relieve pain or demonstrate their courage. He was now placed on a broad plank, and carried by six men into the woods, where I was invited to accompany them. I could not conjecture what would be the end of this ceremony, particularly as I saw one man carry fire, another an axe, and a third dry wood. I was, indeed, disposed to suspect that, as it was their custom to burn the dead, they intended to relieve the poor man from his pain, and perform the last sad duty of surviving affection. When they had advanced a short distance into the wood, they laid him upon a clear spot, and kindled a fire against his back, when the physician began to scarify the ulcer with a very blunt instrument, the cruel pain of which operation the patient bore with incredible resolution. The scene afflicted me and I left it.

On my return to our lodge, I observed before the door of the chief's residence, four heaps of salmon, each of which consisted of between three and four hundred fish. Sixteen women were employed in cleaning and preparing them. They first separate the head from the body, the former of which they boil; they then cut the latter down the back on each side of the bone, leaving one third of the fish adhering to it, and afterwards take out the guts. The bone is roasted for immediate use, and the other parts are dressed in the same manner, but with more attention, for future provision. While they are before the fire, troughs are placed under them to receive the oil. The roes are also carefully preserved, and form a favourite article of their food.

After I had observed these culinary preparations, I paid a visit to the chief, who presented me with a roasted salmon; he then opened one of his chests, and took out of it a garment of blue cloth, decorated with brass buttons; and another of a flowered cotton, which I supposed were Spanish; it had been trimmed with leather fringe, after the fashion of their own cloaks. Copper and brass are in great estimation among them, and of the former they have great plenty: they point their arrows and spears with it, and work it up into personal ornaments; such as collars, ear-rings, and bracelets, which they wear on their wrists, arms, and legs. I presume they find it the most advantageous article of trade with the more inland tribes. They also abound in iron. I saw some of their twisted collars of that metal which weighed upwards of twelve pounds. It is generally beat in bars of fourteen inches in length, and one inch three quarters wide. The brass is in thin squares: their copper is in larger pieces, and some of it appeared to be old stills cut up. They have various trinkets; but their manufactured iron consists only of poniards and daggers. Some of the former have very neat handles, with a silver coin of a quarter or eighth of a dollar fixed on the end of them. The blades of the latter are from ten to twelve inches in length, and about four inches broad at the top, from which they gradually lessen into a point.

When I produced my instruments to take an altitude, I was desired not to make use of them. I could not then discover the cause of this request, but I experienced the good effect of the apprehension which they occasioned, as it was very effectual in hastening my departure. I had applied several times to the chief to prepare canoes and people to take me and my party to the sea, but very little attention had been paid to my application till noon; when I was informed that a canoe was properly equipped for my voyage, and that the young chief would accompany me. I now discovered that they had entertained no personal fear of the instruments, but were apprehensive that the operation of them might frighten the salmon from that part of the river. The observation taken in this village gave me 52. 25. 52 North latitude.

In compliance with the chief's request I desired my people to take their bundles, and lay them down on the bank of the river. In the mean time I went to take the dimensions of his large canoe, in which, it was signified to me, that about ten winters ago he went a considerable distance towards the mid-day sun, with forty of his people, when he saw two large vessels full of such men as myself, by whom he was kindly received: they were, he said, the first white people he had seen. They were probably the ships commanded by Captain Cook.[1] This canoe was built of

[1] Captain James Cook had explored the north Pacific Coast on his famous voyage of discovery of 1776–78.—ED.

cedar, forty-five feet long, four feet wide, and three feet and a half in depth. It was painted black and decorated with white figures of fish of different kinds. The gunwale, fore and aft, was inlaid with the teeth of the sea-otter.*

When I returned to the river, the natives who were to accompany us, and my people, were already in the canoe. The latter, however, informed me, that one of our axes was missing. I immediately applied to the chief, and requested its restoration; but he would not understand me till I sat myself down on a stone, with my arms in a state of preparation, and made it appear to him that I should not depart till the stolen article was restored. The village was immediately in a state of uproar, and some danger was apprehended from the confusion that prevailed in it. The axe, however, which had been hidden under the chief's canoe, was soon returned. Though this instrument was not, in itself, of sufficient value to justify a dispute with these people, I apprehended that the suffering them to

*As Captain Cook has mentioned, that the people of the sea-coast adorned their canoes with human teeth, I was more particular in my inquiries; the result of which was, the most satisfactory proof, that he was mistaken: but his mistake arose from the very great resemblance there is between human teeth and those of the sea-otter.

keep it, after we had declared its loss, might have occasioned the loss of every thing we carried with us, and of our lives also. My people were dissatisfied with me at the moment; but I thought myself right then, and, I think now, that the circumstances in which we were involved, justified the measure which I adopted.

Chapter 11

Renew our voyage. Circumstances of the river. Land at the house of a chief. Entertained by him. Carried down the river with great rapidity to another house. Received with kindness. Occupations of the inhabitants on its banks. Leave the canoe at a fall. Pass over land to another village. Some account of it. Obtain a view of an arm of the sea. Lose our dog. Procure another canoe. Arrive at the arm of the sea. Circumstances of it. One of our guides returns home. Coast along a bay. Some description of it. Meet with Indians. Our communication with them. Their suspicious conduct towards us. Pass onwards. Determine the latitude and longitude. Return to the river. Dangerous encounter with the Indians. Proceed on our journey.

July, 1793.

FRIDAY, 19. At one in the afternoon we renewed our voyage in a large canoe with four of the natives. We found the river almost one continued rapid, and in half an hour we came to an house, where, however, we did not land, though invited by the inhabitants. In about an hour we arrived at two houses, where we were, in some degree, obliged to go on shore, as we were informed that the owner of them was a person of consideration. He indeed received and regaled us in the same manner as at the last village; and to increase his consequence, he produced many European articles, and amongst them were at least forty pounds weight of old copper stills. We made our stay as short as possible, and our host embarked with us. In a very short time we were carried by the rapidity of the current to another house of very large dimensions, which was partitioned into different apartments, and whose doors were on the side. The inhabitants received us with great kindness; but instead of fish, they placed a long, clean, and well made trough before us full of berries. In addition to those which we had already seen, there were some black, that were larger than the huckle berry, and of a richer flavour; and others white, which resembled the blackberry in every thing but colour. Here we saw a woman with two pieces of copper in her under lip, as described by Captain Cook. I continued my usual practice of making these people presents in return for their friendly reception and entertainment.

The navigation of the river now became more difficult, from the numerous channels into which it was divided, without any sensible diminution in the velocity of its current. We soon reached another house of the common size, where we were well received;

but whether our guides had informed them
that we were not in want of any thing, or
that they were deficient in inclination, or
perhaps the means, of being hospitable to us,
they did not offer us any refreshment. They
were in a state of busy preparation. Some of
the women were employed in beating and
preparing the inner rind of the cedar bark,
to which they gave the appearance of flax.
Others were spinning with a distaff and spin-
dle. One of them was weaving a robe of it,
intermixed with stripes of the sea-otter skin,
on a frame of adequate contrivance that was
placed against the side of the house. The
men were fishing on the river with drag-nets
between two canoes. These nets are forced
by poles to the bottom, the current driving
them before it; by which means the salmon
coming up the river are intercepted, and give
notice of their being taken by the struggles
they make in the bag or sleeve of the net.
There are no weirs in this part of the river, as
I suppose, from the numerous channels into
which it is divided. The machines, therefore,
are placed along the banks, and consequently
these people are not so well supplied with
fish as the village which has been already described, nor do they appear to possess the
same industry. The inhabitants of the last
house accompanied us in a large canoe. They

recommended us to leave ours here, as the next village was but at a small distance from us, and the water more rapid than that which we had passed. They informed us also, that we were approaching a cascade. I directed them to shoot it, and proceeded myself to the foot thereof, where I re-embarked, and we went on with great velocity, till we came to a fall, where we left our canoe, and carried our luggage along a road through a wood for some hundred yards, when we came to a village, consisting of six very large houses, erected on palisades, rising twenty-five feet from the ground, which differed in no one circumstance from those already described, but the height of their elevation. They contained only four men and their families. The rest of the inhabitants were with us and in the small houses which we passed higher up the river.* These people do not seem to enjoy the abundance of their neighbours, as the men who returned from fishing had no more than five salmon; they refused to sell one of them, but gave me one roasted of a very indifferent kind. In the houses there were several chests or boxes containing different articles that belonged to the people whom we had lately passed. If

* Mr. Johnstone came to these houses the first day of the preceding month.

I were to judge by the heaps of filth beneath these buildings, they must have been erected at a more distant period than any which we had passed. From these houses I could perceive the termination of the river, and its discharge into a narrow arm of the sea.

As it was now half past six in the evening, and the weather cloudy, I determined to remain here for the night, and for that purpose we possessed ourselves of one of the unoccupied houses. The remains of our last meal, which we brought with us, served for our supper, as we could not procure a single fish from the natives. The course of the river is about West, and the distance from the great village upwards of thirty-six miles. There we had lost our dog, a circumstance of no small regret to me.

Saturday, 20. We rose at a very early hour this morning, when I proposed to the Indians to run down our canoe, or procure another at this place. To both these proposals they turned a deaf ear, as they imagined that I should be satisfied with having come in sight of the sea. Two of them peremptorily refused to proceed; but the other two having consented to continue with us, we obtained a larger canoe than our former one, and though it was in a leaky state we were glad to possess it.

At about eight we got out of the river, which discharges itself by various channels into an arm of the sea. The tide was out, and had left a large space covered with sea-weed. The surrounding hills were involved in fog. The wind was at West, which was a-head of us, and very strong; the bay appearing to be from one to three miles in breadth. As we advanced along the land we saw a great number of sea-otters. We fired several shots at them, but without any success from the rapidity with which they plunge under the water. We also saw many small porpoises or divers. The white-headed eagle, which is common in the interior parts; some small gulls, a dark bird which is inferior in size to the gull, and a few small ducks, were all the birds which presented themselves to our view.

At two in the afternoon the swell was so high, and the wind, which was against us, so boisterous, that we could not proceed with our leaky vessel, we therefore landed in a small cove on the right side of the bay. Opposite to us appeared another small bay, in the mouth of which is an island, and where, according to the information of the Indians, a river discharges itself that abounds in salmon.

Our young Indians now discovered a very evident disposition to leave us; and, in the evening, one of them made his escape. Mr. Mackay, however, with the other, pursued and brought him back; but as it was by no means necessary to detain him, particularly as provisions did not abound with us, I gave him a small portion, with a pair of shoes, which were necessary for his journey, and a silk handkerchief, telling him at the same time, that he might go and inform his friends, that we should also return in three nights. He accordingly left us, and his companion, the young chief, went with him.

When we landed, the tide was going out, and at a quarter past four it was ebb, the water having fallen in that short period eleven feet and an half. Since we left the river, not a quarter of an hour had passed in which we did not see porpoises and sea-otters. Soon after ten it was high water, which rendered it necessary that our baggage should be shifted several times, though not till some of the things had been wetted.

We were now reduced to the necessity of looking out for fresh water, with which we were plentifully supplied by the rills that ran down from the mountains.

When it was dark the young chief returned to us, bearing a large porcupine on his back. He first cut the animal open, and having disencumbered it of the entrails, threw them into the sea; he then singed its skin, and boiled it in separate pieces, as our kettle was not sufficiently capacious to contain the whole: nor did he go to rest, till, with the assistance of two of my people who happened to be awake, every morsel of it was devoured.

I had flattered myself with the hope of getting a distance of the moon and stars, but the cloudy weather continually disappointed me, and I began to fear that I should fail in this important object; particularly as our provisions were at a very low ebb, and we had, as yet, no reason to expect any assistance from the natives. Our stock was, at this time, reduced to twenty pounds weight of pemmican, fifteen pounds of rice, and six pounds of flour, among ten half-starved men, in a leaky vessel, and on a barbarous coast. Our course from the river was about West-South-West, distance ten miles.

Sunday, 21. At forty minutes past four this morning it was low water, which made fifteen feet perpendicular height below the high-water mark of last night. Mr. Mackay collected a quantity of small muscles which we boiled. Our people did not partake of this regale, as they are wholly unacquainted with sea shell-fish. Our young chief being missing, we imagined that he had taken his flight, but, as we were preparing to depart, he fortunately made his appearance from the woods, where he had been to take his rest after his feast of last night. At six we were upon the water, when we cleared the small bay, which we named Porcupine Cove, and steered West-South-West for seven miles, we then opened a channel about two miles and an half wide at South-South-West, and had a view of ten or twelve miles into it. As I could not ascertain the distance from the open sea, and being uncertain whether we were in a bay or among inlets and channels of islands, I confined my search to a proper place for taking an observation. We steered, there-fore, along the land on the left, West-North-West a mile and an half; then North-West one fourth of a mile, and North three miles to an island; the land continuing to run North-North-West, then along the island, South-South-West half a mile, West a mile and an half, and from thence directly across to the land on the left, (where I had an alti-tude,) South-West three miles.* From this position a channel, of which the island we left appeared to make a cheek, bears North by East.

*The Cape or Point Menzies of Vancouver.

Under the land we met with three canoes, with fifteen men in them, and laden with their moveables, as if proceeding to a new situation, or returning to a former one. They manifested no kind of mistrust or fear of us, but entered into conversation with our young man, as I supposed, to obtain some information concerning us. It did not appear that they were the same people as those we had lately seen, as they spoke the language of our young chief, with a different accent. They then examined every thing we had in our canoe, with an air of indifference and disdain. One of them in particular made me understand, with an air of insolence, that a large canoe had lately been in this bay, with people in her like me, and that one of them, whom he called *Macubah*, had fired on him and his friends, and that *Bensins*[1] had struck him on the back, with the flat part of his sword. He also mentioned another name, the articulation of which I could not determine. At the same time he illustrated these circumstances by the assistance of my gun and sword; and I do not doubt but he well deserved the treatment which he described.

[1] It seems apparent that "Bensins" was Archibald Menzies, botanist and surgeon of Vancouver's expedition. "Macubah" may have been Thomas Manby, master's mate.—ED.

He also produced several European articles, which could not have been long in his possession. From his conduct and appearance, I wished very much to be rid of him, and flattered myself that he would prosecute his voyage, which appeared to be in an opposite direction to our course. However, when I prepared to part from them, they turned their canoes about, and persuaded my young man to leave me, which I could not prevent.

We coasted along the land* at about West-South-West for six miles, and met a canoe with two boys in it, who were dispatched to summon the people on that part of the coast to join them. The troublesome fellow now forced himself into my canoe, and pointed out a narrow channel on the opposite shore, that led to his village, and requested us to steer towards it, which I accordingly ordered. His importunities now became very irksome, and he wanted to see every thing we had, particularly my instruments, concerning which he must have received information from my young man. He asked for my hat, my handkerchief, and, in short, every thing that he saw about me. At the same time he frequently repeated the unpleasant intelligence that he had been shot at by people of

* Named by Vancouver King's Island.

my colour. At some distance from the land a channel opened to us, at South-West by West, and pointing that way, he made me understand that *Macubah* came there with his large canoe. When we were in mid-channel, I perceived some sheds, or the remains of old buildings, on the shore; and as, from that circumstance, I thought it probable that some Europeans might have been there, I directed my steersman to make for that spot. The traverse is upwards of three miles North-West.

We landed, and found the ruins of a village, in a situation calculated for defence. The place itself was over grown with weeds, and in the centre of the houses there was a temple, of the same form and construction as that which I described at the large village. We were soon followed by ten canoes, each of which contained from three to six men. They informed us that we were expected at the village, where we should see many of them. From their general deportment I was very apprehensive that some hostile design was meditated against us, and for the first time I acknowledged my apprehensions to my people. I accordingly desired them to be very much upon their guard, and to be prepared if any violence was offered to defend themselves to the last.

Voyage to the Pacific Ocean

We had no sooner landed, than we took possession of a rock, where there was not space for more than twice our number, and which admitted of our defending ourselves with advantage, in case we should be attacked. The people in the three first canoes, were the most troublesome, but, after doing their utmost to irritate us, they went away. They were, however, no sooner gone, than an hat, an handkerchief, and several other articles, were missing. The rest of our visitors continued their pressing invitations to accompany them to their village, but finding our resolution to decline them was not to be shaken, they', about sun-set relieved us from all further importunities, by their departure.

Another canoe, however, soon arrived, with seven stout, well-looking men. They brought a box, which contained a very fine sea-otter skin, and a goat skin, that was beautifully white. For the former they demanded my hanger, which, as may well be supposed, could not be spared in our present situation, and they actually refused to take a yard and an half of common broad cloth, with some other articles, for the skin, which proves the unreflecting improvidence of our European traders. The goat-skin was so bulky that I did not offer to purchase it.

These men also told me that *Macubah* had
been there, and left his ship behind a point of
land in the channel, South-West from us;
from whence he had come to their village in
boats, which these people represented by
imitating our manner of rowing. When I
offered them what they did not choose to
accept for the otter-skin, they shook their
heads, and very distinctly answered "No,
no." And to mark their refusal of any thing
we asked from them, they emphatically employed the same British monosyllable. In
one of the canoes which had left us, there
was a seal, that I wished to purchase, but
could not persuade the natives to part with
it. They had also a fish, which I now saw for
the first time. It was about eighteen inches
in length, of the shape and appearance of a
trout, with strong, sharp teeth. We saw great
numbers of the animals which we had taken
for sea otters, but I was now disposed to
think that a great part of them, at least,
must have been seals.

The natives having left us, we made a fire
to warm ourselves, and as for supper, there
was but little of that, for our whole daily
allowance did not amount to what was sufficient for a single meal. The weather was
clear throughout the day, which was succeeded by a fine moon-light night. I directed

the people to keep watch by two in turn, and laid myself down in my cloak.

Monday, 22. This morning the weather was clear and pleasant; nor had any thing occurred to disturb us throughout the night. One solitary Indian, indeed, came to us with about half a pound of boiled seal's flesh, and the head of a small salmon, for which he asked an handkerchief, but afterwards accepted a few beads. As this man came alone, I concluded that no general plan had been formed among the natives to annoy us, but this opinion did not altogether calm the apprehensions of my people.

Soon after eight in the morning, I took five altitudes for time, and the mean of them was 36° 48′ at six in the afternoon, 58. 34. time, by the watch, which makes the achrometer slow apparent time 1ʰ 21ᵐ 44ˢ.

Two canoes now arrived from the same quarter as the rest, with several men, and our young Indian along with them. They brought a very few small sea-otter skins, out of season, with some pieces of raw seal's flesh. The former were of no value, but hunger compelled some of my people to take the latter, at an extravagant price. Mr. Mackay lighted a bit of touch wood with a burning-glass, in the cover of his tobacco-box, which so surprised the natives, that they exchanged

the best of their otter skins for it. The young
man was now very anxious to persuade our
people to depart, as the natives, he said, were
as numerous as musquitoes, and of very malignant character. This information produced some very earnest remonstrances to
me to hasten our departure, but as I was determined not to leave this place, except I
was absolutely compelled to it, till I had ascertained its situation, these solicitations
were not repeated.

While I was taking a meridian, two canoes, of a larger size, and well manned, appeared from the main South-West channel.
They seemed to be the fore-runners of others,
who were coming to co-operate with the people of the village, in consequence of the message sent by the two boys, which has been
already mentioned; and our young Indian,
who understood them, renewed his entreaties
for our departure, as they would soon come
to shoot their arrows, and hurl their spears
at us. In relating our danger, his agitation
was so violent that he foamed at the mouth.
Though I was not altogether free from apprehensions on the occasion, it was necessary
for me to disguise them, as my people were
panic struck, and some of them asked if it
was my determination to remain there to
be sacrificed? My reply was the same as their

former importunities had received, that I
would not stir till I had accomplished my object; at the same time, to humour their fears,
I consented that they should put every thing
into the canoe, that we might be in a state of
preparation to depart. The two canoes now
approached the shore, and in a short time
five men, with their families, landed very
quietly from them. My instruments being
exposed, they examined them with much apparent admiration and astonishment. My
altitude, by an artificial horizon, gave
$52° 21' 33''$; that by the natural horizon was
$52° 20' 48''$ North latitude.*

These Indians were of a different tribe
from those which I had already seen, as our
guide did not understand their language. I
now mixed up some vermilion in melted
grease, and inscribed, in large characters, on
the South-East face of the rock on which we
had slept last night, this brief memorial—
"Alexander Mackenzie, from Canada, by
land, the twenty-second of July, one thousand seven hundred and ninety-three."

As I thought that we were too near the
village, I consented to leave this place,
and accordingly proceeded North-East three
miles, when we landed on a point, in a

* This I found to be the cheek of Vancouver's Cascade
Canal.

small cove, where we should not be readily seen, and could not be attacked except in our front.

Among other articles that had been stolen from us, at our last station, was a sounding-line, which I intended to have employed in this bay, though I should not probably have found the bottom, at any distance from the shore, as the appearance both of the water and land indicated a great depth. The latter displayed a solid rock, rising, as it appeared to me, from three to seven hundred feet above high water mark. Where any soil was scattered about, there were cedars, spruce-firs, white birch, and other trees of large growth. From its precipices issued streams of fine water, as cold as ice.

The two canoes which we had left at our last station, followed us hither, and when they were preparing to depart, our young chief embarked with them. I was determined, however, to prevent his escape, and compelled him, by actual force, to come on shore, for I thought it much better to incur his displeasure, than to suffer him to expose himself to any untoward accident among strangers, or to return to his father before us. The men in the canoe made signs for him to go over the hill, and that they would take him on board at the other side of it. As I was necessarily engaged in other matters, I desired my people to take care that he should not run away; but they peremptorily refused to be employed in keeping him against his will. I was, therefore, reduced to the necessity of watching him myself.

I took five altitudes, and the mean of them was 29. 23. 48. at 3. 5. 53. in the afternoon, by the watch, which makes it slow apparent time 1^h 22^m 38^s

In the forenoon
it was   .   .   1   21   44   2   44   22

Mean of both   .   1   22   11

Difference nine hours going of
the time-piece slow   .   .   .   8

1   22   19

I observed an emersion of Jupiter's third satellite, which gave 8° 32′ 21″ difference of longitude. I then observed an emersion of Jupiter's first satellite, which gave 8. 31. 48. The mean of these observations is 8° 32′ 2″ which is equal to 128. 2. West of Greenwich.

I had now determined my situation, which is the most fortunate circumstance of my long, painful, and perilous journey, as a few cloudy days would have prevented me from ascertaining the final longitude of it.*

At twelve it was high water, but the tide did not come within a foot and an half of the high water mark of last night. As soon as I had completed my observations, we left this place: it was then ten o'clock in the afternoon. We returned the same way that we came, and though the tide was running out very strong, by keeping close in with the rocks, we proceeded at a considerable rate, as my people were very anxious to get out of the reach of the inhabitants of this coast.

Tuesday, 23. During our course we saw several fires on the land to the Southward, and after the day dawned, their smokes were visible. At half past four this morning we

---

*Mr. Meares was undoubtedly wrong in the idea, so earnestly insisted on by him in his voyage, that there was a North-West passage to the Southward of sixty-nine degrees and an half of latitude, as I flatter myself has been proved by my former voyage. Nor can I refrain from expressing my surprise at his assertion, that there was an inland sea or archipelago of great extent between the islands of Nootka and the main, about the latitude where I was at this time. Indeed I have been informed that Captain Grey, who commanded an American vessel, and on whose authority he ventured this opinion, denies that he had given Mr. Meares any such information. Besides, the contrary is indubitably proved by Captain Vancouver's survey, from which no appeal can be made.

arrived at our encampment of the night of the 21st, which had been named Porcupine Cove. The tide was out, and considerably lower than we found it when we were here before; the high water mark being above the place where we had made our fire. This fluctuation must be occasioned by the action of the wind upon the water, in those narrow channels.

As we continued onwards, towards the river, we saw a canoe, well manned, which at first made from us with great expedition, but afterwards waited, as if to reconnoitre us; however, it kept out of our way, and allowed us to pass. The tide being much lower than when we were here before, we were under the necessity of landing a mile below the village. We observed that stakes were fixed in the ground along the bay, and in some places machines were fastened to them, as I afterwards learned, to intercept the seals and otters. These works are very extensive, and must have been erected with no common labour. The only bird we saw to-day was the white-headed eagle.*

Our guide directed us to draw the canoe out of the reach of the tide and to leave it. He would not wait, however, till this operation was performed, and I did not wish to let him go alone. I therefore followed him

* This bay was now named Mackenzie's Outlet.

through a bad road encumbered with under-wood. When we had quitted the wood, and were in sight of the houses, the young man being about fifteen or twenty paces before me, I was surprised to see two men running down towards me from one of the houses, with daggers in their hands and fury in their aspect. From their hostile appearance, I could not doubt of their purpose. I therefore stopped short, threw down my cloak, and put myself in a posture of defence, with my gun presented towards them. Fortunately for me, they knew the effect of fire-arms, and instantly dropped their daggers, which were fastened by a string to their wrists, and had before been held in a menacing attitude. I let my gun also fall into my left hand, and drew my hanger. Several others soon joined them, who were armed in the same manner; and among them I recognised the man whom I have already mentioned as being so trou-blesome to us, and who now repeated the names of Macubah and Bensins, signifying at the same time by his action, as on a former occasion, that he had been shot at by them. Until I saw him my mind was undisturbed; but the moment he appeared, conceiving that he was the cause of my present perilous sit-uation, my resentment predominated, and, if he had come within my reach, I verily believe, that I should have terminated his insolence for ever.

The rest now approached so near, that one of them contrived to get behind me, and grasped me in his arms. I soon disengaged myself from him; and, that he did not avail himself of the opportunity which he had of plunging his dagger into me, I cannot conjecture. They certainly might have overpowered me, and though I should probably have killed one or two of them, I must have fallen at last.

One of my people now came out of the wood. On his appearance they instantly took to flight, and with the utmost speed sought shelter in the houses from whence they had issued. It was, however, upwards of ten minutes before all my people joined me; and as they came one after the other, these people might have successively dispatched every one of us. If they had killed me, in the first instance, this consequence would certainly have followed, and not one of us would have returned home to tell the horrid fate of his companions.

After having stated the danger I had encountered, I told my people that I was determined to make these natives feel the impropriety of their conduct toward us, and compel them to return my hat and cloak which they had taken in the scuffle, as well as the articles previously purloined from us; for most of the men who were in the three canoes that we first saw, were now in the village. I therefore told my men to prime their pieces afresh, and prepare themselves for an active use of them, if the occasion should require it.

We now drew up before the house, and made signs for some one to come down to us. At length our young chief appeared, and told us that the men belonging to the canoes had not only informed his friends, that we had treated him very ill, but that we had killed four of their companions whom we had met in the bay. When I had explained to them as well as it was in my power, the falsehood of such a story, I insisted on the restoration of every thing that had been taken from us, as well as a necessary supply of fish, as the conditions of my departure; accordingly the things were restored, and a few dried fish along with them. A reconciliation now took place, but our guide or young chief was so much terrified that he would remain no longer with us, and requested us to follow with his father's canoe, or mischief would follow. I determined, however, before my departure, to take an observation, and at noon got a meridian altitude, making this place,

which I named Rascal's Village, 52. 23. 43.
North latitude.

On my informing the natives that we
wanted something more to eat, they brought
us two salmons; and when we signified that
we had no poles to set the canoe against the
current, they were furnished with equal alac-
rity, so anxious were they for our departure.
I paid, however, for every thing which we
had received, and did not forget the loan of
the canoe.

Chapter 12

July, 1793.

THE current of the river was so strong, that I should have complied with the wishes of my people, and gone by land, but one of my Indians was so weak, that it was impossible for him to perform the journey. He had been ill some time; and, indeed, we had been all of us more or less afflicted with colds on the sea coast. Four of the people therefore set off with the canoe, and it employed them an hour to get half a mile. In the mean time the native, who has been already mentioned as having treated us with so much insolence, and four of his companions, went up the river in a

320

canoe, which they had above the rapid, with as many boxes as men in her. This circumstance was the cause of fresh alarm, as it was generally concluded that they would produce the same mischief and danger in the villages above, as they had in that below. Nor was it forgotten that the young chief had left us in a manner which would not be interpreted in our favour by his father and friends.

At length the canoe arrived, and the people declared in the most unreserved terms, that they would proceed no further in her; but when they were made acquainted with the circumstances which have just been described, their violence increased, and the greater part of the men announced their determination to attempt the mountains, and endeavour, by passing over them, to gain the road by which we came to the first village. So resolved were they to pursue this plan, that they threw every thing which they had into the river, except their blankets. I was all this time sitting patiently on a stone, and indulging the hope that, when their frantic terror had subsided, their returning reason would have disposed them to perceive the rashness of their project; but when I observed that they persisted in it, I no longer remained a silent listener to their passionate declarations, but proceeded to employ such arguments as I trusted would turn them from their senseless and impracticable purpose. After reproving my young Indian in very severe terms, for encouraging the rest to follow their mad design of passing the mountains, I addressed myself generally to them, stating the difficulty of ascending the mountains, the eternal snows with which they were covered, our small stock of provisions, which two days would exhaust, and the consequent probability that we should perish with cold and hunger. I urged the folly of being affected by the alarm of danger which might not exist, and if it did, I encouraged them with the means we possessed of surmounting it. Nor did I forget to urge the inhumanity and injustice of leaving the poor sick Indian to languish and die. I also added, that as my particular object had been accomplished, I had now no other but our common safety; that the sole wish of my heart was to employ the best means in my power, and to pursue the best method which my understanding could suggest, to secure them and myself from every danger that might impede our return.

My steersman, who had been with me for five years in that capacity, instantly replied that he was ready to follow me wherever I should go, but that he would never again enter that canoe, as he had solemnly sworn he would not, while he was in the rapid. His example was followed by all the rest, except two, who embarked with Mr. Mackay,* myself, and the sick Indian. The current, however, was so strong, that we dragged up the greatest part of the way, by the branches of trees. Our progress, as may be imagined, was very tedious, and attended with uncommon labour; the party who went by land being continually obliged to wait for us. Mr. Mackay's gun was carried out of the canoe and lost, at a time when we appeared to stand in very great need of it, as two canoes, with sixteen or eighteen men, were coming down the stream; and the apprehensions which they occasioned did not subside till they shot by us with great rapidity.

At length we came in sight of the house, when we saw our young Indian with six others, in a canoe coming to meet us. This was a very encouraging circumstance, as it satisfied us that the natives who had preceded, and whose malignant designs we had every reason to suspect, had not been able to prejudice the people against us. We, therefore, landed at the house, where we were received in a friendly manner, and having procured some fish, we proceeded on our journey.

* It is but common justice to him, to mention in this place that I had every reason to be satisfied with his conduct.

It was almost dark when we arrived at the next house, and the first persons who presented themselves to our observation were the turbulent Indian and his four companions. They were not very agreeable objects; but we were nevertheless well received by the inhabitants, who presented us with fish and berries. The Indians who had caused us so much alarm, we now discovered to be inhabitants of the islands, and traders in various articles, such as cedar-bark, prepared to be wove into mats, fish-spawn, copper, iron, and beads, the latter of which they get on their own coast. For these they receive in exchange roasted salmon, hemlock-bark cakes, and the other kind made of salmon roes, sorrel, and bitter berries. Having procured as much fish as would serve us for our supper, and the meals of the next day, all my people went to rest except one, with whom I kept the first watch.

Wednesday, 24. After twelve last night, I called up Mr. Mackay, and one of the men, to relieve us, but as a general tranquillity appeared to prevail in the place, I recommended them to return to their rest. I was the first to awake in the morning, and sent Mr. Mackay to see if our canoe remained where we left it; but he returned to inform me that the Islanders had loaded it with their articles of traffic, and were ready to depart. On this intelligence I hurried to the water side, and seizing the canoe by the stem, I should certainly have overset it, and turned the three men that were in it, with all their merchandise, into the river, had not one of the people of the house, who had been very kind to us, informed me that this was their own canoe, and that my guide had gone off with ours. At the same moment the other two Indians who belonged to the party, jumped nimbly into it, and pushed off with all the haste and hurry that their fears may be supposed to dictate.

We now found ourselves once more without a guide or a canoe. We were, however, so fortunate as to engage, without much difficulty, two of these people to accompany us; as, from the strength of the current, it would not have been possible for us to have proceeded by water without their assistance. As the house was upon an island, we ferried over the pedestrian party to the main bank of the river, and continued our course till our conductors came to their fishing ground, when they proposed to land us, and our small portion of baggage; but as our companions were on the opposite shore, we could not acquiesce, and after some time persuaded them to proceed further with us. Soon after we met the chief, who had regaled us in our voyage down the river. He was seining between two canoes, and had taken a considerable quantity of salmon. He took us on board with him, and proceeded upwards with great expedition. These people are surprisingly skilful and active in setting against a strong current. In the roughest part they almost filled the canoe with water, by way of a sportive alarm to us.

We landed at the house of the chief, and he immediately placed a fish before me. Our people now appeared on the opposite bank, when a canoe was sent for them. As soon as they had made their meal of fish, they proceeded on their route, and we followed them, the chief and one of the natives having undertaken to conduct us.

At five in the afternoon we came to two houses, which we had not seen in going down. They were upon an island, and I was obliged to send for the walking party, as our conductors, from the lateness of the hour, refused to proceed any further with us till the next day. One of our men, being at a small distance before the others, had been attacked by a female bear, with two cubs, but another of them arrived to his rescue, and shot her. Their fears probably prevented them from killing the two young ones. They brought a part of the meat, but it was very indifferent. We were informed that our former guide, or young chief, had passed this place, at a very early hour of the morning, on foot.

These people take plenty of another fish, besides salmon, which weigh from fifteen to forty pounds. This fish is broader than the salmon, of a greyish colour, and with an hunch on its back; the flesh is white, but neither rich nor well flavoured. Its jaw and teeth are like those of a dog, and the latter are larger and stronger than any I had ever seen in a fish of equal size: those in front bend inwards, like the claws of a bird of prey. It delights in shallow water, and its native name is Dilly.

We received as many fish and berries from these people as completely satisfied our appetites. The latter excelled any of the kind that we had seen. I saw, also, three kinds of gooseberries, which, as we passed through the woods, we found in great abundance.

Thursday, 25. I arose before the sun, and the weather was very fine. The men who were to accompany us went to visit their machines, and brought back plenty of fish, which they strung on a rope, and left them in the river. We now embarked thirteen in a canoe, and landed my men on the South bank, as it would have been impracticable to have stemmed the tide with such a load. The under-wood was so thick that it was with great difficulty they could pass through it. At nine we were under the necessity of waiting to ferry them over a river from the South, which is not fordable. After some time we came to two deserted houses, at the foot of a rapid, beyond which our boatmen absolutely refused to conduct us by water. Here was a road which led opposite to the village. We had, however, the curiosity to visit the houses, which were erected upon posts; and we suffered very severely for the indulgence of it; for the floors were covered with fleas, and we were immediately in the same condition, for which we had no remedy but to take to the water. There was not a spot round the houses, free from grass, that was not alive, as it were, with this vermin.

Our guides proposed to conduct us on our way, and we followed them on a well-beaten track. They, however, went so fast, that we could not all of us keep up with them, particularly our sick Indian, whose situation was very embarrassing to us, and at length they contrived to escape. I very much wished for these men to have accompanied us to the village, in order to do away any ill impressions which might have arisen from the young chief's report to his father, which we were naturally led to expect would not be in our favour.

This road conducted us through the finest wood of cedar trees that I had ever seen. I measured several of them that were twenty-four feet in the girth, and of a proportionate height. The alder trees are also of an uncommon size; several of them were seven feet and an half in circumference, and rose to forty feet without a branch; but my men declared that they had, in their progress, seen much larger of both kinds. The other wood was hemlock, white birch, two species of spruce-firs, willows, &c. Many of the large cedars appeared to have been examined, as I suppose by the natives, for the purpose of making canoes, but finding them hollow at heart, they were suffered to stand. There was but little underwood, and the soil was a black rich mould, which would well reward the trouble of cultivation. From the remains of bones on certain spots, it is probable that the natives may have occasionally burned their dead in this wood.

As it was uncertain what our reception might be at the village, I examined every man's arms and ammunition, and gave Mr. Mackay, who had unfortunately lost his gun, one of my pistols. Our late conductors had informed us that the man whom we left in a dying state, and to whom I had administered some Turlington's balsam, was dead; and it was by no means improbable that I might be suspected of hastening his end.

At one in the afternoon we came to the bank of the river, which was opposite to the village, which appeared to be in a state of perfect tranquillity. Several of the natives were fishing above and below the weir, and they very readily took us over in their canoes. The people now hurried down to the water side, but I perceived none of the chief's family among them. They made signs to me to go to his house; I signified to them not to crowd about us, and indeed drew a line, beyond which I made them understand they must not pass. I now directed Mr. Mackay, and the men to remain there, with their arms in readiness, and to keep the natives at a distance, as I was determined to go alone to the chief's house; and if they should hear the report of my pistols, they were ordered to make the best of their way from these people, as it would then be equally fruitless and dangerous to attempt the giving me any assistance, as it would be only in the last extremity, and when I was certain of their intention to destroy me, that I should discharge my pistols. My gun I gave to Mr. Mackay, when, with my loaded pistols in my belt, and a poniard in my hand, I proceeded to the abode of the chief. I had a wood to

pass in my way thither, which was intersected by various paths, and I took one that
led to the back instead of the front of the
house; and as the whole had been very much
altered since I was here before, I concluded
that I had lost my way. But I continued to
proceed, and soon met with the chief's wife,
who informed me, that he was at the next
house. On my going round it, I perceived
that they had thrown open the gable ends,
and added two wings, nearly as long as the
body, both of which were hung round with
salmon as close as they could be placed. As
I could discover none of the men, I sat down
upon a large stone near some women who
were supping on salmon roes and berries.
They invited me to partake of their fare, and
I was about to accept their invitation, when
Mr. Mackay joined me, as both himself and
all my party were alarmed at my being alone.
Nor was his alarm lessened by an old man
whom he met in the wood, and who made
use of signs to persuade him to return. As he
came without his gun, I gave him one of my
pistols. When I saw the women continue
their employment without paying the least
attention to us, I could not imagine that
any hostile design was preparing against
us. Though the non-appearance of the men
awakened some degree of suspicion that I

should not be received with the same welcome as on my former visit. At length the
chief appeared, and his son, who had been
our guide, following him: displeasure was
painted in the old man's countenance, and
he held in his hand a bead tobacco pouch
which belonged to Mr. Mackay, and the
young chief had purloined from him. When
he had approached within three or four
yards of me, he threw it at me with great in-
dignation, and walked away. I followed him,
however, until he had passed his son, whom
I took by the hand, but he did not make any
very cordial return to my salutation; at the
same time he made signs for me to discharge
my pistol, and give him my hanger which Mr.
Mackay had brought me, but I did not pay
the least attention to either of his demands.

We now joined the chief, who explained to
me that he was in a state of deep distress for
the loss of his son, and made me understand
that he had cut off his hair and blackened
his face on the melancholy occasion. He also
represented the alarm which he had suffered
respecting his son who had accompanied us;
as he apprehended we had killed him, or had
all of us perished together. When he had finished his narrative, I took him and his son by
their hands, and requested them to come
with me to the place where I had left my

people, who were rejoiced to see us return, having been in a state of great anxiety from our long absence. I immediately remunerated the young chief for his company and assistance in our voyage to the sea, as well as his father, for his former attentions. I gave them cloth and knives, and, indeed, a portion of every thing which now remained to us. The presents had the desired effect of restoring us to their favour; but these people are of so changeable a nature, that there is no security with them. I procured three robes and two otter-skins, and if I could have given such articles in exchange as they preferred, I should probably have obtained more. I now represented the length of the way which I had to go, and requested some fish to support us on our journey, when he desired us to follow him to the house, where mats were immediately arranged and a fish placed before each of us.

We were now informed, that our dog, whom we had lost, had been howling about the village ever since we left it, and that they had reason to believe he left the woods at night to eat the fish he could find about the houses. I immediately dispatched Mr. Mackay, and a man, in search of the animal, but they returned without him.

When I manifested my intention to proceed on my journey, the chief voluntarily sent for ten roasted salmon, and having attended us with his son, and a great number of his people, to the last house in the village, we took our leave. It was then half past three in the afternoon.

I directed Mr. Mackay to take the lead, and the others to follow him in Indian file, at a long and steady pace, as I determined to bring up the rear. I adopted this measure from a confusion that was observable among the natives which I did not comprehend. I was not without my suspicions that some mischief was in agitation, and they were increased from the confused noise we heard in the village. At the same time a considerable number came running after us; some of them making signs for us to stop, and others rushing by me. I perceived also, that those who followed us were the strangers who live among these people, and are kept by them in a state of awe and subjection; and one of them made signs to me that we were taking a wrong road. I immediately called out to Mr. Mackay to stop. This was naturally enough taken for an alarm, and threw my people into great disorder. When, however, I was understood, and we had mustered again, our Indian informed us, that the noise we heard was occasioned by a debate among the natives, whether they should stop us or not.

Voyage to the Pacific Ocean

When, therefore, we had got into the right road, I made such arrangements as might be necessary for our defence, if we should have an experimental proof that our late and fickle friends were converted into enemies.

Our way was through a forest of stately cedars, beneath a range of lofty hills, covered with rocks, and without any view of the river. The path was well beaten, but rendered incommodious by the large stones which lay along it.

As we were continuing our route, we all felt the sensation of having found a lost friend at the sight of our dog; but he appeared, in a great degree, to have lost his former sagacity. He ran in a wild way backwards and forwards; and though he kept our road, I could not induce him to acknowledge his master. Sometimes he seemed disposed to approach as if he knew us; and then, on a sudden, he would turn away, as if alarmed at our appearance. The poor animal was reduced almost to a skeleton, and we occasionally dropped something to support him, and by degrees he recovered his former sagacity.

When the night came on we stopped at a small distance from the river, but did not venture to make a fire. Every man took his tree, and laid down in his clothes, and with his arms, beneath the shade of its branches.

We had removed to a short distance from the path; no centinel was now appointed, and every one was left to watch for his own safety.

Friday, 26. After a very restless, though undisturbed night, we set forward as soon as day appeared, and walked on with all possible expedition, till we got to the upper, which we now called Friendly Village, and was the first we visited on our outward journey.

It was eight in the morning of a very fine day when we arrived, and found a very material alteration in the place since we left it. Five additional houses had been erected and were filled with salmon: the increase of inhabitants was in the same proportion. We were received with great kindness, and a messenger was dispatched to inform the chief, whose name was Soocomlick, and who was then at his fishing-weir, of our arrival. He immediately returned to the village to confirm the cordial reception of his people; and having conducted us to his house, entertained us with the most respectful hospitality. In short, he behaved to us with so much attention and kindness, that I did not withhold any thing in my power to give, which might afford him satisfaction. I presented him with two yards of blue cloth, an axe, knives, and various other articles. He gave me in return a large shell which resembled

the under shell of a Guernsey oyster, but
somewhat larger. Where they procure them
I could not discover, but they cut and polish
them for bracelets, ear-rings, and other personal ornaments. He regretted that he had
no sea-otter skins to give me, but engaged to
provide abundance of them whenever either
my friends or myself should return by sea;
an expectation which I thought it right to encourage among these people. He also earnestly requested me to bring him a gun and
ammunition. I might have procured many
curious articles at this place, but was prevented by the consideration that we must
have carried them on our backs upwards of
three hundred miles through a mountainous
country. The young chief, to his other acts of
kindness, added as large a supply of fish as
we chose to take.

Our visit did not occasion any particular
interruption of the ordinary occupation of
the people; especially of the women, who
were employed in boiling sorrel, and different
kinds of berries, with salmon-roes, in large
square kettles of cedar wood. This pottage,
when it attained a certain consistency, they
took out with ladles, and poured it into
frames of about twelve inches square and one
deep, the bottom being covered with a large
leaf, which were then exposed to the sun till

their contents became so many dried cakes.
The roes that are mixed up with the bitter
berries, are prepared in the same way. From
the quantity of this kind of provision, it
must be a principal article of food, and probably of traffic. These people have also port-
able chests of cedar, in which they pack
them, as well as their salmon, both dried and
roasted. It appeared to me, that they eat no
flesh, except such as the sea may afford
them, as that of the sea-otter and the seal.
The only instance we observed to the contrary, was in the young Indian who accompanied us among the islands, and has been
already mentioned as feasting on the flesh of
a porcupine: whether this be their custom
throughout the year, or only during the season of the salmon fishery; or, whether there
were any castes of them, as in India, I cannot
pretend to determine. It is certain, however,
that they are not hunters, and I have already
mentioned the abhorrence they expressed at
some venison which we brought to their village. During our former visit to these people,
they requested us not to discharge our fire-
arms, lest the report should frighten away
the salmon, but now they expressed a wish
that I should explain the use and management of them. Though their demeanour to
us was of the most friendly nature, and they

appeared without any arms, except a few who accidentally had their daggers, I did not think it altogether prudent to discharge our pieces; I therefore fired one of my pistols at a tree marked for the purpose, when I put four out of five buck-shot, with which it was loaded, into the circle, to their extreme astonishment and admiration.

These people were in general of the middle stature, well-set, and better clothed with flesh than any of the natives of the interior country. Their faces are round, with high cheek bones, and their complexion between the olive and the copper. They have small grey eyes with a tinge of red; they have wedge heads, and their hair is of a dark brown colour, inclining to black. Some wear it long, keep it well combed, and let it hang loose over their shoulders, while they divide and tie it in knots over the temples. Others arrange its plaits, and bedaub it with brown earth, so as to render it impervious to the comb; they, therefore, carry a bodkin about them to ease the frequent irritation, which may be supposed to proceed from such a state of the head. The women are inclined to be fat, wear their hair short, and appear to be very subject to swelled legs, a malady that, probably, proceeds from the posture in which they are always sitting: as they are

chiefly employed in the domestic engage-
ments of spinning, weaving, preparing the
fish, and nursing their children, which did
not appear to be numerous. Their cradle differed from any that I had seen; it consisted
of a frame fixed round a board of sufficient
length, in which the child, after it has been
swathed, is placed on a bed of moss, and a
conductor contrived to carry off the urinary
discharge. They are flung over one shoulder
by means of a cord fastened under the other,
so that the infant is always in a position to be
readily applied to the breast, when it requires
nourishment. I saw several whose heads were
inclosed in boards covered with leather, till
they attain the form of a wedge. The women
wear no clothing but the robe, either loose
or tied round the middle with a girdle, as the
occasion may require, with the addition of a
fringed apron, already mentioned, and a cap,
in the form of an inverted bowl or dish. To
the robe and cap, the men add, when it rains,
a circular mat with an opening in the middle
sufficient to admit the head, which extending over the shoulders, throws off the wet.
They also occasionally wear shoes of dressed
moose-skin, for which they are indebted to
their neighbours. Those parts, which among
all civilized nations are covered from familiar
view, are here openly exposed.

They are altogether dependent on the sea and rivers for their sustenance, so that they may be considered as a stationary people; hence it is that the men engage in those toilsome employments, which the tribes who support themselves by the chase, leave entirely to the women. Polygamy is permitted among them, though, according to my observation, most of the men were satisfied with one wife, with whom, however, chastity is not considered as a necessary virtue. I saw but one woman whose under lip was split and disfigured with an appendant ornament. The men frequently bathe, and the boys are continually in the water. They have nets and lines of various kinds and sizes, which are made of cedar bark, and would not be known from those made of hemp. Their hooks consist of two pieces of wood or bone, forming when fixed together, an obtuse angle.

Their spears or darts are from four to sixteen feet in length; the barb or point being fixed in a socket, which, when the animal is struck, slips from it: thus the barb being fastened by a string to the handle, remains as a buoy; or enables the aquatic hunter to tire and take his prey. They are employed against sea-otters, seals, and large fish.

Their hatchets are made principally of about fourteen inches of bar-iron, fixed into a wooden handle, as I have already described them; though they have some of bone or horn: with these, a mallet and wooden wedge, they hew their timbers and form their planks. They must also have other tools with which they complete and polish their work, but my stay was so short, my anxiety so great, and my situation so critical, that many circumstances may be supposed to have escaped me.

Their canoes are made out of the cedar tree, and will carry from eight to fifty persons.

Their warlike weapons, which, as far as I could judge, they very seldom have occasion to employ, are bows and arrows, spears, and daggers. The arrows are such as have been already described, but rather of a slighter make. The bows are not more than two feet and an half in length; they are formed of a slip of red cedar; the grain being on one side untouched with any tool, while the other is secured with sinews attached to it by a kind of glue. Though this weapon has a very slender appearance, it throws an arrow with great force, and to a considerable distance. Their spears are about ten feet long, and pointed with iron. Their daggers are of various kinds, being of British, Spanish, and American manufacture.

Their household furniture consists of boxes, troughs, and dishes formed of wood, with different vessels made of watape. These are employed, according to their several applications, to contain their valuables and provisions, as well as for culinary purposes, and to carry water. The women make use of muscle-shells to split and clean their fish, and which are very well adapted to that purpose.

Their ornaments are necklaces, collars, bracelets for the arms, wrists, and legs, with ear-rings, etc.

They burn their dead, and display their mourning, by cutting their hair short, and blackening their faces. Though I saw several places where bodies had been burned, I was surprised at not seeing any tomb or memorial of the dead, particularly when their neighbours are so superstitiously attentive to the erection and preservation of them.

From the number of their canoes, as well as the quantity of their chests and boxes, to contain their moveables, as well as the insufficiency of their houses, to guard against the rigours of a severe winter, and the appearance of the ground around their habitations, it is evident that these people reside here only during the summer or salmon season, which does not probably last more than three months. It may be reasonably inferred, therefore, that they have villages on the sea-coast, which they inhabit during the rest of the year. There it may be supposed they leave the sick, the infirm, and the aged; and thither they may bear the ashes of those who die at the place of their summer residence.

Of their religion I can say but little, as my means of observation were very contracted. I could discover, however, that they believed in a good and an evil spirit: and that they have some forms of worship to conciliate the protection of one, and perhaps to avert the enmity of the other, is apparent from the temples which I have described; and where, at stated periods, it may be presumed they hold the feasts, and perform the sacrifices, which their religion, whatever it may be, has instituted as the ceremonials of their public worship.

From the very little I could discover of their government, it is altogether different from any political regulation which had been remarked by me among the savage tribes. It is on this river alone that one man appears to have an exclusive and hereditary right to what was necessary to the existence of those who are associated with him. I allude to the salmon weir, or fishing place, the sole right to which confers on the chief an arbitrary power. Those embankments could not have been formed without a very great and associated labour; and, as might be supposed, on the condition that those who assisted in constructing it should enjoy a participating right in the advantages to be derived from it. Nevertheless, it evidently appeared to me, that the chief's power over it, and the people, was unlimited, and without control. No one could fish without his permission, or carry home a larger portion of what he had caught, than was set apart for him. No one could build an house without his consent; and all his commands appeared to be followed with implicit obedience. The people at large seemed to be on a perfect equality, while the strangers among them were obliged to obey the commands of the natives in general, or quit the village. They appear to be of a friendly disposition, but they are subject to sudden gusts of passion, which are as quickly composed; and the transition is instantaneous, from violent irritation to the most tranquil demeanour. Of the many tribes of savage people whom I have seen, these appear to be the most susceptible of civilization. They might soon be brought to cultivate the little ground about them which is capable of it. There is a narrow border of a rich black soil, on either side of the river, over a bed of gravel, which would yield any grain or fruit, that are common to similar latitudes in Europe.

The very few words which I collected of their language, are as follows:—

Zimilk,	Salmon.
Dilly,	A fish of the size of a salmon, with canine teeth.
Sepnas,	Hair of the head.
Kietis,	An axe.
Clougus,	Eyes.
Itzas,	Teeth.
Ma-acza,	Nose.
Ich-yeh,	Leg.
Shous-shey,	Hand.
Watts,	Dog.
Zla-achle,	House.
Zimnez, ·	Bark mat robe.
Couloun,	Beaver or otter ditto.
Dichts,	Stone.
Neach,	Fire.
Ulkan,	Water.
Gits com,	A mat.
Shiggimia,	Thread.
Till-kewan,	Chest or box.
Thlogatt,	Cedar bark.
Achimoul,	Beads got upon their coast.
Il-caiette,	A bonnet.
Couny,	A clam shell.
Nochasky,	A dish composed of berries and salmon roes.
Caiffre,	What?

Chapter 13

July, 1793.

FRIDAY, 26. At eleven in the morning we left this place, which I called Friendly Village, accompanied by every man belonging to it, who attended us about a mile, when we took a cordial leave of them; and if we might judge from appearances, they parted from us with regret.

In a short time we halted, to make a division of our fish, and each man had about twenty pounds weight of it, except Mr. Mackay and myself, who were content with shorter allowance, that we might have less weight to carry. We had also a little flour, and some pemmican. Having completed this arrangement with all possible expedition, we proceeded onwards, the ground rising gradually, as we continued our route. When we were clear of the wood, we saw the mountain towering above, and apparently of impracticable ascent. We soon came to the fork of the river, which was at the foot of the precipice, where the ford was three feet deep, and very rapid. Our young Indian, though much recovered, was still too weak to cross the water, and with some difficulty I carried him over on my back.

It was now one in the afternoon, and we had to ascend the summit of the first mountain before night came on, in order to look for water. I left the sick Indian, with his companion and one of my men, to follow us, as his strength would permit him. The fatigue of ascending these precipices I shall not attempt to describe, and it was past five when we arrived at a spot where we could get water, and in such an extremity of weariness, that it was with great pain any of us could crawl about to gather wood for the necessary purpose of making a fire. To relieve our anxiety, which began to increase every moment for the situation of the Indian, about seven he and his companions arrived; when we consoled ourselves by sitting round a blazing fire, talking of past dangers, and indulging the delightful reflection that we were thus far advanced on our homeward journey. Nor was it possible to be in this situation without contemplating the wonders of it. Such was the depth of the precipices below, and the height of the mountains above, with the rude and wild magnificence of the scenery around, that I shall not attempt to describe such an astonishing and awful combination of objects; of which, indeed, no description can convey an adequate idea. Even at this place, which is only, as it were, the first step towards gaining the summit of the mountains, the climate was very sensibly changed. The air that fanned the village which we left at noon, was mild and cheering; the grass was verdant, and the wild fruits ripe around it. But here the snow was not yet dissolved, the ground was still bound by the frost, the herbage had scarce begun to spring, and the crowberry bushes were just beginning to blossom.

Saturday, 27. So great was our fatigue of yesterday, that it was late before we proceeded to return over the mountains, by the same route which we had followed in our outward journey. There was little or no change in the appearance of the mountains since we passed them, though the weather was very fine.

Sunday, 28. At nine this morning we arrived at the spot, where we slept with the natives on the 16th instant, and found our pemmican in good condition where we had buried it.

The latitude of this place, by observation, when I passed, I found to be 52. 46. 32. I now took time, and the distance between sun and moon. I had also an azimuth, to ascertain the variation.

August, 1793. We continued our route with fine weather, and without meeting a single person on our way, the natives being all gone, as we supposed, to the Great River. We recovered all our hidden stores of provisions, and arrived about two in the afternoon of Sunday, August the 4th, at the place which we had left a month before.

A considerable number of Indians were encamped on the opposite side of the small river, and in consequence of the weather, confined to their lodges: as they must have heard of, if not seen, us, and our arms being out of order from the rain, I was not satisfied with our situation; but did not wish to create an alarm. We, therefore, kept in the edge of the wood, and called to them, when they turned out like so many furies, with their arms in their hands, and threatening destruction if we dared to approach their habitations. We remained in our station till their passion and apprehensions had subsided, when our interpreter gave them the necessary information respecting us. They proved to be strangers to us, but were the relations of those whom we had already seen here, and who, as they told us, were upon an island at some distance up the river. A messenger was accordingly sent to inform them of our arrival.

Monday, 5. On examining the canoe, and our property, which we had left behind, we found it in perfect safety; nor was there the print of a foot near the spot. We now pitched our tent, and made a blazing fire, and I treated myself, as well as the people, with a dram; but we had been so long without tasting any spirituous liquor, that we had lost all relish for it. The Indians now arrived from above, and were rewarded for the care they had taken of our property with such articles as were acceptable to them.

At nine this morning I sent five men in the canoe, for the various articles we had left below, and they soon returned with them, and except some bale goods, which had got wet, they were in good order, particularly the provisions, of which we were now in great need.

Many of the natives arrived both from the upper and lower parts of the river, each of whom was dressed in a beaver robe. I purchased fifteen of them; and they preferred large knives in exchange. It is an extraordinary circumstance, that these people, who might have taken all the property we left behind us, without the least fear of detection, should leave that untouched, and purloin any of our utensils, which our confidence in their honesty gave them a ready opportunity of taking. In fact, several articles were missing, and as I was very anxious to avoid a quarrel with the natives, in this stage of our journey, I told those who remained near us, without any appearance of anger, that their relations who were gone, had no idea of the mischief that would result to them from taking our property. I gravely added, that the salmon, which was not only their favourite food, but absolutely necessary to their existence, came from the sea which belonged to us white men; and that as, at the entrance of the river, we could prevent those fish from coming up it, we possessed the power to starve them and their children. To avert our anger, therefore, they must return all the articles that had been stolen from us. This finesse succeeded. Messengers were dispatched to order the restoration of every thing that had been taken. We purchased several large salmon of them and enjoyed the delicious meal which they afforded.

At noon this day, which I allotted for repose, I got a meridian altitude, which gave 53. 24. 10. I also took time. The weather had been cloudy at intervals.

Tuesday, 6. Every necessary preparation had been made yesterday for us to continue our route to day; but before our departure, some of the natives arrived with part of the stolen articles; the rest, they said, had been taken by people down the river, who would be here in the course of the morning, and recommended their children to our commiseration, and themselves to our forgiveness.

The morning was cloudy, with small rain, nevertheless I ordered the men to load the canoe, and we proceeded in high spirits on finding ourselves once more so comfortably together in it. We landed at an house on the first island, where we procured a few salmon, and four fine beaver skins. There had been much more rain in these parts than in the country above, as the water was pouring down the hills in torrents. The river consequently rose with great rapidity, and very much impeded our progress.

The people on this river are generally of the middle size, though I saw many tall men among them. In the cleanliness of their persons they resemble rather the Beaver Indians than the Chepewyans. They are ignorant of the use of fire arms, and their only weapons are bows and arrows, and spears. They catch the larger animals in snares, but though their country abounds in them, and the rivers and lakes produce plenty of fish, they find a difficulty in supporting themselves, and are never to be seen but in small bands of two or three families. There is no regular government among them; nor do they appear to have a sufficient communication or understanding with each other, to defend themselves against an invading enemy, to whom they fall an easy prey. They have all the animals common on the West side of the mountains, except the buffalo and the wolf; at least we saw none of the latter, and there being none of the former, it is evident that their progress is from the South-East. The same language is spoken, with very little exception from the extent of my travels down this river, and in a direct line from the North-East head of it in the latitude 53° or 54° to Hudson's Bay; so that a Chepewyan, from which tribe they have all sprung, might leave Churchill River, and proceeding in every direction to the North-West of this line without knowing any language except his own, would understand them all: I except the natives of the sea coast, who are altogether a different people. As to the people to the Eastward of this river, I am not qualified to speak of them.

At twelve we ran our canoe upon a rock, so that we were obliged to land in order to repair the injury she had received; and as the rain came on with great violence, we remained here for the night. The salmon were now driving up the current in such large shoals, that the water seemed, as it were, to be covered with the fins of them.

Wednesday, 7. About nine this morning the weather cleared, and we embarked. The shoals of salmon continued as yesterday. There were frequent showers throughout the day, and every brook was deluged into a river. The water had risen at least one foot and an half perpendicular in the last twenty-four hours. In the dusk of the evening we landed for the night.

Thursday, 8. The water continued rising during the night; so that we were disturbed twice in the course of it, to remove our baggage. At six in the morning we were on our way, and proceeded with continual and laborious exertion, from the increased rapidity of the current. After having passed the two carrying places of Rocky Point, and the Long Portage, we encamped for the night.

Friday, 9. We set off at five, after a rainy night, and in a foggy morning. The water still retained its height. The sun, however, soon beamed upon us; and our clothes and baggage were in such a state that we landed to dry them. After some time we re-embarked, and arrived at our first encampment on this river about seven in the evening. The water fell considerably in the course of the day.

Saturday, 10. The weather was cloudy with slight showers, and at five this morning we embarked, the water falling as fast as it had risen. This circumstance arises from the mountainous state of the country on either side of the river, from whence the water rushes down almost as fast as it falls from the heavens, with the addition of the snow it melts in its way. At eight in the evening we stopped for the night.

Sunday, 11. At five this morning we proceeded with clear weather. At ten we came to the foot of the long rapid, which we ascended with poles much easier than we expected. The rapids that were so strong, and violent in our passage downwards, were now so reduced, that we could hardly believe them to be the same. At sun-set we landed and encamped.

Monday, 12. The weather was the same as yesterday, and we were on the water at a very early hour. At nine we came to a part of the river where there was little or no current. At noon we landed to gum the canoe, when I took a meridian altitude, which gave 54. 11. 36. North latitude. We continued our route nearly East, and at three in the afternoon approached the fork, when I took time, and the distance between the sun and moon. At four in the afternoon we left the main branch. The current was quite slack, as the water had fallen six feet, which must have been in the course of three days. At sunset we landed and took our station for the night.

Tuesday, 13. There was a very heavy rain in the night, and the morning was cloudy; we renewed our voyage, however, at a very early hour, and came to the narrow gut between the mountains of rock, which was a passage of some risk; but fortunately the state of the water was such, that we got up without any difficulty, and had more time to examine these extraordinary rocks than in our outward passage. They are as perpendicular as a wall, and give the idea of a succession of enormous Gothic churches. We were now closely hemmed in by the mountains, which have lost much of their snow since our former passage by them. We encamped at a late hour, cold, wet, and hungry: for such was the state of our provisions, that our necessary allowance did not answer to the active cravings of our appetites.

Wednesday, 14. The weather was cold and raw, with small rain, but our necessities would not suffer us to wait for a favourable change of it, and at half past five we arrived at the swampy carrying-place, between this branch and the small river. At three in the afternoon the cold was extreme, and the men could not keep themselves warm even by their violent exertions which our situation required; and I now gave them the remainder of our rum to fortify and support them. The canoe was so heavy that the lives of two of them were endangered in this horrible carrying place. At the same time it must be observed, that from the fatiguing circumstances of our journey, and the inadequate state of our provisions, the natural strength of the men had been greatly diminished. We encamped on the banks of the bad river.

Thursday, 15. The weather was now clear, and the sun shone upon us. The water was much lower than in the downward passage, but as cold as ice, and, unfortunately, the men were obliged to be continually in it to drag on the canoe. There were many embarras, through which a passage might have been made, but we were under the necessity of carrying both the canoe and baggage.

About sun-set we arrived at our encampment of the 13th of June, where some of us had nearly taken our eternal voyage. The legs and feet of the men were so benumbed, that I was very apprehensive of the consequences. The water being low, we made a search for our bag of ball, but without success. The river was full of salmon, and another fish like the black bass.

Friday, 16. The weather continued to be the same as yesterday, and at two in the afternoon we came to the carrying-place which leads to the first small lake; but it was so filled with drift wood, that a considerable portion of time was employed in making our way through it. We now reached the high land which separates the source of the Tacoutche Tesse, or Columbia River, and Unjigah, or Peace River: the latter of which, after receiving many tributary streams, passes through the great Slave Lake, and disembogues itself in the Frozen Ocean, in latitude 69½ North, longitude 135. West from Greenwich; while the former, confined by the immense mountains that run nearly

parallel with the Pacific Ocean, and keep it
in a Southern course, empties itself in 46. 20.
North latitude and longitude 124. West from
Greenwich.

If I could have spared the time, and had
been able to exert myself, for I was now
afflicted with a swelling in my ankles, so that
I could not even walk, but with great pain
and difficulty, it was my intention to have
taken some salmon alive, and colonised them
in the Peace River, though it is very doubt-
ful whether that fish would live in waters
that have not a communication with the sea.

Some of the inhabitants had been here
since we passed; and I apprehend, that on
seeing our road through their country, they
mistook us for enemies, and had therefore
deserted the place, which is a most convenient station; as on one side, there is great
plenty of white fish, and trout, jub, carp, &c.
and on the other, abundance of salmon, and
probably other fish. Several things that I had
left here in exchange for articles of which I
had possessed myself, as objects of curiosity,
were taken away. The whirtle berries were
now ripe, and very fine of their kind.

Saturday, 17. The morning was cloudy,
and at five we renewed our progress. We
were compelled to carry from the lake to the
Peace River, the passage, from the falling of

the water, being wholly obstructed by drift-
wood. The meadow through which we passed
was entirely inundated; and from the state
of my foot and ankle, I was obliged, though
with great reluctance, to submit to be carried over it.

At half past seven we began to glide along
with the current of the Peace River; and
almost at every canoe's length we perceived
beaver roads to and from the river. At two
in the afternoon, an object attracted our notice at the entrance of a small river, which
proved to be the four beaver skins, already
mentioned to have been presented to me by
a native, and left in his possession to receive
them on my return. I imagine, therefore, that
being under the necessity of leaving the
river, or, perhaps, fearing to meet us again,
he had taken this method to restore them to
me; and to reward his honesty, I left three
times the value of the skins in their place.
The snow appeared in patches on the mountains. At four in the afternoon we passed the
place where we found the first natives, and
landed for the night at a late hour. In the
course of the day we caught nine outards, or
Canada geese, but they were as yet without
their feathers.

Sunday, 18. As soon as it was light we proceeded on our voyage, and drove on before

the current, which was very much diminished in its strength, since we came up it. The water indeed was so low, that in many parts it exposed a gravelly beach. At eleven we landed at our encampment of the seventh of June, to gum the canoe and dry our clothes: we then re-embarked, and at half past five arrived at the place, where I lost my book of memorandums, on the fourth of June, in which were certain courses and distances between that day and the twenty-sixth of May, which I had now an opportunity to supply. They were as follows:

North-North-West half a mile, East by North half a mile, North by East a quarter of a mile, North-West by West a quarter of a mile, West-South-West half a mile, North-West a mile and a quarter, North-North-West three quarters of a mile, North by East half a mile, North-West three quarters of a mile, West half a mile, North-West three quarters of a mile, West-North-West one mile and a quarter, North three quarters of a mile, West by North one quarter of a mile, North-West one mile and an half, West-North-West half a mile, North-North-West three quarters of a mile, West one quarter of a mile, North-North-East half a mile, North-North-West two miles, and North-West four miles.

We were seven days in going up that part
of the river which we came down to-day; and
it now swarmed, as it were, with beavers and
wild fowl. There was rain in the afternoon,
and about sun-set we took our station for the
night.

Monday, 19. We had some small rain
throughout the night. Our course to-day was
South-South-West three quarters of a mile,
West-North-West half a mile, North half a
mile, North-West by West three quarters of
a mile, North by West half a mile; a small
river to the left, South-West by West three
quarters of a mile, West-North-West a mile
and an half, North-West by North four
miles, a rivulet on the right, West-North-
West three quarters of a mile; a considerable river from the left, North-North-West
two miles, North half a mile, West-North-
West one mile and an half; a rivulet on the
right, North-West by West one mile and a
quarter, West-North-West one mile, West-
South-West a quarter of a mile, North-
North-West half a mile, North-West half a
mile, West-South-West three quarters of a
mile, North-West by West three miles,
West-South-West three quarters of a mile,
North-West by West one mile; a small river
on the right, South-West a quarter of a mile,
West-North-West, islands, four miles and

an half, a river on the left, North half a mile,
West a quarter of a mile, North a quarter of
a mile, North-West by West three quarters
of a mile, North-North-East three quarters
of a mile, North-West by North half a mile,
West-North-West a mile and an half, and
North-West by North half a mile. The
mountains were covered with fresh snow,
whose showers had dissolved in rain before
they reached us. North-West three quarters
of a mile, South-West a quarter of a mile,
North a mile and three quarters, West-
North-West a mile and a quarter, North-
West a mile and an half, North-North-West
half a mile, West-North-West a quarter of a
mile, North half a mile; here the current was
slack: North-West by North half a mile,
North-West by West a quarter of a mile,
North-North-West a quarter of a mile,
North-West by West one mile and a quarter, North half a mile, North-East by North
one mile and three quarters, South-West one
mile and a quarter, with an island, North by
East one mile, North-West. Here the other
branch opened to us, at the distance of three
quarters of a mile.

I expected from the slackness of the current in this branch, that the Western one
would be high, but I found it equally low. I
had every reason to believe that from the

upper part of this branch, the distance could not be great to the country through which I passed when I left the Great River; but it has since been determined otherwise by Mr. J. Finlay, who was sent to explore it, and found its navigation soon terminated by falls and rapids.

The branches are about two hundred yards in breadth, and the water was six feet lower than on our upward passage. Our course, after the junction, was North-North-West one mile, the rapid North-East down it three quarters of a mile, North by West one mile and a quarter, North by East one mile and an half, East by South one mile, North-East two miles and an half, East-North-East a quarter of a mile; a rivulet; East by South one mile and an half, North-East two miles, East-North-East one mile, North-North-East a quarter of a mile, North-East by East half a mile, East-South-East a quarter of a mile, East-North-East half a mile, North-East two miles, North-East by East two miles and a quarter, South-East by East a quarter of a mile; a rivulet from the left; East by North a mile and an half, East by South one mile, East-North-East one mile and three quarters; a river on the right; North-North-East three quarters of a mile, North-East a mile and an half, North-East by East a mile and a quarter, East-North-East half a mile, and North-East by North half a mile. Here we landed at our encampment of the 27th of June, from whence I dispatched a letter in an empty keg, as was mentioned in that period of my journal, which set forth our existing state, progress, and expectation.

Tuesday, 20. Though the weather was clear, we could not embark this morning before five, as there was a rapid very near us, which required day-light to run it, that we might not break our canoe on the rocks. The baggage we were obliged to carry. Our course was North by East a mile and an half, North-North-East a mile and an half down another rapid on the West side; it requires great care to keep directly between the eddy current, 'and that which was driving down with so much impetuosity. We then proceeded North-North-West, a river from the right; a mile and a quarter, North-North-East a mile and an half, a river from the left; North one mile and three quarters, North-East two miles, North-East by East two miles and a quarter, East by North one mile, North-East by East four miles, a river from the left, and East by South a mile and an half. Here was our encampment on the 26th of May, beyond which it would be altogether superfluous for me to take the courses, as they are inserted in their proper places.

As we continued our voyage, our attention was attracted by the appearance of an Indian encampment. We accordingly landed, and found there had been five fires, and within that number of days, so that there must have been some inhabitants in the neighbourhood, though we were not so fortunate as to see them. It appeared that they had killed a number of animals, and fled in a state of alarm, as three of their canoes were left carelessly on the beach, and their paddles laying about in disorder. We soon after came to the carrying-place called the Portage de la Montagne de Roche. Here I had a meridian altitude, which made the latitude 56. 3. 51. North.

The water, as I have already observed, was much lower than when we came up it, though at the same time, the current appeared to be stronger from this place to the forks; the navigation, however, would now be attended with greater facility, as there is a stony beach all the way, so that poles, or the towing line, may be employed with the best effect, where the current overpowers the use of paddles.

We were now reduced to a very short allowance; the disappointment, therefore, at not seeing any animals was proportioned to our exigencies, as we did not possess at this time more than was sufficient to serve us for two meals. I now dispatched Mr. Mackay and the Indians to proceed to the foot of the rapids, and endeavour in their way to procure some provisions, while I prepared to employ the utmost expedition in getting there; having determined, notwithstanding the disinclination of my people, from the recollection of what they had suffered in coming that way, to return by the same route. I had observed, indeed, that the water which had fallen fifteen feet perpendicular, at the narrow pass below us, had lost much of its former turbulence.

As dispatch was essential in procuring a supply of provisions, we did not delay a moment in making preparation to renew our progress. Five of the men began to carry the baggage, while the sixth and myself took the canoe asunder, to cleanse her of the dirt, and expose her lining and timbers to the air, which would render her much lighter. About sun-set Mr. Mackay and our hunters returned with heavy burdens of the flesh of a buffalo: though not very tender, it was very acceptable, and was the only animal that they had seen, though the country was covered with tracks of them, as well as of the moose-deer and the elk. The former had done rutting, and the latter were beginning to run. Our people returned, having left their loads mid-way on the carrying place. My companion and myself completed our undertaking, and the canoe was ready to be carried in the morning. An hearty meal concluded the day, and every fear of future want was removed.

Wednesday, 21. When the morning dawned we set forwards, but as a fire had passed through the portage, it was with difficulty we could trace our road in many parts; and with all the exertion of which we were capable, we did not arrive at the river till four in the afternoon. We found almost as much difficulty in carrying our canoe down the mountain as we had in getting it up; the men being not so strong as on the former occasion, though they were in better spirits; and I was now enabled to assist them, my ankle being almost well. We could not, however, proceed any further till the following day, as we had the canoe to gum, with several great and small poles to prepare; those we had left here having been carried away by the water, though we had left them in a position from fifteen to twenty feet above the water-mark, at that time. These occupations employed us till a very late hour.

Thursday, 22. The night was cold, and though the morning was fine and clear, it was seven before we were in a state of preparation to leave this place, sometimes driving with the current, and at other times shooting the rapids. The latter had lost much of their former strength; but we, nevertheless, thought it necessary to land very frequently, in order to examine the rapids before we could venture to run them. However, the canoe being light, we very fortunately passed them all, and at noon arrived at the place where I appointed to meet Mr. Mackay and the hunters: there we found them, with plenty of excellent fat meat, ready roasted, as they had killed two elks within a few hundred yards of the spot where we then were. When the men had satisfied their appetites, I sent them for as much of the meat as they could carry. In coming hither, Mr. Mackay informed me, that he and the hunters kept along the high land, and did not see or cross the Indian path. At the same time, there can be no doubt but the road from this place to the upper part of the rapids is to be preferred to that which we came, both for expedition and safety.

After staying here about an hour and an half, we proceeded with the stream, and landed where I had forgotten my pipe-tomahawk and seal, on the eighteenth of May. The former of them I now recovered.

On leaving the mountains we saw animals grazing in every direction. In passing along an island, we fired at an elk, and broke its leg; and, as it was now time to encamp, we landed; when the hunters pursued the wounded animal, which had crossed over to the main land, but could not get up the bank. We went after it, therefore, in the canoe, and killed it. To give some notion of our appetites, I shall state the elk, or at least the carcass of it, which we brought away, to have weighed two hundred and fifty pounds; and as we had taken a very hearty meal at one o'clock, it might naturally be supposed that we should not be very voracious at supper; nevertheless, a kettle full of the elk flesh was boiled and eaten, and that vessel replenished and put on the fire. All that remained, with the bones, &c. was placed, after the Indian fashion, round the fire to roast, and at ten next morning the whole was consumed by ten persons and a large dog, who was allowed his share of the banquet. This is no exaggeration; nor did any inconvenience result from what may be considered as an inordinate indulgence.

Friday, 23. We were on the water before day-light; and when the sun rose a beautiful country appeared around us, enriched and animated by large herds of wild cattle. The weather was now so warm, that to us, who had not of late been accustomed to heat, it was overwhelming and oppressive. In the course of this day we killed a buffalo and a bear; but we were now in the midst of abundance, and they were not sufficiently fat to satisfy our fastidious appetites, so we left them where they fell. We landed for the night, and prepared ourselves for arriving at the Fort on the following day.

Saturday, 24. The weather was the same as yesterday, and the country increasing in beauty; though as we approached the Fort, the cattle appeared proportionably to diminish. We now landed at two lodges of Indians, who were as astonished to see us, as if we had been the first white men whom they had ever beheld. When we had passed these people not an animal was to be seen on the borders of the river.

At length, as we rounded a point, and came in view of the Fort, we threw out our flag, and accompanied it with a general discharge of our fire-arms; while the men were in such spirits, and made such an active use of their paddles, that we arrived before the two men whom we left here in the spring, could recover their senses to answer us. Thus we landed at four in the afternoon, at the place which we left on the ninth of May.——

Voyage to the Pacific Ocean

Here my voyages of discovery terminate. Their toils and their dangers, their solicitudes and sufferings, have not been exaggerated in my description. On the contrary, in many instances, language has failed me in the attempt to describe them. I received, however, the reward of my labours, for they were crowned with success.

As I have now resumed the character of a trader, I shall not trouble my readers with any subsequent concern, but content myself with the closing information, that after an absence of eleven months, I arrived at Fort Chepewyan, where I remained, for the purposes of trade, during the succeeding winter.

Index

Index

ALDER, trees, size noted, 329.

Alexandria, significance of site, 193.

Anah-yoe Tesse, Indian designation for river, 258.

Annah, Chipewyan name for Knisteneaux Indians, 252.

Arrowsmith, ——, supplies map, xxxviii-xxxix.

Assiniboine (Red) River, habitat of red deer, 160.

Athabaska Lake, significance of name, 5.

Athabaska (Elk) River, Mackenzie stationed on, xix; as boundary, 5; gardening operations, 15.

Atnah (Chin) Indians, vocabulary, 188-89; visit explorers, 215; resemble Bella Coola River natives, 276.

BARK, of trees, as food, 254, 282.

Basins, geological formations, described, 240-41.

Bears, seen, 15, 56, 63-64, 105; killed, 326; dens, 56, 105. See also Grizzly Bears.

Bear River, mouth passed, 58.

Beauchamp, Jacques, member of Mackenzie's expedition, 46.

Beaulieux, François, member of Mackenzie's expedition, 45.

Beavers, hunted, 30; seen, 60, 71, 93-94, 96, 129, 232, 243, 363; skins purchased, 352-53.

Beaver Indians, relations with Knisteneaux, 5-6, 37-38; with Rocky Mountain Indians, 30; described, 37; chastity of women, 42; visit Mackenzie, 50-52.

Bella Coola River, explorers reach, 268; descend, 278-300; ascend, 320-46.

"Bensins," identified, 304; mentioned, 316.

Birds, described, 21-22.

Bisson, Baptiste, member of Mackenzie's expedition, 45.

377

Index

Blackwater (West Road) River, Mackenzie ascends, 222–25; seen, 234, 291.

Bois-picant tree, described, 83.

Bonaparte, Napoleon, interest in Mackenzie's narrative, xxix.

Boyer, ———, builds Old Establishment, 7.

Buffaloes, seen, 15, 60–62, 65, 371–72; killed, 368; migrations, 43.

CABBAGES, cultivated, 14.

Cancre, The, member of Mackenzie's expedition, 46; explains emblem, 85–86; ascends mountain 98–102; sent in search of guide, 147; companion of Mackenzie, 234.

Canoes, Mackenzie's, described, 45; wrecked, 133–38; repaired, 138–42; new canoe built, 164, 175–76, 209–18; stored, 225; of natives, described, 120–21, 292–93, 342.

Canoe Island, explorers leave, 219.

Carrots, cultivated, 14.

Cartier, Jacques, explores St. Lawrence River, xx.

Cascade Canal, identified, 311.

Cedar trees, size noted, 329.

Chinook, described, 27–28.

Chipewyan Indians, widespread use of language, 354–55.

Churchill River, Mackenzie stationed on, xviii.

Colby, C. W., edits Mackenzie's narrative, xxix.

Columbia (Tacoutche Tesse) River, confused with Fraser River, xxvi, 186; explorers reach watershed, 359–60.

Cook, James, explores Northwest Coast, xxiv, 292, 296.

Cormorants, seen, 64.

Courtois, François, member of Mackenzie's expedition, 46.

Currant bushes, seen, 83.

DEER, inhabit Deer Mountain, 16; Assiniboine River, 160; seen, 160; hunted, 266–67. See also Reindeer.

Deer Mountain, described, 16.

Index

Index

Grande Isle, explorers pass, 7.

Grand Portage, as fur trade capital, xvii–xviii.

Graves, Indians preserve, 239, 243; described, 268; burial customs, 256–57.

Gray (Grey), Capt. Robert, repudiates report of Northwest Passage, 314.

Gregory, John, fur trade relations described, xvi.

Gregory, McLeod, and Company, as rival of North West Company, xvi–xviii.

Grizzly bears, Indians fear, 57; encountered on Peace River, 56, 61.

Ground hogs, seen, 64; eaten, 266.

HEMLOCK trees, use of bark as food, 281–82.

Hudson, Henry, explores Hudson River, xx.

INDIANS, of Peace River Establishment, described, 9–11; of Parsnip River, 107–21; of Fraser River, 157–59, 161–63, 167–76, 178–86; of Bella Coola River, 276–77; of Blackwater River, 354; of Friendly Village, 337–46; women described, 10–11, 117–18, 259, 337–41; births among, 31; status of, 38–40, 245; domestic labors, 297; polygamy among, 11, 36, 38, 235, 245, 341; medical practices, 20, 40, 289–90; drinking habits, 29, 37; mourning customs, 28–29, 41, 44, 343; quarrels, 32, 35–36; games, 32, 261; superstitions, 33, 275, 283–84, 291–92; destroy property of deceased, 34, 41; give geographical information, 115–16, 172–73, 175, 182–85, 189–90, 228, 237; habitations described, 161–63, 255–56, 271, 284–86, 298; vocabularies, 188–89, 346; conjuring exploit described, 230; respect for aged, 236; preserve graves of kindred, 239, 243; graves described, 268; burial customs, 256–57; house of worship described, 286–87; skill as canoeists, 279, 326; steal from explorers, 293–94, 307, 312, 332, 352–53; hostile toward, 304–19, 320–24, 330–31, 334–35; engage in trade, 324.

JOHNSTONE, ——, visits Indian village, 298.

380

Index

381

Index

Index

Parsnips, cultivated, 14. See also Wild Parsnips.
Parsnip River, Mackenzie explores, xxv, 91–127, 361–64; Indian gives geographical information, 54.
Partridges, killed, 243.
Peace Point, gives name to Peace River, 5; treaty made, 37.
Peace (Unjigah) River, explored, xx, xxiv–xxv, 3–13, 47–91, 365–73; origin of name, 5; Mackenzie winters on, 17–44; Indians described, 9–11; gardening operations, 14–15; source reached, 129. See also Parsnip River.
Peace River City, site of Mackenzie's winter quarters, 13.
Perez, Juan, explores Northwest Coast, xxiv.
Pine River, route via, 4.
Point Menzies, identified, 303.
Polygamy, among Indians, 11, 36, 38, 235, 245, 341.
Pond, Peter, activities in fur trade, xvi–xix; career sketched, 15.
Porcupine, killed, 105; eaten, 301–02.
Porcupine Cove, named, 303.
Portage de la Montagne de Roche, explorers pass, 367.
Potatoes, cultivated, 14.
QUADRA, ——, explores Northwest Coast, xxiv.
REINDEER, migration of, 43. See also Deer.
Religion, house of worship described, 286–87; customs of Friendly Village Indians, 344.
Rocky Mountain Indians, supply geographical information, 29–30, 54; Knisteneaux prey upon, 37–38; visit Mackenzie, 53–56; repute as liars, 262.
SALMON, eaten, 272–73; superstitions concerning, 274–75, 283–84, 291–92; weir described, 273–74; method of preserving, 290; caught, 327; project to plant in Peace River, 360.
Sand-flies, afflict explorers, 219, 221.
Scots, migrate to Canada, xv.